steven berkoff

AND THE THEATRE
OF SELF-PERFORMANCE

Published in our
centenary year

~ **2004** ~

MANCHESTER

steven berkoff

AND THE THEATRE
OF SELF-PERFORMANCE

robert cross

Manchester University Press

Manchester and New York

distributed exclusively in the USA by Palgrave

Copyright © Robert Cross 2004

The right of Robert Cross to be identified as the author of this work has been asserted by him in accordance with the Copyright, Designs and Patents Act 1988

Published by Manchester University Press
Oxford Road, Manchester M13 9NR, UK
and Room 400, 175 Fifth Avenue, New York, NY 10010, USA
www.manchesteruniversitypress.co.uk

Distributed exclusively in the USA by
Palgrave, 175 Fifth Avenue, New York, NY 10010, USA

Distributed exclusively in Canada by
UBC Press, University of British Columbia, 2029 West Mall, Vancouver, BC, Canada V6T 1Z2

British Library Cataloguing-in-Publication Data
A catalogue record for this book is available from the British Library

Library of Congress Cataloging-in-Publication Data applied for

ISBN 0 7190 6253 5 *hardback*
ISBN 0 7190 6254 3 *paperback*

First published 2004

11 10 09 08 07 06 05 04   10 9 8 7 6 5 4 3 2 1

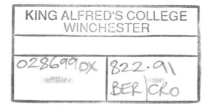
Typeset in Scala and Scala Sans
by Koinonia, Manchester
Printed in Great Britain
by Bell & Bain Ltd, Glasgow

for Stan, who planted the seeds

L'homme est à inventer chaque jour. (Jean-Paul Sartre)

   All the world's a stage
   And all the men and women merely players;
   They have their exits and their entrances;
   And one man in his time plays many parts.
                           (William Shakespeare)

I am just a cocktail of emotions. I am Herod. Harlequin.
The golem. Hamlet. I am a man in search of a soul.
                           (Steven Berkoff)

CONTENTS

LIST OF FIGURES

PREFACE

The prehistory of this book was an acting workshop at the Albany Empire in New Cross more than twenty years ago. That was where I had my first taste of Berkoff. I recall vividly my excitement at hearing the instructor intone the punk poetry of the Herald's report from *Agamemnon*. That day I started to track down anything I could find by Berkoff. *East*, with its daring juxtaposition of profane Cockney and cod-Shakespeare, was a revelation. Theatre, I discovered, could be as scabrous as stand-up comedy, as hard-hitting as a prize fight, and as spectacular as a circus.

As I became more familiar with Berkoff's plays, watched him in action performing in his productions, and read his interviews, I saw that he was not only inviting but also challenging his readers and audiences to look for 'Steven Berkoff' in his writings and in his performances both on and off-stage. "The evolution of my life goes through my plays", he declared in one newspaper article. When I made the decision to write a study of his work, Berkoff's 'self' was the logical point of entry. This book is an examination of how his life has evolved, or rather how he has *constructed* and *projected* his life, through his plays and his other non-dramatic works.

Before launching into my narrative, it is necessary that I should say a word or two about what this book is *not*. First of all, it is neither a traditional biography nor a psychological examination of what I shall be referring to here as the 'Berkoff phenomenon'. Furthermore, although I am principally interested in Berkoff's theatrical work, this book does not aspire to be a complete study of his plays. My purpose is to examine the dynamic processes of his identity formation, thus I concentrate on those key works that he has used as vehicles or strategies for self-projection. For that reason, I do not touch on plays such as *Acapulco*, *The Tell-Tale Heart*, *Sturm and Drang* and *Oedipus* that have little direct bearing on my theme. Nor do I deal in detail with his revivals of works by other playwrights. An analysis of his physical interpretations of Shakespeare's plays, for example, would form the subject matter of an entirely separate book.

Finally, I do not claim to be an innocent, disinterested academic observer. A study such as this, which sets out to examine the constructed nature of Berkoff's subjectivity – and the socially constructed nature of human identity in general – throws into sharp relief my own subjectivity and the assumptions embedded in my perspectives. What follows below, then, is necessarily a coproduction between my own 'self' as the researcher and Berkoff's 'self' as the object of my investigation. Since I share Berkoff's working-class upbringing in the East End of London, I have almost certainly reacted to certain strategies employed by him—the 'in-yer-face' use of profane Cockney in certain plays, for example—in a way that is different from, let us say, a person born into the middle or upper classes and educated at private institutions. Inevitably, I have filtered his account of leaving the East End to enter the largely middle-class world of the theatre through my own experience of leaving the East End to enter the largely middle-class world of academia. I state this not to excuse any possible lapses in objectivity (if objectivity exists at all) but to signal that I am in the text that follows as much as is Berkoff.

ACKNOWLEDGEMENTS

This book, in the words of the song, has been a long time comin'. An earlier version of this text was presented as a PhD thesis at the University of Lancaster. The single person to whom I remain indebted, therefore, is my supervisor at that time, Baz Kershaw (now at Bristol University). Baz's challenging and stimulating guidance along the arduous doctoral trek encouraged me to venture along many new paths in my research, and this book would not exist without the kind and unstinting support and assistance he showed me then. It goes without saying, of course, that I bear sole responsibility for any errors or wayward judgements expressed in the pages that follow.

I could not have completed this book without the kind co-operation and support of many people and institutions. First off, I wish to thank Mr Steven Berkoff himself for having stimulated me with his works to the extent that I was moved to undertake this project. In addition, I would like to record my gratitude to him for generously allowing me to interview him when he visited Japan in 1992, and for answering my numerous subsequent letters.

I would like to extend my thanks to Jim Haynes for replying so fully to my questions about Berkoff's first production at the London Arts Lab; to Roland Rees for telling me of his experiences as a director in the alternative theatre scene of the 1960s; to Petra Markham and Steve Dixon for sharing with me their recollections of acting under Berkoff's direction; and to Professor Emeritus John Pick for answering my questions about unemployment in the theatre profession.

I also wish to thank the Institute of Language and Culture at Doshisha University, Kyoto, Japan, for providing me with a secure and stimulating base during the past seven years and for kindly granting me the study leave in England which enabled me to complete the final work on this book. I would like to thank my colleagues at Doshisha for all the kind support and encouragement they have extended to me over the years.

For their permission to reproduce photographs in this book, I would like to offer my sincere thanks to David Gamble, Richard Mildenall and, most particularly, Cordelia Weedon. For images reproduced from newspaper articles I would like to thank the *Evening Standard*, the *Observer* and the *Guardian*. For permission to reproduce movie stills, I wish to thank Universal Pictures (UK) Limited and Metro-Goldwyn-Mayer Studios Inc. For permission to use images from archives, I offer my thanks to Getty Images, the Folger Shakespeare Library and the Houghton Library at Harvard University.

For their unstinting support, patience and understanding throughout the process of getting this book into print, I would like to record my gratitude to all the staff at Manchester University Press.

Finally, my greatest and warmest thanks are reserved for my beloved Kyoko and our very own J-League, Jethro, Jamie and Jasmine, who not only granted me the freedom and space to complete this book but also steered me away from the reefs of madness with their love, understanding and tireless support.

LIST OF ABBREVIATIONS

INTRODUCTION

Theatre can and should hold the mirror up to ourselves in the hope
that we will dislike the reflection sufficiently to wish to change it, or
else to show an image which is so desirable that we would wish to
become it. (Glenda Jackson)[1]

The reception of Berkoff and his *œuvre*

The *œuvre*, career and personality of the contemporary London-born
playwright, writer, actor-manager and director Steven Berkoff have consistently defied easy categorisation. Seemingly out-of-place in, or at least
on the fringes of, both the mainstream and the alternative sectors of
modern theatre, he is what I should like to term a 'threshold figure' or, as
one commentator has put it, "an odd-man-out in the British theatre"
(Elder 1978: 37). Few would disagree that the man who has described
academics as "intellectuals who fart with their mouths at conferences"
(*CID* 142),[2] theatre critics as "sadists and worn-out old tarts" (Lister
1989), and British theatre audiences as "the most pretentious, hypo-
critical, cynical theatregoers in the entire planet" (Reynolds 1998); who
has disparaged his fellow theatre workers relentlessly; and whose
working methods as a director have bordered on the dictatorial, has been
singularly adept at making enemies. One journalist, expressing a view
held by many people, has described him as "temperamental, arrogant,
disdainful, contemptuous, iconoclastic [and] savage" (Hicklin 1997).
Berkoff is, quite simply, a *difficult* person to deal with, as this writer
knows from the tense interview conducted with him backstage at the
Ginza Saison Theatre, Tokyo, in 1992. His liminal position in the theatre
and the often contradictory ways in which he has projected himself both
on the stage and in public life, together with his well-documented
abrasiveness and aggressive responses to perceived insults and rejections,
have discouraged a thorough and balanced scholarly assessment of
Berkoff and his work and significance.

Orthodox scholars of contemporary British theatre and drama have mostly chosen to ignore Berkoff's achievement. Cave's *New British Drama in Performance on the London Stage 1970–1985* (1987), Innes's *Modern British Drama, 1800–1990* (1992), and Demastes's *British Playwrights, 1956–1995* (1996), to cite three prominent examples, pass over him completely. Similarly, the *Oxford Companion to the Theatre* (Hartnoll 1993), to name one authoritative reference work, contains no entry on Berkoff. Those who mention him do so in a cursory fashion. Shepherd and Womack, for example, make just two passing references to Berkoff's satirical comedy *Decadence* in their *English Drama: A Cultural History* (1996), and Shellard devotes only one paragraph of his *British Theatre Since the War* (1999) to a thumbnail sketch of Berkoff's career, compared, for example, to the eight pages and numerous scattered references concerning Howard Brenton. Berkoff's career is very briefly surveyed in Eyre and Wright's *Changing Stages: A View of British Theatre in the Twentieth Century* (2000). In the worst cases, Berkoff has been treated with undisguised hostility by certain orthodox scholars. Ruby Cohn's three pages on Berkoff in her *Retreats from Realism in Recent English Drama* (1991), for example, add up to a sweeping rejection of his work.

The earliest chroniclers of the 1960s alternative theatre scene have dealt unevenly with Berkoff and his work. He and his London Theatre Group (henceforth abbreviated to LTG) are accorded equal space to other artists and companies in *Time Out*'s seminal 'Guide to Underground Theatre' (1971), the first attempt to map the contours of the new theatre. By contrast, Jonathan Hammond (1973: 45) makes only the briefest mention of Berkoff and the LTG in his 'A Potted History of the Fringe', despite the fact that during the preceding four-to-five years the company had staged three well-received Kafka adaptations at the Arts Lab, the Round House and the Oval House, the most prominent alternative venues in London at that time. Shortly after this, however, *Plays and Players* did publish Hammond's (1974) thoughtful and detailed double review of *Agamemnon* and *The Trial*. Berkoff is conspicuous by his absence, however, in such prominent surveys of the alternative theatre scene as Peter Ansorge's *Disrupting the Spectacle* (1975), Clive Barker's 'From Fringe to Alternative Theatre' (1978), and Catherine Itzin's *Alternative Theatre Handbook 1975–76* (1976) and *Stages in the Revolution* (1980). This 'silent treatment' is almost certainly due to these writers' recognition of Berkoff's publicly stated ambivalence towards the alternative theatre scene and his espousal, at least five years in advance of Mrs Thatcher's first election victory in May 1979, of a brand of neo-conservative individualism entirely antithetical to the counter-cultural spirit of the non-mainstream theatre world of the late 1960s and early 1970s.

Two articles based around interviews that offer interesting glimpses of a young and idealistic Berkoff in the first flush of success are Mary Benson's 'Steven Berkoff: what theatre can be', which appeared in the *London Magazine* in the winter of 1976/77, and Bruce Elder's '"Doing the inexpressible uncommonly well": the theatre of Steven Berkoff', published in the *Theatre Quarterly* in the summer of 1978. Whilst one might find fault with the gushing admiration of both writers for their subject, their sympathetic leading questions did give one 'angry young man' an opportunity to ventilate his contempt for mainstream theatre practice and set out his own evolving conception of physical theatre.

Berkoff and his work have received passing mentions in academic studies of alternative British theatre and drama with regard to specific contexts. Hewison (1987: 204) and Kershaw (1992: 101) refer to him in the context of the London Arts Lab (1968–69) and its place in the development of alternative theatre; Elsom (1979: 149) and Chambers (1980: 109) briefly mention his work in connection with the new actor-based theatre that emerged during the 1960s; Birch (1991: 25–6; 68–73) discusses Berkoff's linguistic shock tactics in his study of dramatic language; Chambers and Prior (1987: 51–2) touch on his depiction of the working classes; Paget (1992: 166–7; 175–6) examines Berkoff's drama *Sink the Belgrano!* in his article on plays about the Falklands War; Bigsby (1981: 33; 45) includes Berkoff in his survey of the theatrical treatment of Britain's postwar decline; Sinfield (1988: 133) briefly discusses Berkoff's play *West* in the context of the appropriation and subversion of Shakespeare's iconicity in recent British drama; Dunn (1996: 25–9) offers a refreshingly balanced but short overview of Berkoff's work; Vigouroux-Frey (1997: 6) discusses his play *Greek* in her article about Greek myth in modern English drama; Peacock, in his book *Thatcher's Theatre: British Theatre and Drama in the Eighties*, confines his analysis of Berkoff's work to a one-paragraph discussion of *Metamorphosis* (Peacock 1999: 209); and Sierz (2001: 25–6), in his study of radical British drama in the 1990s, briefly discusses Berkoff's impact as "a pioneer of in-yer-face theatre".

The appearance over the past decade of a small number of studies devoted solely to Berkoff and his work suggests that scholarly interest in him may gradually be picking up. In his doctoral thesis entitled 'The Theatre of Steven Berkoff' (1991), Paul Currant traces Berkoff's career from the 1950s to the 1990s in order, as he puts it, "to find the essentials of his theatre". Proceeding chronologically through Berkoff's career,

Currant's traditional biographical approach is to locate parallels between the playwright's life and work. However, this study, which relies almost exclusively on newspaper interviews and reviews for background material, lacks any theoretical position that might have enabled Currant to analyse or interpret the relationship between Berkoff's life and creative work in a more meaningful fashion. Similarly, theatre director Craig Rosen's undated essay entitled 'Creating the "Berkovian" Aesthetic: an Analysis of Steven Berkoff's Performance Style' lacks a theoretical framework and fails to contextualise Berkoff and his work by offering any analysis of his relationship with his influences or with the broader theatrical scene.[3] The merit of this descriptive piece, though, lies in the fairly detailed picture it records of Berkoff's theatrical style, and in Rosen's interesting interview with Berkoff that is included in an appendix.

Two articles that appeared in the same 1996 issue of the *Contemporary Theatre Review* are Monique Prunet's 'The outrageous 80s: Conservative policies and the Church of England under fire in Steven Berkoff's *Sink the Belgrano!* and David Hare's *The Secret Rapture* and *Racing Demon*' and Nicole Boireau's 'Steven Berkoff's orgy: the four-letter ecstasy'. Prunet's uncritical reading of *Belgrano!* as self-evidently a satirical attack on the policies of Margaret Thatcher suffers from her evident consideration of the play in isolation and not in the broader context of Berkoff's other works, which, as I argue below in chapter 6, show that his relationship with Thatcherism has been considerably more problematic and ambiguous. Boireau's article posits that Berkoff's dramatic art represents a "mythical journey back to origins" (Boireau 1996: 77). The subversive quality of Berkoff's dramaturgy, for that writer, lies in his use of grotesque images, both in mime and language, to undermine received notions of Western culture. Boireau's argument, however, tends to lose itself in the obscure mysticism of her language. Her rather naive and, I suggest, erroneous conclusion is that a "plea for an archaic return to the love of nature, to man degree zero [*sic*], emerges from Berkoff's work" (88).

Journalists, in stark contrast to scholars, have been willing to lavish attention on Berkoff. Yet their concern has been less with the playwright, actor and director than with the 'notorious' public figure. In short, Berkoff has made for good copy. The titles alone of some of the many sensational profiles and interviews that have appeared throughout his career – 'Steve Berkoff's cultural assault' (Chaillet 1980), 'Bovver craft' (McAfee 1989), 'Beware of Berkoff' (Appleyard 1989), 'Anti-hero with an East side story' (Walsh 1991), and 'Noble Savage' (Hicklin 1997), for instance – show clearly that the authors of these pieces have seized upon his 'dangerous' public image. Some writers – Lambert (1989), Phillips (1991), Iley (1993) and Church (1994), for example – have taken a different though no less sensational tack by attempting to look behind the 'hard man' persona. One of them, indeed, has gone so far as to speculate that "[a]t the heart of bovver-boy actor, writer and director Steven Berkoff is a small frightened man" (McAfee 1991). It is not too much to say that journalists have generally helped to thicken the fog of hype and mis-information that swirls around their interviewee. In so doing, they have contributed actively to the creation of Berkoff's public 'notoriety' and diverted the public's attention away from his work as an artist in the theatre. Deborah Ross (2001) is one journalist who has shown her aware-ness of this problem by expressing the hope that "Steven Berkoff, the PR disaster, [would not] ever totally eclipse Steven Berkoff the actor (impos-sible to take your eyes off him), director (startingly original, particularly his Shakespeare and Kafka adaptations), and playwright."

With regard to his treatment at the hands of theatre critics, Berkoff has, like any playwright, actor or director, received both good and bad notices during his career. What is notably different in his particular case, however, is the manner in which some critics, especially those writing for the less progressive newspapers and journals, appear to have had their sharpened nibs out for him. One example among countless others is Charles Spencer, who begins his review of Berkoff's autobiography in the *Sunday Telegraph* (4 April 1996) with the following personal attack: "Steven Berkoff, for so long the *enfant terrible* of British theatre, is now in danger of becoming its Grumpy Old Man. Next year he celebrates his 60th birthday, but his splenetic arrogance shows little sign of abating. When he collects his bus pass, one imagines it will be with the scowling petulance of the adolescent." In a similarly caustic manner, his review in the *Daily Telegraph* (17 September 1999) of the 1999 revival of *East* at the Vaudeville Theatre, London demonstrates a personal antagonism towards the playwright/director despite a reluctant acceptance of the merits of the production:

> I have been rude about Steven Berkoff in the past, and in a minute I'm going to be rude about him again. But I have to admit that *East* is a drama of vitality and far-reaching influence ... Yet although it is easy to admire *East*, I find it impossible to like it.

Thus this particular critic obstinately refuses to like a production he professes to admire because he is unable or unwilling to overcome his disdain for its creator. Sadly, a similar lack of objectivity and fairminded-ness is shared by quite a number of Spencer's colleagues in the print media.

Despite his unhappy relations with orthodox scholars, conservative critics, sensation-seeking journalists, and even his fellow theatre workers, it is possible to say of Berkoff, after more than four troubled decades in the theatre profession, that he has finally achieved a certain grudging recognition. In 1991 he garnered the prestigious Evening Standard Award for best comedy with his play *Kvetch*. His own performance in the American premiere of his play *Massage* (Odyssey Theatre, Los Angeles) in 1997 earned him a nomination for Best Actor in the L. A. Weekly Theatre Awards. In the same year he was honoured at the Edinburgh Festival with a Total Theatre Lifetime Achievement Award, and in 2000 he was the most performed playwright at that festival. In addition, Faber and Faber published his *Collected Plays* (Volumes I and II in 1994, and Volume III in 2000) and his autobiography, *Free Association* (1996), and he has directed revivals of his dramas on the stages of the National Theatre.[4] In 1988 he was appointed as a member to the Artistic Directorate of the International Shakespeare Globe Centre, and in 2001 the British Council sponsored a production of his play *Messiah* in Croatia. Given that he is clearly a figure of some significance and influence in contemporary British theatre, therefore, a fact that may partially explain the silence and hostility from some quarters, a thorough assessment of Berkoff's achievement and significance is long overdue. This book is modestly offered as an attempt to address that lack.

Aims and methodology

A key point to be emphasised about this book, despite its concern with looking at Berkoff's life and work, is that it is not a biography in any traditional sense. I am interested less in the facts of Berkoff's life than in what Berkoff has *made* of his 'life' across a variety of media. This book is an investigation into the ever-shifting interplay between Berkoff's *œuvre* and his publicly constructed self, a dynamic process of identity formation that I refer to as the 'Berkoff phenomenon'. Before proceeding further, it is necessary for me to clarify my use of the key terms *œuvre* and *self*, since they are crucial to my whole argument and theoretical position.

I understand Berkoff's *œuvre* (a more broadly inclusive term than *work*) to refer to a wide-ranging multimedia project. It includes primarily, of course, his writings. These consist of his dramatic adaptations and original plays (both published and unpublished), together with his short stories, polemical essays on theatre, production diaries, newspaper articles, travelogues and autobiography. Yet Berkoff is also an actor, director, voice artist and photographer. Thus I understand his *œuvre* in a more comprehensive way to embrace his stage, film, radio and TV performances; his direction of his own plays and of revivals of dramas by Shakespeare, Albee and Wilde; his voice-over and narration work on TV commercials and videos, on a disco song ('Mind of the Machine' by N-Trance), and as the reader of works by Franz Kafka for the Penguin Audiobooks series; his exhibition of his own photographs of the Jewish East End; and his self-promotion and commodification through his website (www.east-productions.demon.co.uk). Crucially, I also understand it to include what I shall call his 'social performances' as a public figure, particularly in interviews conducted with him in newspapers, magazines and on television and radio, and in the well-documented cases of his aggressive behaviour.

Turning now to the concept of *self*, it is important to establish both how Berkoff appears to conceive of his own self and how I understand and use the term in what follows. To judge from his scattered statements regarding the nature of his identity/subjectivity, Berkoff appears to invest himself – or rather his 'self' – with psychological stability, coherence and continuity. In the preface to his autobiography, for example, he states:

> When I started to write these memoirs I had in mind all those I had waded through in the past and my impatience with their order of events. I was keen to get to the personality I knew, to bite into the mature fruit rather than be made to wait. (*FA*: ix)

Berkoff, as we shall see, has overtly made the uncovering and expression of this 'personality' the primary subject matter of his dramatic works (indeed, of his entire *œuvre*). He has declared confidently that "I very rarely need to 'research' to find my themes or seek for 'subjects', since take it or leave it the subject has been myself" (*FA*: 4). In his 'Three Theatre Manifestos' he maintains that "[w]hat is vital to the spectator is your core, the inner part of you" (*TTM*: 8). His dramas are, he writes, implying a process of signification that unproblematically achieves closure, the "living embodiments of my life" (*FA*: 391). This is reinforced by Berkoff's *physically* living embodiment of his alter-ego protagonists on stage in the original productions of most of these works. Even when, at one point in his autobiography, Berkoff briefly describes himself as a kind of multiple personality, as an individual who has projected himself 'through' other people, such as Franz Kafka, Antonin Artaud, Norman Mailer and others (see chapter 2), he nevertheless finds the security of apparent self-knowledge in the existence of "plain dull and ordinary me" (*FA*: 177), the core 'self' that he assumes he can know, describe, explain, thematise in his *œuvre*, and, finally, perform on stage and in public life.

The underlying procedure of this investigation is my questioning of Berkoff's (indeed, anyone's) assumption of a coherent, unitary and stable selfhood. Instead, I posit a notion of 'self' that is fluid, multiple, unstable and provisional. My primary aim here is to interrogate the supposedly self-referential quality of Berkoff's *œuvre*, and to critique his ability to achieve closure in the representation of himself/his 'self'. The term *self* (together with words related to it, such as *himself, myself, self-construction, self-empowerment* and so on) is linguistically and philosophically problematic, particularly in a study such as this which sets out to question the very ground of selfhood. In my text I separate out and signal two key ways in which I approach the concept here. Mostly, I place the word within single quotation marks – 'self' – in order to indicate that I am questioning the notion of selfhood as a stable and unified entity. In various places in this text, however, when it is appropriate to my argument, I provisionally adopt what appears to be Berkoff's unitary view of his identity/subjectivity in order to discuss a subject position or discursive strategy from his point of view. I signal this by using the word *self* in the customary fashion without quotation marks.

An exploration of a protean and unstable entity such as the 'Berkoff phenomenon' requires a methodological approach that can account for its dynamic, non-unitary and paradoxical qualities. In this study I primarily use the theoretical insights offered by social constructionism, together with various strands of poststructuralism, notably certain ideas and methods of Barthes, Derrida and Foucault, to examine the ways in which Berkoff has attempted to construct and project his 'self' through his *œuvre*. This 'self' has not emerged in isolation, however, but across a diverse range of media and within the broad contexts of the theatrical world and socio-political climate of Britain since the mid-1950s. Thus I support my arguments where appropriate with concepts and ideas developed in postmodernist theories of literature and performance; cultural materialism; social, cultural and political history; theories of popular culture; and theatre semiotics. I also employ most particularly Bakhtin's theory of the carnivalesque and Callois's notions of play and ludism.

Social constructionism, which draws upon the work of sociologists, psychologists, linguists, discourse analysts and poststructuralists, examines such concepts as personality, identity, behaviour, language, ideology and power in ways that depart radically from the positivist assumptions of Western liberal humanism. Two key studies that contributed to the establishment of social constructionism as a discipline were Berger and Luckmann's *The Social Construction of Reality* (1966), and K. J. Gergen's paper 'Social psychology as history' (1973), both of which set out the view that human and social reality are not pre-existing but are generated through social interaction. Social constructionism approaches all social interactions as dynamic *processes* in which different versions of reality may be represented, contested and negotiated. Crucially, it is concerned with investigating how power and resources are distributed among institutions and individuals in society; with how the imbalances in this distribution serve to promote or inhibit such social and cultural practices as identity formation and creative activity; and with how people become both the agents and the products of the strategies they adopt in the ongoing construction of their subjectivities. Thus, in this study I examine Berkoff's formation of the LTG (see chapter 3), for example, and his carnivalesque raids on the Shakespearean canon in his play *East* (see chapter 5) as strategies designed to empower his 'self' *vis-à-vis* what he has characterised as a hegemonic theatre Establishment.

Two further important and closely related terms that are crucial to this discussion are *discourse* and *text*, and it is necessary to clarify my use of them here. Discourses are understood, to use Foucault's (1972: 49) succinct formulation, as "practices which form the objects of which they speak". Simply put, all cultural practice, including all linguistic communication, *creates* reality or realities. Thus as Davies and Harré (1990: 46) put it, a discourse is understood as a "multi-faceted public process through which meanings are progressively and dynamically achieved". And Burr (1995: 48), elaborating on this notion, writes that a

> discourse refers to a set of meanings, metaphors, representations, images, stories, statements and so on that in some way together produce a particular version of events. It refers to a particular picture that is painted of an event (or person or class of persons), a particular way of representing it or them in a certain light.

Thus people and institutions employ discourses in the unceasing processes of constituting and re-constituting their 'selves' and in the accounts they offer of events. One of my primary concerns here is to explore the diverse discourses – 'Jewish victim', 'East End villain', and 'un-English physical performer', for example – that Berkoff's 'self', as a constructionist process, has evolved through the production of the 'Berkoff phenomenon' through the *œuvre*.

Text is a much debated term. In this investigation I mainly encounter the 'Berkoff phenomenon' through conventional texts (playscripts, stories, autobiography, published interviews, and so on). As noted above, though, Berkoff's *œuvre* operates across a wide range of media, including, for example, his 'social performances'. Thus texts are understood here in a more comprehensive sense to refer to the infinite ways in which discourses are *realised*. As Burr (1995: 50–1) explains:

> A discourse about an object is said to manifest itself in texts – in speech, say a conversation or interview, in written material such as novels, newspaper articles or letters, in visual images like magazine advertisements or films, or even in the 'meanings' embodied in the clothes people wear or the way they do their hair. In fact, anything that can be 'read' for meaning can be thought of as being a manifestation of one or more discourses and can be referred to as a 'text'.

In this way I view the 'Berkoff phenomenon' as a flexible network of discourses that manifest themselves in and through a wide variety of texts that may be conventional or non-conventional in character. His 'East End villain' discourse, to take one example, is constituted through a diverse array of texts (discussed in chapter 1) that include his drama *East*; his performance as the thuggish hero Mike in the original production of that play; the closely cropped 'convict' hairstyle he has adopted; his 'threat' to murder a theatre critic; his screen performances as an East End villain in such films as *McVicar* and *The Krays*; and the anecdotes he recounts in his autobiography about growing up among real-life villains in the East End. Here I follow Barthes (1977) in seeing texts as open "methodological fields", as evolving processes of signification, rather than closed works or products.

I now need to explain my approach to the key issue underlying this investigation, namely the nature and operation of human subjectivity. Liberal humanism has rested to a very large extent upon the notion of the autonomous individual as a unified, coherent and rational agent who is the sole author of her or his own experience and its meaning. As Celia Kitzinger (1992: 229) explains:

> The individuated self concept is a powerful influence in the West – one of our most cherished values, structuring our vision of the world in our everyday lives, in our political thought, and in our formal psychological theorizing. Individualism can be described as the liberal belief, emerging with, or at least consolidated by, the bourgeois

revolution, that persons exist in the form of discrete bounded units coincident with the biological human body. The 'individual' is conceptualized as a relatively autonomous, self-contained and distinctive entity, who is affected by external variables like 'socialization' and 'social context' but is in some sense separate from these 'influences'.

Social constructionism and recent postmodernist theories of culture, society and gender challenge this entrenched concept of the stable and unified individual and posit instead the notion of a decentred and elusive *subject* that lacks any fixed or essential presence and/or existence.

This 'postmodern subject', ever in flux, emerges through the processes of social interaction, "not as a relatively fixed end-product but as one who is constituted and reconstituted through the various discursive practices in which they participate" (Davies and Harré 1990: 46). People, crucially, are simultaneously the producers and products of discourses and texts through the complex operation of "interactive positioning" (48). As "discourse users" (Gergen 1989) they take up what are termed "subject positions" (Davies and Harré 1990: 53) by adopting the discourses that are culturally available to them such as those determined by their age, gender, class, ethnicity, sexual orientation, and so on. Conversely, people are also "positioned" (43) by the discursive practices (which they may reject, accept or negotiate) that are employed by other people or institutions. Subjectivity, conceived of in this way as fluid, ephemeral and multiple, is also frequently contradictory (58–9). An example of this in Berkoff's case is his adoption of the seemingly opposed 'Jewish victim' and 'East End villain' subject positions.

Such a fluid approach to selfhood challenges classic role theory,[5] which argues that in her or his social interactions a person continually adopts roles that mask an essential primary self. These roles may be seen as "pre-ordained societal 'slots' that come with a pre-written script or set of expected behaviours, which people somehow 'slip on', like an overcoat, over their real selves" (Burr 1995: 140). The dynamic subject positions posited by social constructionism, by contrast, permit us to think ourselves as "choosing subjects" (Davies and Harré 1990: 52) and as determiners of our own identity. Choice implies human agency. And here we encounter what appears to be a paradox: How can a "choosing subject", by definition cognisant of strategies that it wishes or intends to employ in order to effect change, select and adopt subject positions if it is assumed to possess no essential or stable existence? The social constructionist view, which I take as the basis of my approach here, is that the subject at any given moment is both 'self-knowing' and provisional.

As Paul Smith (1988: xxxv) argues in *Discerning the Subject*, the human subject is constituted by "the series or the conglomeration of *positions*, subject-positions, provisional and not necessarily indefeasible, in which a person is momentarily called by the discourses and the world he/she inhabits". In other words, the continually shifting subject, defined by the ever-changing sum total of the subject positions temporarily adopted, is always aware of the positions she or he takes up and subsequently retains or discards. The qualities of this process are nicely expressed in Gergen's (1989: 72) formulation that a person's "vocabulary of self shifts as pragmatic exigencies dictate". Thus the 'self', always provisional and shifting, is capable and conscious, as agent, of adopting the necessary strategies for its further reconstitution.

People, particularly the disenfranchised in society, will frequently improvise strategies and subject positions through acts of *bricolage*, a term coined by the anthropologist Claude Lévi-Strauss in *The Savage Mind* (1962). In that work he distinguished between the modern human who, like an engineer, makes use of specialised tools and materials, and the so-called 'primitive' human, who like an 'odd-job man' or *bricoleur*, makes use of the means at hand in improvisatory acts. Recent theorists of popular culture (e. g. Hebdige 1979; Fiske 1989a, 1989b) have taken over this concept of 'making do' to refer to the ways in which in capitalist societies the disempowered subversively construct their own culture out of the resources of the empowered. This may be seen, as Fiske (1989b: 150) points out, in subcultural dress,

> where punks, for instance, can combine workingmen's boots with bits of military uniform and mix Nazi and British insignia into a 'new' style that does not 'mean' anything specific, but rather signifies their power to make their own style and to offend their 'social betters' in the process.

In a similar fashion, I shall argue, Berkoff, who has characterised himself as a Jewish working-class outsider in British theatre and society, has employed *bricolage* with the aim of empowering himself and offending his 'social betters' in the theatre hierarchy. One example of this, I suggest, is the way he appropriated Shakespeare's language and combined it with Cockney slang in his play *East* (see chapter 5) to create his own style of polyphonic dramatic speech. Berkoff's staging of the 25th anniversary revival of that play in 1999 on the stage of the Vaudeville Theatre in the West End may be seen as a further act of *bricolage*, involving the 'occupation' and 're-signposting' of the 'territory' of the mainstream theatre. Here I approach the 'Berkoff phenomenon' as a vast network of such acts – what Marvin Carlson (1996: 49), in his explication of the social constructionist view of the 'self', terms "a pragmatic piecing-together of pre-existing scraps of material".

The human subject, ephemeral, provisional, decentred and multiple, is characterised both by presence and absence. Jacques Derrida, the founder of deconstructionism, has shown through his concept of *différance* how meaning is continually deferred, how the identity of any object of our consciousness lies not merely in that object itself but also in all the things that it is not, in absence as well as presence (Derrida 1978: 8–9). As Sampson (1989: 8) notes:

> Through [Derrida's] close reading of texts, he seeks to discover *within* the meaning of any single term its opposite member: e.g. to discover within A the meaning of its presumed opposite, Not-A. This challenges the notions of identity, opposition and entity because A is *both* A *and* not-A.

To assign anything an identity, to say what it is, is necessarily also to say what it is not, thus presence contains absence and vice versa. If we apply this idea to the human subject, then it follows that the nature and identity of what is meant by the 'self' are functions both of itself and of what it is not.

In what follows I do not engage in any thoroughgoing way with Derrida's analyses but rather employ one key aspect of his textual methodology, namely the device of placing certain terms *sous rature* or "under erasure" (Derrida 1977: 19). In simple terms, this strategy involves printing a word and crossing it out, and then printing the word and its deletion. For example, the word *subjectivity*, under erasure, would be printed thus: ~~subjectivity~~. Norris (1991: 69) explains the effect of this: "The marks of erasure acknowledge both the *inadequacy* of the terms employed – their highly provisional status – and the fact that thought simply cannot manage without them in the work of deconstruction. By this graphic means ... concepts are perpetually shaken and dislodged." Throughout this investigation, I consider the term 'Berkoff phenomenon' as well as the proper name 'Steven Berkoff' and all personal pronouns referring to it, to stand under erasure. Thus I invite the reader to understand these terms to be implicitly crossed out – viz. ~~Berkoff phenomenon~~, ~~Steven Berkoff~~, ~~he~~, ~~him~~, etc. – since they are inappropriate but nevertheless necessary. To spare my readers any undue distress, however, they will be written in the conventional way in my text.

Berkoff's primary field of creative activity – acting, writing and directing in the theatre – focuses attention on the performed qualities of the 'Berkoff phenomenon'. *Performance* is another tricky concept that needs to be clarified here. Steven Connor, writing in the context of postmodern performance, makes the following distinction between two meanings of the word:

> The closeness of the word 'perform' to the word 'act' ... may alert us to a certain tremor of equivocation in the word. For, if to perform means to act, make or do something, it also means to dissimulate or to pretend to act, to feign action. The difference between the two meanings of performance corresponds closely to the difference between 'acting', in the sense of doing something, and 'enacting', in the sense of playing out, or impersonating. (Connor 1996: 108)

On the one hand, then, Connor understands performance in the sense that J. L. Austin conceived of in his speech-act theory of doing or achieving something;[6] on the other hand, Connor also understands it in the theatrical sense of impersonating or playing a character. In this investigation, I am particularly interested in examining the loci in the 'Berkoff phenomenon' where these two uses of the word appear to merge – where *act* elides into *enact* and vice versa. In other words, I am concerned with the intersections at which Berkoff performs his 'self' into presence/absence before becoming a new transitory manifestation of 'self' that is constituted by a different sum total of subject positions.

Performance, in the sense both of acting and enacting, pervades the entire Berkoff's *œuvre* and all the processes involved in his construction of 'self'. It goes without saying that his 'self-referential' work in the theatre, as playwright and actor, is where he may be most easily seen to be performing his 'self' into fleeting existence. The performativity of the 'Berkoff phenomenon' is not limited to his *physical* enactments, however, whether theatrical, cinematic or social, but pervades all the media he has employed. This is particularly so in his autobiography, *Free Association*, a work that I use as a constant point of reference throughout this investigation and which I examine in detail in chapter 7. A number of literary theorists (Bruss 1976; Renza 1977; Jay 1984; Sturrock 1993 and others) have examined the performative qualities of autobiography. In her aptly titled study *Autobiographical Acts*, Elizabeth Bruss draws upon speech-act theory to show how autobiography is a dynamic genre that not only states but also *performs*. John Sturrock, too, analyses the performative qualities of the genre. The autobiographer, he writes, is "engaged on an exhibition of self" (Sturrock 1993: 291). Berkoff's autobiography, I suggest, is such an exhibition of 'self'; and the 'Berkoff phenomenon', working across diverse media, is what I should like to call a *macro-exhibition* of 'self'.

Some further notes on terminology

There are some key terms and concepts connected with theatre and performance that are used throughout this investigation which I should like to clarify here. All other definitions that are necessary will be given in the text in the situations in which they arise.

The theatre Establishment – In British society great political, economic, cultural and religious power lies in the hands of what is commonly referred to as 'the Establishment', an elite and mostly male grouping that hails disproportionately from the upper class and frequently receives its education at top public schools and Oxbridge. One component of this is what I shall term the theatre Establishment. The list compiled by Bigsby (1981: 13–14) of leading contemporary playwrights, directors and critics active in Britain during the years 1956–81 demonstrates convincingly the dominance of what he calls the "Oxbridge axis". The theatre Establishment is understood here to refer to the hegemonic network of 'top people' who exercise comprehensive control over mainstream theatre through their homogeneous background, as well as through the machinery of the Arts Council and the drama schools which they largely steer.

Mainstream theatre – This is a contested term. For present purposes it will be understood to refer to the structures (companies and venues) of the subsidised and commercial theatre sectors, namely the National Theatre, the Royal Shakespeare Company, the West End, the provincial theatres which contain repertory companies for at least part of the year, and the fifteen or so substantial provincial theatres which, lacking permanent companies, take in commercial and subsidised productions. Mainstream theatre, certainly during the 1960s, when Berkoff was a beginning actor in regional repertory, and the 1970s, when he was establishing his independent career, was a predominantly middle-class institution in terms of the plays produced, the playwrights who wrote them, the theatre professionals who staged them, and the audiences who filled the auditoria (Jackson and Rowell 1984). Whilst this situation changed considerably during the 1980s with the growth of new minority constituencies, such as gay, women's and Black theatre, and the shift towards more heterogeneous audiences, the funding of mainstream theatre has remained within the grasp of the theatre Establishment, particularly during Mrs Thatcher's second term of office.

Alternative theatre – This term, also much argued about, is understood here to encompass the various types of non-mainstream theatre that emerged from the 1960s counter-culture. Alternative theatre defined itself through its opposition to the aesthetics, values and working practices of mainstream theatre and/or the socio-political *status quo* (Rees 1992). Whilst it was imbued with a counterhegemonic spirit that challenged the sociopolitical and cultural Establishment of the time, I do not follow Itzin (1976), Craig (1980b) and others in assuming that alternative theatre was always and necessarily synonymous with radical political theatre, since, as Kershaw (1992: 47) observes, "it is by no means always easy to distinguish between groups that were 'alternative' in the sense of being simply theatrically different from mainstream practices, and those that were 'alternative' because they pursued an ideologically oppositional policy". Berkoff, as we shall see, has occupied, and continues to occupy, a liminal position that slips between mainstream and alternative theatre.

French total theatre – The term *total theatre* has been applied to a bewildering range of diverse theatrical traditions and styles from *kabuki* to Wagner (see Kirby 1969). Here I will make specific reference to 'French total theatre', about which Innes (1993: 100) writes that:

> The search for 'totality' in one form or another was one of the major motifs in French theatre between the wars. From Barrault the line runs back not only to Artaud with his concept of a theatre that could totally involve the audience, both physically and emotionally: it can be traced through Charles Dullin, Barrault's first mentor ... to the symbolists, and to Copeau's Vieux Colombier, where Dullin received his training. Copeau united a visual stylization derived from Gordon Craig with Adolphe Appia's concepts of rhythmic movement, sculptural lighting and 'musical space' in which actor and setting are united in a single plastic and expressive image.

Since the Second World War the tradition may be traced through to the teaching of Jacques Lecoq, with whom Berkoff studied mime. 'French total theatre', particularly the ideas and practices associated with Artaud, Barrault and Lecoq, as Berkoff has repeatedly emphasised, inspired his own brand of un-English 'total theatre'.

Metatheatre – This term is understood quite simply to mean theatre which is *about* theatre (Counsell 1996: 138). A play or performance that is metatheatrical draws attention to its own status *as* theatricality, and blurs or erases the dividing line between play and real life (Pavis 1998: 210).

Here I use this term in an extended sense to describe how Berkoff has used his work in the theatre to say something about the extra-theatrical 'drama' of his own social life. Thus I approach the play *Metamorphosis*, for example, as metatheatre since it may be seen as an enactment of his troubled relationship with the theatre Establishment (see chapter 4).

Mise-en-scène – This term is commonly translated into English as 'staging'. A useful definition, which I accept for present purposes, is offered by Veinstein (1955):

> In the broad sense, the term *mise-en-scène* refers to all of the resources of stage performance: décor, lighting, music and acting ... In a narrower sense, the term *mise-en-scène* refers to the activity that consists in arranging, in a particular time and space, the various elements required for the stage performance of a dramatic work.[7]

Thus I take *mise-en-scène* here to refer to the elements (and to Veinstein's list one could add sound effects, stage properties, costumes, masks and, in the case of Berkoff's work, mime and choreography) and the deployment of those elements that, taken together, transform a dramatic text into a fully realised theatrical event.

Dramaturgy – Another much debated term. For present purposes, I take it to mean the overall ideology informing a dramatic and theatrical work, namely the intention, design and intended purpose of the playwright and/or director. In this sense I understand it as a form of logocentricism. The term *logocentrism* describes that form of rationalism that presupposes a 'presence' in the form of an idea, an intention, a truth, a meaning or a reference behind language and text. The concept derives, as Counsell notes, from Derrida's idea that "within any discourse or ideology there is one founding principle that is deemed beyond interrogation. It is from this, the Logos [reason], that all the discourse's other claims and formulations derive their status as 'truth'" (Counsell 1996: 93). When I refer to Berkoff's dramaturgy here, therefore, I mean an approach to the conception and staging of a theatrical event that is determined by his intentions and designs as playwright, director, producer and actor; that is grounded, in other words, in the logocentricism of his artistic purpose.

Use of the term *logocentric* in the context of theatre and drama has tended to focus disproportionate attention on the playwright's script as the "the primary element, the deep structure, and the essential content of dramatic art" (Pavis 1998: 384) of the event on stage. However, as Philip Auslander argues, "the *logos* of the performance need not take the form of a playwright's or creator's text. Other grounding concepts include the director's concept and, more interesting, the actors' self" (Auslander 1997: 29). Thus I wish to stress that I do not use the term *logocentric* here merely to describe a dramaturgy that privileges the script (although a script may be one form of logocentricism). In such cases I employ the term *text-based*. My approach to Berkoff's dramaturgy is to see it as logocentric but not (entirely) text-based.

The structure of this book

This book is divided into seven main chapters and a concluding chapter that examine in different ways how the 'Berkoff phenomenon' has been constituted through the discursive strategies employed by Berkoff in the construction of his 'self' and in the creation of his *œuvre*. As I mentioned above, I assume no absolute demarcation line between his creative work and his 'life', since his *œuvre* and his representations of his 'self' flow and blur over any putative divisions between these spheres. Each chapter is concerned with the shifting and often paradoxical or contradictory strategies with which Berkoff has set out publicly to construct and project his 'self'. Within Berkoff's multimedia *œuvre* I will focus mostly on his plays and his autobiography.

The chapters of this book follow a broadly linear chronology, starting with his youth in the East End of London, his drama training, his early years as an actor in repertory, and his establishment of the LTG. Following that, they progress chronologically through his plays and career, and culminate in a discussion of his autobiography, one of his more recent works that offers Berkoff's own best gloss on his career and his 'self'. I do not wish to suggest by this chronological organisation, however, that there is a modernist teleology operating either in Berkoff's construction of 'self' or in his *œuvre*; rather the opposite, namely that the 'Berkoff phenomenon' has come about through expedient acts of *bricolage* on his part. Thus Berkoff may be said to have largely *improvised* his career and the construction of his 'self'.

Chapter 1, 'Jewish East End roots', examines two of Berkoff's key representations of his 'self', namely as a 'Jew' and an 'East Ender'. Having abandoned the proletarian Jewish world in which he grew up, Berkoff pragmatically re-embraced, appropriated and resignified his Jewish and Cockney roots at two key moments in his early career: the staging of *In the Penal Colony* in 1968 and *East* in 1975. He has elaborated these subject positions throughout his career as two of his chief modes of representing his 'self'. In chapter 2, 'Berkoff's interpersonal "self"', I analyse Berkoff's strategy of projecting his 'self' in proximity to certain iconic individuals. I take as two case studies his interaction with the textualised 'lives' of the British actors Edmund Kean and Sir Laurence Olivier, and demonstrate how as a beginning actor he adopted aspects of their physical and intense performance styles in order to authenticate his own approach to acting. In chapter 3, 'The London Theatre Group', I look at how Berkoff, frustrated by his unemployment during the 1960s and his 'marginalisation' by the theatre Establishment, launched his independent career with the formation of the LTG. In particular, I examine his autocratic working style as a director and show how this separated him from the egalitarian spirit of the alternative theatre scene in the late 1960s. Chapter 4 'Confinement and escapology', explores how Berkoff challenged what he has characterised as the naturalistic text-based dramaturgy of main-stream theatre with his own brand of mime-centred 'total theatre'. Using *Metamorphosis* as a case study, I show how he metatheatrically enacted his escape from the 'straitjacket' of mainstream theatre practices prevalent before and during the 1960s. In chapter 5, 'Berkoff's Cockney carnival', I discuss how Berkoff created what, at the risk of employing a seemingly contradictory term, I should like to call linguistically spectacular theatre with his plays *East* and *West*. I show how, with these works, he moved on from primarily physical performance, as in *Metamorphosis*, to claim space for himself as a playwright. I also demonstrate how the language that he synthesised from Cockney slang and Shakespearean pastiche enabled him to create notoriety for himself through its shock-effects and through his carnivalesque parody of the Bard. Chapter 6, 'Berkoff and Thatcher-ism', looks at the shifts in Berkoff's attitude towards Margaret Thatcher and her impact on British life and culture during the 1980s. I examine the three plays *Greek*, *Decadence* and *Sink the Belgrano!* in order to demonstrate how Berkoff, despite expressing 'anti-Maggie' sentiments, has displayed crypto-Thatcherite tendencies as an entrepreneurial producer and purveyor of 'Berkoff', his commodified 'self'. Chapter 7, 'Berkoff's "inner self"', examines how more recently Berkoff turned away from his hitherto accretive adoption of subject positions and set out to reveal what he apparently considers to be his essential 'self' through his writing of and his performances in the two plays *Kvetch* and *Harry's Christmas* and through the text of his autobiography. In the final chapter, entitled 'Conclusions', I argue that the irony and paradox of Berkoff's 'self-revelatory' project is that his attempt to establish the 'pure' presence of his 'inner self' is undone, wittingly or otherwise, by the logocentric strategies he has consistently employed as omniscient Author. I finish with my own assessment of Berkoff's achievement in the light of what he has tried to say about his 'self' in and through his *œuvre*.

Notes

1 Quoted from David Nathan, *Glenda Jackson* (Tunbridge Wells: Spellmount, 1984), 30.
2 Quotations from Berkoff's primary works are cited in the text with abbreviations as listed on p. xiii above.
3 This essay can be accessed from the Berkoff fan site at www.iainfisher.com/berkoff.html, where it is described as a "dissertation by Craig Rosen, Ph.D." No details regarding date or university are provided, however, and neither the Library of Congress nor the British Library has any catalogue entry for this title or its author.
4 Berkoff staged *Metamorphosis*, *East* and *The Fall of the House of Usher* at the Cottesloe Theatre in 1977, and *The Trial* at the Lyttelton Theatre in 1991.
5 Role theory is closely associated with the work of the American sociologist Erving Goffman, in particular his landmark study *The Presentation of Self in Everyday Life* (1959).
6 Speech act theory was developed by the Oxford philosopher J. L. Austin, whose 1955 lectures at Harvard University were published posthumously as *How to Do Things with Words* (1962).
7 Quoted in Pavis (1998: 363).

1

JEWISH EAST END ROOTS

> Above all he began to miss Jews. He had imagined that he was thoroughly anglicized, but only now that he was separated from them did he realize how strong a hold his people had on him. He had never been religious, had rarely attended a synagogue, but this early environment had so seeped into his subconscious that he longed for the sight of a swarthy hook-nosed face, and the loud unabashed sound of a fruity Jewish voice. (Simon Blumenfeld, *Phineas Kahn – Portrait of an Immigrant*)

In this first chapter I focus my attention on two key discursive strategies employed by Berkoff in his construction of 'self' during the greater part of his career, namely his adoption of working-class 'Jewish' and 'East Ender' subject positions. He first elaborated these interrelated and sometimes overlapping discourses at two pivotal moments early on in his career with the apparent intention of validating the public personæ he was projecting through his dramas and productions. His 'Jewish' subject position was first taken up in 1968 through the link he created to the writer Franz Kafka with his first independent production, *In the Penal Colony*, which he had adapted from the latter's story. His adoption of the proletarian 'East Ender' subject position followed swiftly on the heels of the sudden and unexpected success in 1975 of his first original play to be staged, *East*. These two productions and the subject positions associated with them are key elements in Berkoff's construction of his 'self' at the outset of his independent theatrical career, and many of his other subsequent subject positions may be seen as variants of, or as being related to or determined by, these two fundamental discourses.

It is necessary that I recount briefly some of the relevant biographical facts of Berkoff's childhood and youth in the Jewish East End and the relocated Jewish working-class community in Stamford Hill, north London before going on to consider what he later 'made' of his early background. Berkoff was born Leslie Steven Berkovitch on 3 August 1937 and grew up in Stepney. His grandparents were Jewish *émigrés* from Russia who had come to Britain in the 1890s at the height of the mass exodus of mostly proletarian Ashkenazi Jews fleeing the pogroms in eastern Europe (FA: 131, 210–11). Like many of their co-religionists, they settled close to the docks where they had first set foot on English soil in what rapidly became a Jewish ghetto.[1] Berkoff lived in this teeming quarter as a child, but his stay there was discontinuous and short: he was evacuated to Luton in 1942 to escape the Blitz, and stayed one year with his extended family in New York in 1947 (FA: 73–94). In 1950 his family was moved out of the East End permanently to a housing estate in Stamford Hill (FA: 30–46) as part of the London County Council's slum clearance policy. Berkoff's recollections of his early years demonstrate a clear ambivalence towards his Jewish and working-class background, in so far as they chart the radical shift from his initial rejection as a child and a youth of his proletarian Jewish background (whether in Stepney or Stamford Hill) to a later overt embracing of his roots during the early years of his independent career in the theatre as he evolved new working-class 'Jewish' and 'East Ender' subject positions.

Berkoff evidently harboured mixed feelings about his environment as a child. A leitmotif running through his accounts of his early years in the Jewish quarter is the desire or need he felt to escape from it. A typical expression of this is his recollection that as "a youngster living in a two-roomed East End slum I wrote myself a letter about all the things I hoped I might be, so I did feel that there was a destiny somewhere over the horizon. It can't all be like this I thought" (FA: 195). Such sentiments, Berkoff points out, intensified during his adolescence, as he became increasingly aware, through eye-opening spells of work as a salesman in (West) Germany (FA: 164–73) and as a shop assistant and waiter in the West End (FA: 135–6), of the possibilities that existed outside his immediate environment for overcoming his doubly disadvantaged position as a working-class Jew. When he first began to entertain the idea of becoming an actor it was primarily with a view to escaping from a background that, as he puts it, he was "getting thoroughly sick of" (FA: 203).

Berkoff embarked upon drama studies, first on a part-time basis at the City Literary Institute in 1957–58, and then as a full-time student at the Webber Douglas Academy in 1958–59. As a result of his contact with this new and predominantly middle-class milieu, he recalls, he went through a complete transformation: "I changed my life when I studied to become an actor and altered everything about myself until I was no longer what I had been; my metamorphosis between old and new Berkoff was no less a change than that which separates Jekyll and Hyde" (FA: 21). This metamorphosis (a telling word in the evolution of the 'Berkoff phenomenon') was most evident in the attempt to expunge his Jewish Cockney accent, perhaps the most conspicuous marker of his social and ethnic background. This strategy was in direct contrast to the manner in which a fellow-East Ender contemporary at Webber Douglas, the screen actor Terence Stamp, positioned himself among his peers. Stamp (1988: 80) recalls in his autobiography that *not* covering up his Cockney accent caused him no trouble at all in the environment at the drama school. Moreover, it is interesting to compare their respective beginnings in the acting profession. Stamp's lack of shame regarding his background enabled him to capitalise upon his Cockney origins and roguish charm to become a highly successful screen actor and "one of the icons of 'swinging London'" (Caughie and Rockett 1996: 152). By contrast, Berkoff, locked in regional repertory or, worse still, unemployment, failed to gain the mainstream success that, like any young, aspiring actor, he desired (*FA*: 246). While Stamp sported his now fashionable Cockney accent,[2] Berkoff became a kind of 'linguistic refugee', caught in a vocal limbo halfway between a Jewish Cockney accent that he apparently wanted to suppress and a new 'educated' mode of speech that he had imperfectly acquired. Recalling the frustration of 'resting' during the early 1960s, he complains: "True, I did not have the pearly vowels of my heroes Ian Richardson or Alec McCowen, but I did not speak like Alf Garnett either" (*FA*: 21).[3] This vocal liminality has stayed with him throughout his career. One journalist observed in an interview with Berkoff that he "speaks with such a passionate and vivid vocabulary, yet there is a constant shift of accent from Jewish Cockney to mid-Atlantic twang to something very actorrrish with lots of rs where he rolls out his tongue like a carpet". The interviewer adds, significantly, that "[p]eople with chameleon accents are always trying to find somewhere to fit" (Iley 1993). These frequent and sudden shifts of accent have been a constant characteristic of Berkoff's social performance style both as a drama student and later as an 'infamous' public figure.

Berkoff's staging of *In the Penal Colony* in 1968 and his subsequent work with the LTG during the years 1969–75 signalled not just the launch of his independent career but also of an entirely new approach in the way that he related publicly to his Jewish East End background. As we shall see, he re-embraced and appropriated his roots in the service of his public persona, remetamorphosing his 'self' back, as it were, to something approaching an "old Berkoff", minus any of the negative feelings, noted above, that he had formerly harboured about his origins. This enabled him additionally to set about constructing a smooth 'teleology' that could explain and validate the 'new Berkoff' who was beginning to make a name for himself. The original productions of the two plays *In the Penal Colony* and *East*, I shall argue, were nexuses where the threads of his renewed 'Jewish' and 'East Ender' subject positions respectively intersected.

The structure of this chapter is as follows. In the first section, I examine how, and plausible reasons why, Berkoff, having turned his back on his ethno-religious heritage, subsequently adopted an overt subject position as a 'Jew'. I concentrate in particular on the two crucial themes taken up by him of Jewish victimhood and Jewish theatricality. The second section deals with Berkoff's 'East Ender' subject position, and I focus here, too, upon two interrelated aspects, namely street theatricality and villainy. In the third section, I examine how Berkoff has employed two strategies, his photography and his residence in Limehouse, in his attempt to authenticate still further his claim to roots and heritage.

Berkoff the 'Jew'

One aspect of the history of the Jewish quarter in the East End that is crucial to this discussion, since it forms a significant part of the background to Berkoff's adoption of his 'Jewish' subject position, is the hostility that continually threatened its existence. Following a centuries-old pattern throughout Europe, Jews living in the East End became scapegoats for economic woes, and were despised by sections of the English working-class population. The newcomers were perceived as a threat to jobs and homes, as "foreigners" guilty of invading England (Bourke 1994: 198–211). This negative perception of Jews was exacerbated by the prosperity that their self-support and industry brought them within a relatively short period after their arrival. In the course of just one or two decades many Jews were able to overcome their initial impoverishment and elevate themselves socially and economically above the indigenous Gentile proletariat.

As anti-Semitism spread during the early 1930s, the Jewish quarter, with its anarchists and socialists, became the target of the fascist Oswald Mosley and his Blackshirt followers. The bloody climax was reached with the so-called Battle of Cable Street in 1936, a year before Berkoff's birth (Fishman 1979; Husbands 1983). Hostility towards Jews during the last one and a half centuries, in particular the pogroms in eastern Europe, the Nazi Holocaust, and, closer to hand, the anti-Semitism in the East End (*FA*: 74), has provided Berkoff with a considerable fund of accumulated racial suffering which he has invested in the projection of himself as a Jewish *victim*. Yet as we shall see, there has been a conspicuous reluctance or failure on his part to engage in any substantial way with this dark side of Jewish history. Rather, he has invoked this history of persecution self-referentially as a personal metaphor for his own 'exclusion' from mainstream theatre in Britain.

One of Berkoff's strategies for projecting himself as a Jewish victim has been his insistence upon a gulf dividing East End Jews and Gentiles. In his autobiography, Berkoff emphasises what he felt as a youngster to be his separateness from "the other side" of the working-class community, namely "the Gentiles, for whom the Jews had such a fascination" (*FA*: 41). He recalls the first time that he personally became aware of the threatening implications of this division when, as a result of being evacuated to Luton in 1942, he found himself living for the first time among the *goyim*. Having learned something of the anti-Semitic policies of the Nazis, he recalls his shock at hearing from a mischievous schoolmate that if the Germans ever succeeded in invading Britain they would exterminate all the Jews (*FA*: 74). This anecdote enabled Berkoff to position himself retrospectively in 'proximity' to the victims of the Holocaust, the boy and girls who, under the same summer sun, "were experiencing the hell on earth of Treblinka" (*FA*: 74), and thereby elaborate a personal discourse of 'Jewish victimhood'. One strand of this is his recollection of being persecuted and bullied at school, both by other children and by the anti-Semitic 'system':

> I became a victim. Perhaps I always felt this and I was being bullied rather appallingly, though for what reason I could never quite work out. Perhaps the potential victim gives out signals of insecurity or need, and this reinforces the other boys' sense of power. (*FA*: 12)

Anti-Semitism was also prevalent in the Christocentric religious instruction classes where the children were taught that "the Jew killed Jesus" (*FA*: 80). As a result, he recalls, "I always had the horrors of school, where I was beginning to feel like an exile or potential devil incarnate" (*FA*: 80).

The desire to avoid persecution and marginalisation has tempted countless Jews over the centuries, in Britain and elsewhere, to renounce their heritage (in public at least) and assimilate themselves into Gentile society. Berkoff's own family had apparently travelled some distance along this path even before his birth. By the time he was a child, he recalls, "we no longer spoke the quaint language of Yiddish nor went to the synagogue and had emasculated our more exotic-sounding names"

STEVEN BERKOFF

(*FA*: 357). Indeed, Berkoff makes no mention in his writings or interviews of having practised Judaism in any form during his childhood and youth, and one finds in his recollections no accounts of his participation in any Jewish ceremonies or festivals, even the *bar mitzvah*, the fundamental rite of passage for Jewish boys. Conversely, Berkoff has neither expressed an abhorrence of Judaism nor discussed what it means for him personally to be a Jew *without* Judaism.

In the late 1950s, Berkoff evidently set out to complete the process of his own secularisation and assimilation by cutting his ties with the Jewish community in Stamford Hill and studying drama "up west" (*FA*: 66) near Covent Garden and in Kensington: "I decided that acting was a suitable form of escapism", he recalls (*TTM*: 7). The secular seeds planted in him by his parents thus bore secular fruit. Forty years after his 'break out' he declared in one newspaper interview: "My Jewishness – such as it is – is cultural. I've absconded from religious affiliation because I'd rather be a humanist and take the best from all ideologies and religions" (Lambert 1989). On the face of it, then, Berkoff's policy of keeping the religion and heritage of his forefathers at arm's length appears to have been consistent. Yet such a conclusion would gloss over the fact that during the second half of the 1960s Berkoff executed a spectacular U-turn, when, having taken up the playwright's pen, he expediently constructed and adopted 'Jewish' subject positions in and 'around' his first four plays.

In 1965, he wrote his first script, *Hep, Hep, Hep*, a drama dealing with the persecution of the Jews of medieval Lincoln.[4] Although the script remained unproduced until its premiere in 2001 at the Nottingham Playhouse under the new title *Ritual in Blood*, it nevertheless indicates the general drift of his attitudes and preoccupations around that time. Following this, during the years 1968–70, he embraced the works of Franz Kafka, by writing and staging three adaptations: *In the Penal Colony* (Arts Lab, 1968), *Metamorphosis* (Round House, 1969) and *The Trial* (Oval House, 1970). As he explained in what was most probably his earliest published interview, "I was drawn to Kafka, this marvellous Jewish man, and the pain of guilt, the lyricism and mysticism which is a Jewish thing" (Benson 1976/77: 84).

Why did Berkoff, to all intents and purposes a completely secularised 'fugitive' from his ethnic and religious background, re-embrace his ancestors' heritage at that particular time and in such a public manner, and become, as one of the disciples in his later play *Messiah* (2000) says of Jesus, a "Superjew"? The answer lies, I believe, in the common theme that links these four works, namely the victimisation and persecution of the Jews, a narrative that Berkoff applied to himself at a time when he considered (or projected) himself as an artist systematically marginalised by the British theatre Establishment. Looking back in his autobiography at the period leading up to the setting-up of his independent company, the LTG, he asks, with some bitterness: "What could I have not done had someone had the wit and perception to employ me? I was a storm of energy and for the life of me I could not understand why I was getting so little work. What was wrong?" (FA: 21). In one interview (Appleyard 1989), Berkoff estimated that during 1960–68, the period spanning the beginning of his professional acting career and the founding of the LTG, he was employed sporadically for a mere eighteen months. Berkoff's response was to gravitate towards a medieval event and the fictional works of a Czech writer that spoke of the troubled history and culture of his ancestral people and resignify them as metaphors for his own struggle during this unhappy stage in his career.

Berkoff wrote Hep, Hep, Hep after coming across a plaque in Lincoln Cathedral commemorating the 'martyrdom' of 8-year-old Little Saint Hugh of Lincoln in 1255, whose accidental death led to the false accusation of murder and subsequent torture and death of many members of the local Jewish community. They were accused of the "blood libel", of using the blood of murdered Christian children in their Passover rituals. Berkoff recalls that :

> In researching this play what struck me most forcibly was the incredible extent to which the poison of anti-Semitism was part of the fabric of the early church and how much the more reactionary elements irrigated the earth for these poisonous shoots to thrive. (CP, III: 4)

Superficially, at least, Berkoff pursued the theme of the victimisation of Jews and dealt with it metaphorically in his three Kafka adaptations. In what follows I concentrate on In the Penal Colony, since this was Berkoff's first independent production and thus the first public 'unveiling' of his new 'Jewish' subject position. I discuss Metamorphosis and, and to a lesser extent, The Trial in chapter 4 in the context of physical performance.

Kafka first published 'In the Penal Colony' in 1919. In this story, an explorer visits the penal colony, where an officer demonstrates to him the Harrow, an instrument used to inflict capital punishment. The Harrow is an extraordinarily elegant instrument: the condemned man lies face-down on a Bed, while a complex system of needles inscribes the commandment he has broken on his back. The needles pierce deeper and deeper until the prisoner dies. In the process of dying, however, the condemned man finally understands the nature of justice and his punishment. His face is transfigured, a sight edifying to all those who watch. The officer begins to demonstrate the Harrow on a prisoner condemned to die because he was sleeping on duty. The machine was conceived and developed by the former Commandant. It soon becomes clear that the explorer does not approve of the death-machine and that he feels morally bound to express this disapproval to the new Commandant, who is already known to have serious questions about using the apparatus as a method of punishment. Suddenly, the officer removes the condemned man from the Bed, strips off, and takes his place. Before doing so, he adjusts the machine to inscribe "BE JUST". Soon after the Writer begins its grisly work on the officer's back, it malfunctions and goes to pieces, but not before the self-condemned officer has died. Although Kafka's grim parable about inhumanity and justice does not deal specifically with any Jewish content, Berkoff, with the benefit of post-Holocaust hindsight, reinscribed it transhistorically as an "accurate prognosis of Nazism" (FA: 107).[5] Furthermore, the timing of the production in 1968 was significant, since it permitted him to construct a parallel between it and what is arguably the most crucial event in post-Second World War Jewish history, the Six Day War.

Berkoff's only 'engagement' with a contemporary political issue related to the Jews is the brief mention he makes in his autobiography of the short but decisive war which broke out between Israel and its Arab neighbours in June 1967. Characteristically, he treated this major event self-referentially, invoking it not to pass comment on what was happening in the modern Jewish world but in order to create an extra-theatrical backdrop to the premiere of his watershed production of In the Penal Colony. He recalls that "In 1967 we [sic] were all in trepidation, fearing the possible end of Israel" (FA: 292). Significantly, this is the first sentence of a section entitled 'In the Penal Settlement – 1967'. Here one finds no considered treatment of this defining historical moment for Jews, however. What becomes apparent instead is the way that Berkoff reinscribed the timing and events of the conflict with the apparent aim of empowering himself vis-à-vis a 'hegemonic' theatre Establishment. The use of the production as a metaphor for Israel is reinforced by his conspicuous replacement of colony with the loaded word settlement, evoking the image of the occupied territories in the West Bank, Sinai and Gaza, and by his strategy of bringing the time forward by one year (In the Penal Colony was actually premiered a year later in April 1968). In his autobiography, therefore, Berkoff retrospectively adopted the subject position of a 'Jew' preparing to fight for his 'survival' in the theatre by means of his physically realised adaptation of a story by arguably the most iconic modern Jewish author – "the Jews' hero of alienation" (*FA*: 99), as he calls Kafka – and against the evocative backcloth of Israel's struggle to retain its territories. "How we [*sic*] cheered", he writes, "how we exulted in the idea of Israel's deliverance from the jaws of death" (*FA*: 127). In recent years, it must be said, since becoming more secure in his fame and success, Berkoff has moderated his views and become more generous towards the plight of the Palestinians.[6]

As a theatrical event, *In the Penal Colony* may be judged to have been successful. When it was revived in July 1969 on a double bill with *Metamorphosis* at the Round House, Harold Hobson (1969) wrote an enthusiastic notice of both plays, and Anthony Hern (1969), referring to Berkoff's multifaceted achievement as writer, director and actor, entitled his review 'Triple Honours for Busy Berkoff'. Thus Berkoff, like the state of Israel, may be said not only to have 'survived' but also to have increased his claim to 'territory' against all the odds by asserting his artistic independence through an aggressive and provocative performance of Kafka-inflected 'Jewishness'. Berkoff's strategy allowed him to incorporate the combined iconic power of Kafka's story, the Holocaust, and Israel's war against its Arab neighbours into his own discourse of 'Jewish victimhood' at the hands of the British theatre Establishment. Significantly, when asked in an interview over three decades after that production if he suffers from self-doubt, Berkoff reprised the strategy by comparing himself with the embattled state of Israel: "I can't really afford to have too many doubts. I'm like a kind of small state surrounded by unsympathetic nations, so I can't relax my vigilance ... I have to protect my little empire" (Ross 2001).

During this early period of his independent career Berkoff's creative involvement with his Jewish heritage appears, at first glance, to have been considerable. The paradox of this strategy, however, is that it avoided any thoroughgoing critical engagement with Judaism, with the morality of Israel's seizure of territory or with Jewishness in the most general sense. Berkoff admits in his autobiography that he gave up the idea of producing his first script, *Hep, Hep, Hep*, because "'Jewy' themes are difficult to set down without falling into the trap of making all the Jews holy, good, decent and the gentiles villains and cold-blooded tyrants" (*FA*: 278). The original script is not in the public domain, but we may guess at its original conception and content from the later version, *Ritual in Blood*. To judge from this, it seems that Berkoff's rather crude and stereotypical characterisation prevented him from any deep confrontation with this episode of Jewish history. This was certainly the view of a number of critics. John Peter, writing in the *Sunday Times* (10 June 2001), opined that "Berkoff has nothing to say about this terrible story except to present the events: any hope that he might tackle their historical or psychological roots is in vain. The persecutors are either primitive, deluded bigots or lying, greedy, prejudiced Jew-haters of the worst kind." Similarly, Rhoda Koenig, whose review appeared in the *Independent* (6 June 2001), thought that the play lacked "any narrative or psychological complexity".

This tendency towards caricature also determined Berkoff's comic treatment of Jewish themes in the plays *East* (1975) and *Kvetch* (1986). In the former play, the Battle of Cable Street is vividly re-enacted in a ranting tea-time speech by Dad, a parody of a *lumpen* Mosleyite. Yet as Currant (1991: 83) observes, "Dad's tirade in favor of fascism ... is more notable for its physical humor and farcical language than the comments it makes on contemporary politics." In *Kvetch*, Berkoff exposes and exploits what he presents as the Jewish tendency to *kvetch* or worry endlessly (see chapter 7). The stereotypical Jewish characters in this play, "superbly gross caricatures" (Nathan 1991), torment themselves about kosher food, sex, circumcision, and mothers-in-law, all staples of Jewish humour. In both plays, Berkoff clearly exploited familiar Jewish material for its comic potential and avoided engaging with any of the possible implications it may have had for his own 'Jewish' subject position.

Berkoff's habitual reluctance to discuss, in public at least, the religious and political significance of having a Jewish background becomes more obvious when one compares his writings and pronouncements with the works of other Jewish East End writers and playwrights such as Emanuel Litvinoff, Simon Blumenfeld, Bernard Kops and Arnold Wesker, all of whom have demonstrated far more thoughtful interactions with their background and heritage.[7] It is with such writers in mind that Michael Woolf (1995: 128) notes the profound pain experienced by anyone revisiting these roots: "Present meets past in uneasy ways. Comfort and security in the present, for example, contradict historical marginality and suffering in the past. In some degree, material success correlates to an uneasy sense of moral failure." By contrast, Berkoff evokes his own 'marginality' as a Jew in British society and theatre in order to emphasise how he as an *individual* has overcome social and cultural obstacles to achieve success in his chosen field. Yet he avoids seriously questioning the nature and ramifications of this exclusion. When he returns to his roots it appears to be with the nostalgic romanticism of the deracinated rather than the anxiety of the spiritually or politically troubled. Far from finding "an uneasy sense of moral failure" in his *œuvre* one is left with a lingering aftertaste of personal triumphalism.

Berkoff's latterly romantised view of the Jewish East End has enabled him to elaborate one further aspect of the Jewish heritage in his construction of 'self', namely the natural theatricality, as he sees it, of the Jews. Berkoff's descriptions of the quirky individuals he remembers from his childhood in the Jewish quarter focus upon their exotic and eccentric performativity. He recalls, for example, their extravagant voices, accents and gestures:

> Hessel Street was like a tributary of Yiddish life, a stream, everybody speaking Yiddish, shouting, screaming, howling and selling bagels in the street. It fascinated me, this tributary, this foreign tributary like a ghetto. I could be inside the Warsaw Ghetto. It was powerful, awesome, this babble of voices shrieking and crying Yiddish sounds. (Hall 1992)

A similar theatricality was displayed, he recalls, by the members of his large extended family: "When we were young there were always people – a room of relatives – playing cards and all talking at once, wonderful voices with accents and intonations that were like singing, pitched in a tone of ecstasy, a rising tone – a joyful opera of voices" (Lambert 1989). As the same interviewer observes, Berkoff's social performance style is similarly histrionic:

> He acts his most vehement sentences, transforming himself into carnival dancer, soccer hooligan or Jewish tailor with the movements of his body. His dominating presence fills the room, and the intensity with which he speaks and performs – even to an audience of one – is thoroughly un-English.

Berkoff's linking of this performative Jewish culture conjured from the East End with that of the Warsaw Ghetto is significant, since it allows him to ground his 'non-English' public persona and acting style both on and off-stage in the rich culture of a distinct and alien ethnicity.

Berkoff has elaborated this eastern European Jewish heritage into a means of staking a privileged claim to 'Kafka' and thereby signalling his distance from British mainstream theatre. In his autobiography, he states that:

> the Brits cannot and have not had a writer like Kafka and our mainstream theatre cannot and does not present his works on stage as Barrault, Welles, Jan Grossman in Poland, Andrzej Wajda and I do, since the Brits seldom have the kind of imagination to enter the interior of man's soul. (FA: 242–3)

Berkoff's evocation of eastern Europe has also enabled him to draw on his Russian ancestry. In a short section in his autobiography entitled 'Jewish Theatre', Berkoff attempts to link himself through his grandparents to the Yiddish Theatre in Whitechapel and through this to the traditions of the old Jewish Russian Theatre, the Habima. This permits him to speculate that "perhaps trickling down through the years, from Moscow, from the last century, from the early stirrings of *The Dybbuk* with its wild ecstasy and mystery, its poetic grandeur, its dance, its expressions of the deepest wonders, this germ came to me" (*FA*: 357). Berkoff's positioning of himself as a *cultural* rather than a religious or political Jew has allowed him to use this romanticised and rather mystical Russian Jewish heritage as a means of validating both his 'self' and his unorthodox (i.e. un-English) approach to theatre and performance.

Berkoff the 'East Ender'

In 1975, Berkoff's public persona suddenly shot off on a new trajectory, when, already known for his adaptations of literary classics by Kafka, Poe, Strindberg and Aeschylus, he staged his first original play, *East*, at the Edinburgh Festival. Berkoff's performance in the original production of this drama about a gang of juvenile delinquents marked the first public appearance of his tough 'East Ender' subject position, a discourse that would have a profound impact upon the whole of his subsequent career, stamping him with a certain notoriety both on and off-stage. Looking back in a 1993 interview Berkoff declared: "I originate from the East End, although I don't *tawk lark Bob 'oskins*. I'm not a professional East Ender like Michael Caine. I have the roots, they have the façade" (Curtis 1993). With his use of the word *façade*, Berkoff hints at artifice and deception on the part of Hoskins and Caine, thereby appearing to dismiss them as 'stage Cockneys'.[8] By contrast, he has set out to validate his own 'East Ender' subject position through this invocation of genuine roots. To this end, Berkoff has appropriated two key strands of East End working-class culture, namely its street theatricality and folkloric villainy, in his attempt to authenticate his 'in-yer-face' style of performance and his own 'notoriety'. As with his 'Jewish' subject position, however, it is a discursive strategy that is not lacking in irony given that he was evidently quite happy to abandon his past when he went 'up west' as a drama student.

In contrast to someone like Arnold Wesker, Berkoff has nothing positive at all to say about such proletarian virtues as a work ethic or a socialistic commitment to the amelioration of the working class. He is contemptuous both of those working-class people who, like his tailor father, remain trapped in lives of endless toil (*FA*: 28), and of those individuals, like the theatre workers he encountered at the Royal Court in the early 1960s, who expressed solidarity with the revolutionary struggle of the proletariat (*FA*: 186–87). Berkoff's admiration is reserved solely for the working-class East Enders who have succeeded in elevating themselves economically, if not socially, through efficacious *performance*, whether as street vendors, villains or, as in Berkoff's case, actors.

Post-*East* Berkoff has romanticised the everyday life of the East End he knew as a youngster by focusing upon its exuberant and sometimes dangerous theatricality. Berkoff's 'East Enders', like his 'Jews', are *natural performers*. Working-class people, he asserts,

> are the most articulate, the most poetic, the most imagistic [*sic*], the most creative, the most interesting, the most fascinating, the most earthy, the most powerful, the most daring. Middle-class people are the most dull-witted, the most boring, the most stupid, the most atrophied, the most impotent. (Kohn 1989)

This mode of projecting himself as a social inferior yet artistic *superior* has been one of Berkoff's chief subject positions *vis-à-vis* the mainstream theatre and the theatre Establishment. This vital creative energy, honed by the vicissitudes and pressures of an underprivileged and oppressed life, Berkoff argues, has always been the basis of what he considers to be 'true' theatre. Like Mikhail Bakhtin, the theorist of the carnivalesque, who argued that the barkers and vendors of the medieval marketplace were "actors in performances at the fair" (Bakhtin 1984: 153), Berkoff finds this 'natural' theatricality in the patter and spiels of the East End market traders that he witnessed in his youth.

He remembers an enterprising street vendor from his early years in the East End, the so-called "Pen King", who offered him a paradigm for success both as a performer and as a purveyor of commodities:

> Once, as a 13-year-old, I stood behind a stall helping the 'Pen King' on Saturdays and watching this magician draw a crowd while he struck the pen onto the Formica saucer like Moses striking the rock ... I could never sell them like the 'Pen King' ... *but he gave me a taste for drama and drawing the crowds.* (My emphasis.) (Kohn 1989)

In his autobiography he elaborates upon this anecdote to construct an explicit 'teleological' link between this commercial street theatricality and his own subsequent economically 'realistic' approach (in the sense associated with Mrs Thatcher) to theatrical performance. The Pen King, he writes,

> was my guide into the realms of teasing an audience, and like it or
> not I was getting my first taste from behind the stall of seeing the
> customers separated from me by a stage. Be it a stall at Whitechapel
> or the stage at a West End theatre, it's still a stall, where you must
> flog your goods with as much aplomb as your will can summon and
> all your heart has to go into those speeches, that patter, the spiel, the
> act, the legerdemain, the persuasive power of your personality plus
> the faith in your goods. (FA: 26)

The financial profit reaped from a day's graft at the market or the theatre
thus depended directly upon how well the vendor or actor had 'performed'
in the task of 'flogging goods'. For Berkoff, the Pen King's economically
driven performance served as a paradigm for the 'marketplace' of the
theatre:

> How many stages are populated by the phony, the spiritless, the
> pretentious, people who would never sell anything to an audience
> which had not paid its money first. The same people, if they could be
> converted into street vendors, would sell sod all to anyone and be left
> at the end of the day without a crust. (FA: 26–7)

Berkoff, by contrast, has been singularly adept at vending. Indeed, his
career has been largely driven by his desire or need to commodify his art
and his 'self', as a visit to his official website may confirm.

The activities of the East End market vendors may slip into illegality.
An example of this is Berkoff's recollection of watching a friend selling
dubiously acquired goods out of a suitcase on Oxford Street (the basis for
Mike's vending scene at the beginning of the second act of *West*, the
sequel to *East*). The anecdote sets up the following rather myopic observation about social class:

> While most kids of seventeen were playing with themselves or
> worrying what new pop shit to buy, Barry was out there grafting like a
> fiend. While still others are sitting back wondering whether to go to
> Oxford or Cambridge or whether to go into law or the BBC, Barry had
> no choice. Get out and struggle or go to the wall. (FA: 35)

The final sentence seems to echo the thinking of the arch-Thatcherite
Conservative Norman Tebbit, "the 'bovver boy' of the Tory Right" (Sked
and Cook 1990: 423), notorious during the period of high unemployment
in the early 1980s for urging the jobless to get on their bikes and look for
work. It seems safe to assume, therefore, that Berkoff's frequently
expressed declarations of love and empathy for the working class have
never extended to a class-wide sense of socialistic solidarity with the

struggle of the proletariat but rather express his admiration for the vital and fierce individuals that are thrown up by the Darwinian struggle to survive. Berkoff's crypto-Thatcherite leanings, as I term them, are discussed at greater length below in chapter 6.

Another key aspect of working-class street theatricality that Berkoff has drawn upon in his construction of 'self' is the spectacular and rebellious performativity of the youth subculture with which he identified as an adolescent, namely the Teddy Boys. His choice of youth cult was most appropriate both ideologically and aesthetically. Cohen and Rock (1970: 288) write that the Teddy Boy was "the most difficult of the problems that had become associated with post-war youth". They argue that the "Teddy Boys were becoming outsiders who required social control. They were subjected to segregation, ostracism and to the campaigns of various agencies. They were a 'grave social evil'" (296). Berkoff's self-alignment with this particular subculture locates him on the rebellious and proletarian side of the dichotomy that the sociologist Michael Brake (1985: 190) delineates between suburban (middle-class, responsible, adult) and street (working-class, irresponsible, adolescent) culture:

> Suburban culture means achievement at school, responsible family and emotional relationships, commitment and the constructive use of leisure. Street culture becomes a mythical antithesis to this. It is desperate, anti-authority, raw and violent, involved in the defence of symbolic territory.

Concerning the latter grouping, Brake further observes that:

> Once youth has separated itself from adulthood, and made a public dramaturgical statement about their difference from adult expectations of them, they feel free to explore and develop what they are. This is why their image is often deliberately rebellious or delinquent. It quite dramatically emphasises their difference ... This is why youth cultures attract those who feel little commitment or investment in the present state of affairs. It [*sic*] attracts those who feel misunderstood, or that they do not fit, or rejected. (Brake 1985: 191)

Berkoff's career-long 'dramaturgical' projection of himself as a misunderstood and rejected outsider within British theatre is predicated upon a similarly subcultural opposition to the dominant culture represented by the bourgeois, adult theatre Establishment.

Aesthetically, too, becoming a Ted opened up a range of 'self-constructive' performance strategies to Berkoff. The defining element of the Teddy Boy 'act' was the dandified costume, comprising the long

Edwardian drape jacket, drainpipe trousers, fancy brocade waistcoat, brothel creeper shoes, and bootlace tie, all topped by the extravagantly greased and quiffed hairstyle. This costume, Berkoff recalls, was an integral part of how he projected himself at that time:

> You also learned the ability to strut your gear and have a talent to amuse by being the joker or clown by your obsession with fashion, since you would always have your suits tailor-made even if it took a year of saving and many months of privation. A suit was your armour and your colours and further defined your sense of aesthetics. (FA: 15)

The 'stage' on which Berkoff enacted his performances as a Teddy Boy was the dance floor. At the Mecca ballroom, he recalls, "you could be who you thought you were. You created yourself. You were the master of your destiny" (FA: 37), and at another Ted venue, the Royal, Tottenham, he recalls that "you were who you wished to be – warrior, lover, Jimmy Cagney, Tony Curtis, villain, spiv, leader, loner, heavy, Beau Brummel. A salesman. Ugh!" (FA: 34). Thus from an early age, Berkoff had become skilful in reinventing himself through shape-shifting performances.

Another key component of the Ted routine was skill with 'verbals', or fighting talk. He describes friends and rivals from that period of his youth as individuals "who were very articulate and very funny. They'd use all kinds of verbal monstrosities to express things; even make up their own language. You could be demolished with words, and you had to fight back with words" (Walsh 1991). These elements of the Teddy Boy act – self-reinvention; rebellion and non-conformity; theatricality in terms of costume, and physical and verbal performance skills – may seen as emblematic for the way Berkoff has projected himself as a theatre artist, particularly in his play *East* (see chapter 5). Berkoff's account of the aesthetic and ideological performance strategies of the Teds forms an early formative stage in the 'teleological' explanation of his own self-positioning *vis-à-vis* the theatre Establishment and the bourgeoisie. The Teddy Boys were outsiders in British society, just as Berkoff has projected himself as an outsider in British theatre. Yet in both cases, I suggest, the 'marginalisation' was a means towards achieving self-definition through adversity.

Serious crime has long formed the bedrock of the myth and folklore of East End life (Fishman 1979: 101–14). According to Berkoff, the 'natural' theatricality of the working-class people of the East End proceeds from an irrepressible energy that, if not dissipated positively, will erupt in dysfunctional or even criminal behaviour. There is, he argues, "no other way out for the person of no education. You either go into the arts or you go into crime – crime is another *metiér* of highly energistic [*sic*], vigorous, ballsy people who can't find an outlet" (Barber 1996). In such a way, he romantically elevates villains to the status of quasi-artists engaged in the creation of their own destiny through the winning of 'territory' and power. In one interview he presents the notion that:

> The villain in our early environment was a hero. He would go *further* than anyone else. He was a luminous, awesome figure who possessed certain powers. It may have been a paradigm for the idea of the Great Actor who in his own way would be daring, would go *further*. (Appleyard 1989)

In his adolescence, Berkoff recalls, he might well have headed down the criminal route. In his autobiography he describes at some length the experience of being sent to borstal for a short spell after being charged with bicycle theft. Characteristically, he dwells on this anecdote in order to relate the opportunity it gave him to *perform*, clad in his grey lag's 'costume', as a villain. Recalling the whole experience, he writes that "it was starting to feel like those gangster movies I was always seeing of the guys holed up in the Pen. Now I could see what was going on inside. Terrific" (*FA*: 138). In passing it is worth noting that the link between villains and performers created by Berkoff here and in his plays echoes, albeit faintly, the work of the French playwright Jean Genet.[9]

East End villainy in the post-Second World War period was symbolised by the notorious Kray twins, Ronnie and Reggie, who were most violently active during Berkoff's late adolescence and his first years in the acting profession.[10] Fishman (1979: 110) makes the point that the Kray brothers were "the first of the local breed who were not drawn to commit crimes through need or childhood insecurity." In other words, they made a career choice. This view is supported by East End playwright Philip Ridley, writer of the screenplay of Peter Majek's 1990 film *The Krays*, who observes: "The criminality of the sixties, as epitomised by the Krays, was the violence of optimism, a desire to further yourself socially" (Kellaway 1994). Their desire for upward social mobility, as with the Mods whose Italian-suited style they adopted, was expressed through their obsessive sartorial perfectionism (see Figure 1). This, as Berkoff observes, was all part of their social performance:

> They were always immaculately turned out in dark suits and ties. There was something awfully macabre about these strange beasts, since their power over people was more than just the threat of

> violence. It was a willing subjugation to the will of the star, a kind of deification of the leader – you relinquish all pretence to any claims yourself and join the serfdom. (FA: 40–1)

Berkoff thus depicts the notorious twins as star 'performers' who manipulated their 'audiences' through personal charisma and/or violence. In his post-*East* career Berkoff has taken great pains to position himself in proximity to the dangerous aura of the two convicted murderers in order, I suggest, to create and project his own 'notoriety'. In addition to getting to act in the 'drama' of the Krays' world by playing the role of the real-life villain George Cornell in Peter Medak's film mentioned above (see Figure 2), Berkoff was a prominent showbiz guest at Reggie Kray's funeral. In addition, he narrated the television documentary *Reggie Kray: The Final Word* (BBC1, 2001), which was made shortly before the gangster's death.

In the context of Berkoff's interaction with real-life Cockney criminals, it is worth mentioning another iconic villain/performer with whom he has conspicuously aligned himself, namely the 'Great Train Robber' Ronnie Biggs. Berkoff, recalling his encounter with him in 1988 in Brazil while filming *A Prisoner in Rio*, describes the Biggs 'routine':

> He relishes telling me the story of his breakout [from Wormwood Scrubs Prison] as if for the first time, and it's not only fascinating but well told, in the way that only a real working class urban villain could. He holds you in the palm of his hand, and it's an act he's perfected since he now regales tourists with it. (PIR: 40)

The most interesting point about this anecdote is how Berkoff uses it to construct an implicit parallel between an iconic working-class villain engaged in commodifying and performing his 'self' (Biggs hawking 'Biggs' to tourists) and a 'villainous' working-class actor doing likewise (Berkoff purveying 'Berkoff' to his theatre audiences and readers).

Berkoff has positioned himself in proximity to certain East End criminals in order, I suggest, to construct a villainous identity for himself in the promotion of his career. The 'surface' quality of this 'gangster' persona is underscored by three factors. First, there is his stated ambivalence towards this subject position. Looking back at his days as a beginning actor, he states that "I never thought I would be playing villains when I started out into the theatrical world after leaving Webber Douglas. The idea would never have occurred to me" (FA: 339). Nor did it occur to him even at the time he created and performed the role of Mike, the juvenile delinquent protagonist of *East*, since he writes that "[m]y archaeological excavations of my childhood were merely an exploration for writing *East* as an affectionate satire on childhood. *Before this event I had never seen myself in this way*" (my emphasis) (*FA*: 223). And he notes further, that "[t]his was almost an eccentric discovery, my writing and playing *East*, but it had the effect of stamping me as a certain type usually played by the energetic Bob Hoskins" (*FA*: 330).[11] Ironically, though, it was on the strength of his 'dangerous' performance in that production that Berkoff was cast as the gangster Charlie Richardson in the musical biopic *McVicar* (1980). After that, he recalls, "I became a 'villain' on the casting books" (*FA*: 331). For all his ambivalence, therefore, it is clear that Berkoff had unexpectedly hit upon a formula for success. This un-doubtedly explains his attempt to repeat the strategy with *West* (Donmar Theatre, 1983), the sequel to *East*, which he began writing in 1978 (*FA*: 63–4).

The second point concerning Berkoff's 'virtual villainy' is his con-scious manipulation of his 'dangerous' appearance and social behaviour. Having been positioned after *East* as an 'East End villain', Berkoff increasingly 'criminalised' his public persona, both on and off-stage. In other words, he began to fill out and inhabit the role. He adopted a severe 'convict' crew cut, for example, because a "cropped-lawn style made me look harder and thus villainous" (*FA*: 331–2). As for his 'criminal' social performance style, he could still be seen acting the 'villain' in public fourteen years after *East* with such self-consciously notorious antics as his supposed threat to murder theatre critic Nicholas de Jongh following the latter's unfavourable review of Berkoff's controversial production of *Hamlet*. Berkoff recalls that:

> Shortly after this review appeared, I met [de Jongh] in a London bar, leaned over and gave him a bit of my old Stamford Hill repertoire, implying some sort of speedy demise. Of course I was only acting, but he took it seriously – so my acting did convince him after all, which was the point I was trying to make. (*FA*: 59)

From this it can be seen that Berkoff was consciously *acting* the part of a Cockney villain.

Finally, there is the 'co-producedness' of this subject position. Berkoff has been heavily dependent upon the willingness of co-agents to underwrite the construction of his 'East End villain' persona. The editor of the *Guardian* newspaper, for example, by requesting police protection for de Jongh (Lister 1989), lent authenticity to Berkoff's 'murder threat'. In a similar state of panic, the critic Matt Wolf, who had been foolish enough to pen a negative review of Berkoff's production of *Salomé* at the

National Theatre, passed on Berkoff's invitation to discuss it over lunch: "I had visions of us meeting in a back alley somewhere in the East End", he writes, "where he would beat me up with ten of his friends" (Stefanova 2000: 136). Countless interviewers, eager to join in the commodification of 'Berkoff', have willingly affirmed the 'menace' in his appearance by dwelling upon such features as "the glint in the eye suggesting the tor-turer's combination of stoicism and fanaticism" (Mick Brown 1986) and the "cheekbones of chiselled granite [and] severe bonehead crop" (Smith 1985). Most tellingly, perhaps, Berkoff has capitalised on the approval that real-life villains have expressed of his stage and screen performances in the roles of criminals. Following his performance in *McVicar*, for example, Berkoff boasts of "being stopped in the street by heavies who claimed to like my interpretation of the notorious Richardson" (FA: 331), and he recalls with obvious satisfaction that when *West* was first staged in 1983 reformed ex-con John McVicar himself turned up and enjoyed it (*FA*: 70). Finally, it is also worth noting that *East*, and thus Berkoff's 'villain' discourse, received what might be regarded as the ultimate seal of underworld approval when the play was performed by lifers in Worm-wood Scrubs (*MOM*: 24).

Speaking of his 'villainous' public image, Berkoff told one inter-viewer: "I don't mind that *either in life or film* [my emphasis]. The gangster is a risk-taker, non-compromiser and outlaw. He is an outsider" (Phillips 1991). Berkoff has been so successful in merchandising his 'criminal' persona in this way that his film and TV appearances have been almost exclusively as arch-rogues. In addition to the performances in *McVicar* and *The Krays* already mentioned, he played an imprisoned East End hood in the BBC's *Crime Doubles* series (2002); sadistic Russians in *Octopussy* (1983) (see Figure 3), *Rambo: First Blood, Part II* (1985) and *Fair Game* (1995); a Russian mafia boss in *Rancid Aluminium* (1999); a thuggish, bullet-headed French Foreign Legion drill sergeant in *Legion-naire* (1998); a crooked British 'businessman' in *Beverly Hills Cop* (1984) and *Under the Cherry Moon* (1986); a sci-fi corporate villain in *Outland* (1981) and an unscrupulous intergalactic arms dealer in *Star Trek: Deep Space Nine* (1993). Moreover, he played the rabid white-supremacist Flicker in *Absolute Beginners* (1986), King Rua, the father of Attilla the Hun, in the mini-series *Atilla* (2000) and without doubt most ironically, given his Jewish background, Adolf Hitler in the television epic *War and Remembrance* (1989). "After him", Berkoff quips in his autobiography, "you can go no further in villainy" (*FA*: 335).

1 Always immaculately turned out: Ronnie (*right*) and Reggie (*left*) Kray

2 George Cornell (Berkoff) meets his maker in *The Krays*

Appropriation of the East End

Since the mid-1980s, Berkoff has taken further steps to validate his 'Jewish' and 'East Ender' subject positions, and thereby the 'teleological' origins of the 'Berkoff phenomenon', by laying claim to his roots through widely varied strategies. An instance of this tendency was his presentation of a video documentary entitled *East End Through the Ages* (2001), in which he sets out nostalgically to create links between his own life and the history of the area, such as his uncle's role in the Battle of Cable Street. In this section, however, I focus upon how Berkoff has attempted to appropriate the culture of the East End by other means, namely through the lens of his camera and through his conspicuous residence in Limehouse.

In 1992 at the Slaughterhouse Art Gallery in Spitalfields Berkoff staged a photographic exhibition entitled 'Images of the East End'. One commentator described it as a "record of [Berkoff's] once-local market on Brick Lane, in the late Sixties and early Seventies" (Hall 1992). Berkoff's photographic re-creation of a Jewish East End that was all but extinct by the time the exhibition took place sheds much light upon the hyper-reality of Berkoff's 'Jewish East Ender' subject positions. A newspaper article by Berkoff describing the exhibition carries the tellingly possessive title 'Berkoff's East Enders' (Berkoff 1992a), thus implying that the inhabitants of the Jewish East End captured by his camera now in some sense belong to him. This is made explicit in one interview dealing with the exhibition in which Berkoff describes his attitude towards his photographic subjects. "With a photographer's eye", he remarks, "you start to become possessive about what you see" (Hall 1992). Thus the photographed Jews have become commodities, part of the cultural capital that he has invested in his self-construction. In theatrical terms, one might say that they have been positioned by him as support players in the 'social drama' that he has constructed out of his life and career.

Another journalist, visiting Berkoff's office in Limehouse and discovering that it was literally a gallery of these same images, now enlarged, enthused:

> On the walls, great framed photographs that Berkoff took in the Seventies: a wizened old pickle-packer; a furtive tailor hanging out crumpled suits in a line. They are wonderful photographs. Berkoff's past and his memory of it is as crucial to his work as his Jewishness, his London-ness, his physicality and uneasiness with intellectual concepts. (Coveney 1996)

What Coveney failed to comment on, however, was the manner in which Berkoff had raided and resignified the culture of the Jewish East End through the creation, reproduction and relocation of these images. Walter Benjamin has argued famously that "[t]he technique of [mechanical] reproduction detaches the reproduced object from the domain of tradition. By making reproductions it substitutes a plurality of copies for a unique existence … [and thereby leads to] the liquidation of the traditional value of the cultural heritage" (Keat *et al.* 1994: 168). Such detachment from tradition may lead, as Frederic Jameson observes in his discussion of the effects of postmodernism, to:

> the disappearance of a sense of history … in which our entire contemporary social system has little by little begun to lose its capacity to retain its own past, has begun to live in a perpetual present and in a perpetual change that obliterates traditions.[12]

In Berkoff's case, I suggest, the objects and individuals captured in his photographs, plucked from their original contexts and positioned in his

3 Berkoff as the sadistic General Orlov in *Octopussy*

4 Berkoff and his Jewish East End

43

office, now serve primarily to signify his own 'East End Jewishness' in a virtual present devoid of any substantial linkage to history and tradition.

This act of *bricolage* is made clear in a newspaper interview (Macdonald 1996) that includes a full-page photograph of Berkoff sitting in an emphatically proprietorial pose before one of these blown-up images of Jewish East End street life (see Figure 4). The result is a telling collage that, one imagines, Berkoff allowed to be used in the article. An image that, in the setting of the photographic exhibition, was a visual narrative in its own right has now become the backdrop for the far more dominant presence of Berkoff in the foreground. Here one may observe two stages of appropriation and resignification: first, Berkoff's initial act of photography in which he isolated, captured and dehistoricised the images; second, the removal of the photographs from the public sphere of the gallery to the private space of Berkoff's Docklands office, where they were made to serve a personal signifying purpose. This office, transformed by the photographic props and his own social performance, has become a personal 'theatre' in which Berkoff projects a virtual Jewish East End culture in the midst, ironically, of the thriving Bangladeshi community beyond its walls. This space and Berkoff's performance in it recalls the stage directions in *East* which stipulate that "[a] large screen upstage centre has projected on it a series of real East End images, commenting and reminding us of the actual world just outside the stage" (*CP*, I: 7). Berkoff used some of the same photographs that he would later display in his exhibition in the original production of this play, and the background photograph in Figure 4 appeared in the programme of the 1976 revival of *East* at the Greenwich Theatre. The projected East End images, as Berkoff points out, act as authenticating conventions that serve to frame the possible world of the play and his theatrical perform- ance in it. Conversely, these same images, removed from the stage on which *East* was enacted to Berkoff's office, now act as extra-theatrical authenticating conventions whose purpose is to frame and validate his social performance as a 'Jewish East Ender'.

In 1985, Berkoff took up residence in Limehouse, not far from where he grew up as a child. He wrote about this relocation in a 1990 newspaper article entitled 'Treasures of the East: Why I live in Limehouse'. In a later interview he states:

> I tend to be a homing pigeon. The area is familiar to me from the past ... That Hampstead idea of lots of people all of one type, and one class, largely, living on top of one another, is anathema to me. The evil squalor of yuppie restaurants. It's ghastly. In the East End you

have, still, a working class and a wonderful ethnic culture. (Cottam 1992: 40)

There are two ironies here to be noted. First, the East End of Berkoff's youth was also an area populated largely by people of one class living very much on top of one another. Second, the "wonderful ethnic [i.e. Jewish] culture" Berkoff knew as a child has been almost entirely replaced by the more recently established Bangladeshi community (Fishman 1979: 93–5). Berkoff has thus returned to his roots in a *geographical* sense alone. Furthermore, the manner in which he has done so, namely in purchasing a luxury riverfront apartment in a gentrified warehouse (see Figure 5) where the late painter Francis Bacon once lived and where his present neighbours, "the glitzy rich of the riverside" (Schwarz 1991: 82), include such luminaries as fellow-actor Sir Ian McKellen and director David Lean, further problematises his 'East Ender' subject position, since, paradoxically, it makes him an active participant in the embourgeoisment – indeed destruction – of large swaths of the working-class East End brought about by the so-called redevelopment of the Docklands in the 1980s, the flagship policy of Margaret Thatcher.

In 1981 the Thatcher government established the London Docklands Development Corporation, charging it ostensibly with the responsibility

5 Berkoff on the balcony of his Docklands penthouse

of overseeing the regeneration of London's defunct docklands, an area that includes Berkoff's Limehouse. In practice, however, it was a project that far from breathing fresh life into the local economy has actually threatened the traditional working-class culture there. As Palmer (1989: 171) observes:

> The LDDC has ... never been popular with the natives of the empire it rules. It is criticised on four main counts: for being an authoritarian rather than a consultative body; for allegedly 'killing local firms' (as the graffitti say) in favour of big names and multi-nationals; for allowing free rein to developers' architects rather than creating a planned city; and for being socially divisive, building homes for the wealthy and thereby destroying the old sense of comradely good neighbourliness.

Palmer's use of the word *empire* here is telling, suggesting, as it does, the way in which the City colonised the territory to its east, obliterated its indigenous culture and drove out families that had lived there for generations. Berkoff's residence in Limehouse, an implicit act of territorial and cultural appropriation, must be seen against this socio-economic and political background, the ethics of which he has evidently been unwilling to confront.

His penthouse apartment is set inside the shell of a riverside warehouse, a building which, but a few years before, would have been the workplace of local stevedores. Berkoff has described these displaced men as they drink in a nearby pub:

> A group of people, mostly dockers, sit quietly enjoying their pints, life seems simple and the group homogenous; there is no foul fruit machine or noisy juke-box in view, just a solemn and working-class group, comforted by each other's existence. (Berkoff 1990e)

Far from being the expression of his closeness to the local working class community that he evidently intended, however, this condescending and romanticised description succeeds in highlighting the gulf that actually separates Berkoff from it. This view is supported by one interviewer who has suggested that Berkoff "really is in love with the idea of the common man, but not the real one who watches football on Sky and goes to Benidorm for a fortnight and lives in a stone-clad semi. His mythical common man comes from the East End of 50 years ago" (Gibb 1999). Indeed, it comes from further back than that, since the Victorian sociologist Charles Booth's depiction of an East End pub scene at the turn of the nineteenth century is almost interchangeable with Berkoff's. Booth describes

46

perhaps half-a-dozen people, men and women chatting together over their beer ... Behind the bar will be a decent middle-aged woman, something above her customers in class, very neatly dressed, respecting herself and respected by them. The whole scene comfortable, quiet and orderly. (Quoted in Keating 1976: 129)

The manner in which Berkoff has resumed residence in the East End and his romanticised and anachronistic statements regarding the dockers align him less with the indigenous working class than with the yuppies who have taken over the area, of whom Bill Schwarz writes the following:

From the moment the prospective purchaser steps into the estate agent's office he or she will be sold Docklands in terms of its not being 'the East End' – not black, not impoverished, not violent ... Thus it is not just in the imaginations of the dispossessed onlookers that the new residents live a segregated existence. Segregation is the cost which must be paid by those newly arrived to protect them from the old. (Schwarz 1991: 89)

Thus Berkoff's residence in this sanitised, depoliticised, dehistoricised and de-ethnicised 'Cockney theme park' represents, I suggest, the ultimate denial, wittingly or otherwise, of his membership of, or any possible affinity with, the working-class culture of his childhood and youth.

Conclusion

In this chapter I have argued that Berkoff has constructed and deployed 'Jewish' and 'East Ender' subject positions in his attempts to project his 'self', his performance style and his position in British theatre in certain ways. Firstly, he has taken great pains to align himself with two sources (as he has seen it) of 'natural' as opposed to 'schooled' theatricality, namely the street theatricality of his romanticised 'East End' and the mystical quasi-religious traditions of the Russian Jewish theatre. He has also identified himself and his animated 'in-yer-face' performance style with the working-class body language of spivs, market traders, Teddy Boys and folkloric villains in order to validate himself as a 'proletarian' struggling against the hegemony of a middle-class theatrical and cultural Establishment. In other words, finding himself rejected by the West End, he re-embraced the *East* End; discovering that he could not relate to 'English' theatre, he projected himself, through his eastern European Jewish heritage, as 'un-English', a 'non-Brit'.

Secondly, he has projected an image of himself as an East End 'hard man' or 'villain' in order to create a highly saleable aura of danger around his celebrity. This is arguably the strategy that has served him best throughout his career as a means of thrusting himself into the limelight. Having stumbled upon this recipe for success with his play *East*, Berkoff has worked assiduously at nurturing his 'virtual villainy' with a wide variety of discursive strategies, including his threats of violence, his 'dangerous' appearance, his conspicuous links to East End gangsters, his villainous roles in films, and his resumed residence in Limehouse. Prior to this, Berkoff had projected himself as a 'Jewish victim'. As he became more and more successful, however, the 'victim' subject position yielded to the aggressive 'hard man' strategy, the bullied mutated into the bully.

For all the sophistication with which these interrelated 'Jewish' and 'East Ender' discourses have been constructed and deployed, however, they explain more about what Berkoff is *not*, since he has not predicated them (publicly at least) upon any substantial examination of or dialogue with his early background. His non-engagement with the religious or political implications of his 'Jewish' discourses, for example, demonstrates his actual distance from the heritage he has sought to appropriate. Similarly, as we saw, his separateness from his proletarian roots is evident in the way in which he has returned to his working-class roots by living in a luxury Docklands apartment. Berkoff's evocation of Jewish history or of the working-class culture of the East End has been consistently self-referential. His appropriation of a romanticised Jewish East End, I suggest, has been an elaborate macro-act of *bricolage* whereby he has taken and resignified aspects of this rich and vibrant heritage in order to construct and project certain crucial aspects of his public identity.

Notes

1 By the outbreak of the First World War, the population of the Jewish quarter in the East End exceeded 142,000 (Palmer 1989: 106). As the immigrants established themselves and moved out of the ghetto, so their numbers began to decline, falling to around 85,000 in the years immediately prior to Berkoff's birth (Lipman 1954: 169).

2 In the chic 'classlessness' of Swinging London, the Cockney accent, natural or manufactured, enjoyed sudden 'street cred' prestige. According to George Melly (1989: 94), both Mick Jagger and the Rolling Stones' manager Andrew Loog Oldham, to cite two famous examples, spoke a contrived "classless cockney", and Robert Hewison (1987: 73) notes that fashion photographers such as David Bailey, Terry Donovan and Terry Duffy "appeared on the scene with cultivated East End backgrounds". Stamp, like Michael Caine, enjoyed iconic status at that time largely as a result of being the 'real thing'.

3 Ian Richardson and Alec McCowen are both associated with their work with

the RSC and with their many performances on stage and screen as upper-crust Englishmen. Alf Garnett was the main character in the immensely popular BBC sitcom *Till Death Us Do Part*, which was written by Johnny Speight and first broadcast in 1964. The racist bigot Garnett, played by the Jewish East End actor Warren Mitchell, delivered his xenophobic rants in a broad Cockney accent.

4 The intriguing title refers, Berkoff explains, to the strange cry "uttered by the crusading knights as they swept down on the unbelievers. The letters are an acronym for 'Hierosolym est perdita'. Jerusalem is lost" (*FA*: 278).

5 In his notes for the programme of the original LAMDA production, Berkoff wrote: "Kafka's vision of a man-destroying machine was to be a terribly accurate premonition of events that were to take place only a few years later. Kafka was spared the agony of seeing his vision coming true in the ovens of TREBLINKA etc."

6 In the section entitled 'Letter from Israel' in his travel diary *Shopping in the Santa Monica Mall* (2000) Berkoff writes: "My opinion is that at the moment those who have the most zeal for our Lord are cracking the very foundations of the Israeli state. With a Palestinian state there is a chance for an ultimate, historic destiny between the Jew and the Arab ... By being generous you win; witness the peace with Egypt after trading Sinai for an historic pact" (p. 183).

7 See, for example, such autobiographical novels as Emanuel Litvinoff's *Journey Through a Small Planet* (1972), Simon Blumenfeld's *Jew Boy* (1986) and *Phineas Kahn – Portrait of an Immigrant* (1988), Bernard Kops's *The World is a Wedding* (1963) and *The Dissent of Dominik Shapiro* (1966), and Arnold Wesker's short stories *Six Sundays in January* (1969) and *Said the Old Man to the Young Man* (1978). Wesker, though a secularised Jew and socialist, has continued to examine his relationship to the Judaism in such plays as *The Old Ones* (1972), *Shylock* (1977), *Caritas* (1980), *When God Wanted a Son* (1986), and *Blood Libel* (1991).

8 In the case of Caine, at least, this is an unfounded criticism, since, as Peter Stead (1989: 201) notes, "Caine had impeccable working-class credentials: he was born in 1933 in an unfashionable area of London's South Bank, his father was a fish porter in a fish market, and his mother was a charlady; before taking up acting he had worked in a meat market." Berkoff's swipe is perhaps motivated by the fact that, as Stead points out, Caine's destiny was to be "the pioneer of new era in the fictional representation of cockneys" (201), the destiny that Berkoff evidently saw as his own.

9 Given that, in the words of one commentator, Genet's "view of theatre as an act of revolt against society has been conditioned by an early life spent largely in correctional institutions and prisons" and his novels glorify the criminal (Hartnoll 1993: 321), it is striking that Berkoff makes no mention of him other than to record briefly in his autobiography that he saw *The Screens* (*FA*: 116) and *The Blacks* (*FA*: 187) staged.

10 The best accounts of the joint career of the Kray twins remain Brian McConnell's *The Rise and Fall of the Brothers Kray* (London: David Bruce & Watson, 1969) and John Pearson's *The Profession of Violence* (London:

Weidenfeld & Nicolson, 1972). Since the deaths of the Kray twins, the folk mythology surrounding them has spawned a thriving cottage industry with relatives and former associates reminiscing in books and on videos. One account that strips away the glamorous mythology is Craig Cabell's *The Kray Brothers: the Image Shattered* (London: Robson Books, 2002).

11 See, for example, Hoskins's performances as East End villains in the films *The Long Good Friday* (1979) and *Mona Lisa* (1986).

12 Quoted from Kershaw (1994: 167).

2

BERKOFF'S INTERPERSONAL 'SELF'

Each one of us is lots and lots of people. Any number, because of all the countless possibilities of being that exist within us. The person you are with me is quite different from the person you are with somebody else. (Luigi Pirandello, *Six Characters in Search of an Author*)

In this chapter I examine one of the discursive strategies most frequently employed by Berkoff in his construction and projection of 'self', namely his tendency to identify with certain iconic individuals, whether fictional or real-life. In his adaptations of works by other people, he has routinely transformed the protagonists into Berkoff-alter egos. Writing about the hero of *The Trial*, for example, he states: "I was K" (*TT*: 5), adding "Joseph K.'s mediocrity was mine and his ordinariness and fears were mine too: the 'under-hero' struggling to find the ego that would lead him to salvation" (5). The protagonist of Poe's *The Fall of the House of Usher* is another example. "To play Roderick Usher", he writes, "is to know him. One cannot approach such a life as Usher's without absorbing his texture" (*AFHU*: 37). As for Berkoff's self-referential resignification of Shakespeare's Danish prince, it is perhaps sufficient to note that he gave his published commentary to that production the title *I Am Hamlet*. As for his own creations, the main characters in most of Berkoff's original plays and stories could be added to this list of 'Berkovian selves' – Les and Mike in *East* and *West*, Harry in *Harry's Christmas*, Eddy in *Greek*, Steve in *Acapulco*, Steve in *Kvetch*, Actor in *Actor*, Harry (H) in the *Gross Intrusion* collection of stories, and so on – since they are all to a greater or lesser extent similarly self-referential. My concern in this chapter is to investigate how and why Berkoff has identifed his 'self' with certain real-life personalities.

There is a crucial passage in his autobiography in which Berkoff appears to conceive of his personality as a network of discourses constructed from identifications with and 'quotations' from the lives, character traits and experiences of various famous individuals:

> I have been many people and changed like a chameleon. Sometimes
> I identify very strongly with Kafka and become absurdly withdrawn,
> cryptic, observing the world from deep within my private body which
> is not accessible. I become like the bug [in *Metamorphosis*]. An out-
> sider, unloved, given to deep probings and guilt and yet with a sense
> somewhere of my superiority in pain. Other times I wish to be Kean
> or Irving, striding important stages and either galvanizing the
> audience like Kean and making myself a sacrifice; being consumed
> by the flames of my own passion, like an Artaud; or like a Wilde,
> sensual, loving, pained by the world's abstruseness and predictability
> and sitting alone on my pedestal of words with which I enchant the
> world. Other times I think of Norman Mailer, a literary pugilist
> stamping on and punching anything that criticizes. Or a Poe who is
> stripped bare to the nerves, skin pulled back and raw. And other
> times plain dull and ordinary me, gripped by indecision and loathing
> my quandary and lack of work. (*FA*: 176–7)

From this statement, it appears that Berkoff's conception of his own
subjectivity conforms to the pattern of classic role theory in two key ways:
firstly, he approaches iconic individuals as roles or personæ that he may,
as a *bricoleur*, appropriate, resignify and embody in order to act out certain
aspects of his 'self'; secondly, he assumes the existence of a core
personality lying constant and unitary beneath these social wrappings:
"plain dull and ordinary me", the 'real' Berkoff, in other words.

In the following discussion I take two of the most significant of
Berkoff's identifications with real-life individuals – his self-alignment
with the English actors Edmund Kean and Laurence Olivier, or rather the
spectral textual constructs that I signal here as 'Kean' and 'Olivier' – as case
studies in order to examine how Berkoff has conceived of, constructed
and projected his subjectivity. Crucially, I approach these interpersonal
subject positions as *performative* rather than descriptive discourses, both
in the sense of how they have made certain things happen in the process
of Berkoff's public construction of 'self' and how they have contributed to
his elaboration and justification of an intense and physical acting style.
The chapter is divided into three parts. The first section deals with
Berkoff's accounts of the early stages of his theatrical career as a student
and as a beginning actor in regional repertory during the years 1957–65.
My purpose in presenting this background material will be to show how
Berkoff, a working-class reject of the education system and an outsider in
mainstream theatre, was compelled, according to the logic of his constructed 'teleology', to adopt new strategies to authenticate his unorthodox
acting style. In the second section, I focus upon Berkoff's identification

with the nineteenth-century tragedian Edmund Kean and show how he used this strategy to validate his social class and aspirations, and to legitimise his maverick position within British theatre as a self-educated and marginalised proponent and exponent of physical performance. Finally, in the third section, I look at how Berkoff expressed his paradoxical desire to be recognised by a theatre Establishment he apparently abhorred through his love for and desire to be loved by one of its greatest figureheads, Sir Laurence Olivier.

Berkoff the beginning actor

Berkoff claims to have been burdened with a sense of alienation and unwantedness during his late adolescence. He recalls having seen himself as a "misfit" and a "weirdo" (McAfee 1991). In addition to what he has characterised as his doubly marginalised position in British society as a working-class Jew, his sense of anomie appears to have been exacerbated by what he has portrayed as his rejection at the hands of the education system. A typical expression of this is the following recollection of his experiences at a school in Manor House, north London:

> For some stupid reason the headmaster saw fit to place me in a 'C' stream, although I had been in an 'A' stream at the famous Raines Foundation School. I was unbelievably depressed and tearful, and remember going home that lunchtime with a fearfully heavy heart. After that demotion I couldn't care less, and no longer took any interest in school. What idiot did this to me, when I was a bright spark – with my proud end-of-term reports? I don't think I fully recovered, and went rapidly on a downward lunge which eventually led to juvenile courts. And I can trace it from that first lunch time [sic] when I crossed Hackney Downs with tears in my eyes and feeling like a stupid shit. (PIR: 180–1)

This theme of his 'exclusion' by the educational system recurs as a powerful leitmotif throughout his autobiographical writings and interviews, prompting one reviewer of his autobiography to assert, correctly in my view, that Berkoff is "positively hag-ridden by intellectual inferiority" (MacDonald 1996). Such inferiority certainly appears to haunt the following wistful recollection of wandering around Cambridge while appearing in repertory in the Arts Theatre there in 1962:

> Punting down the Cam like a Cambridge student. Sniffing out the tea rooms and walking past the great colleges and soaking in the atmosphere of the past. Imagining life at Trinity and hardly being able to conceive it. Liking to walk in the grounds of the college and admiring

the great cathedral [*sic*] with its flying buttresses and the grand
network of arches in its vaulted ceiling. Staring up at it day after day,
with a pull, a tug of some desire for I know not what. (*FA*: 248)

These are manifestly the reflections of a person who was not invited to the party. Berkoff's unhappy relationship with the educational system (at least as he has characterised it) exactly mirrors his career-long relationship with the theatre Establishment, a relationship coloured, on his side, by an abiding sense of exclusion and a futile desire for inclusion. Given this background, Berkoff's decision to commence drama studies in 1957 was, I suggest, a strategy of self-empowerment through the acquisition of education: a characteristically direct and aggressive attempt on his part to storm the bourgeois citadel.

Despite the initial "deep satisfaction" (*FA*: 111) he recalls gaining from studying, and the freedom it offered him of becoming a 'new person' (de Jongh 1989), Berkoff continued to suffer from a sense of dislocation at his two drama schools, the City Literary Institute and the Webber Douglas Academy. This was almost certainly due to his growing awareness of possessing what Paul Willis, in his analysis of how and why young working-class males resist the education system, has termed the "wrong educational decoders" and the "wrong class culture" (Willis 1977: 128). Although, as already noted, Berkoff underwent a "Jekyll and Hyde" metamorphosis upon becoming a drama student, two things appeared to have stayed with him from his early years in the East End and Stamford Hill: an almost total ignorance of dramatic literature and, as compensation for this startling lack, an instinct derived from the street theatricality of the Jewish East End for physical rather than text-based performance practices. Both of these elements greatly influenced how he positioned himself (and how that 'self' was positioned) as a drama student and as a beginning actor in regional repertory. They were also key factors later in the shaping of his body-based dramaturgical style with the LTG.

One incident may be taken as emblematic of the 'conflict' that, according to Berkoff, ensued between himself and the drama schools. A certain teacher at the City Lit, identified by Berkoff simply as "Red Beard", gave his students the task of selecting and memorising a speech from a play for a performance exercise in a later class. This assignment evidently placed Berkoff in a quandary, since he recalls with astonishing frankness that at that time "I had never read a play and had little interest in the ones that I now read" (*FA*: 213). His response was to attempt to circumvent his teacher's requirement that he use a published play text (an approach that, given his self-acknowledged inexperience as a reader of plays, threatened to position him as 'under-educated') and turn to the relative *terra firma* of his favourite writer at that time, Franz Kafka. Specifically, he set about dramatising the short story by the Czech writer entitled "The Bucket Rider" (*FA*: 213–14). Berkoff's strategy was additionally unorthodox in that he experimented with physical acting at a time when drama schools in Britain generally had little or no interest in fostering skills that were based on the expressiveness of the body.[1]

Berkoff has projected his approach to performance, employing the resources of what he has called "the marvellous vocabulary of working-class body language" (*FA*: 2) not merely as a strategy to cover the gaps in his formal education at that time but as a class-inflected challenge to his teacher's bourgeois obsession (as he apparently saw it) with text-based performance. In this context, it is useful to consider the French sociologist Pierre Bourdieu's notion of the disenfranchised working-class body as

> perhaps one of the last refuges of the autonomy of the dominated classes, of their capacity to produce their own representation of the accomplished man [*sic*] and the social world, that is being threatened by all the challenges to working-class identification with the values of virility, which are one of the most autonomous forms of their self-affirmation as a class. (Bourdieu 1984: 384)

One could say, on the basis of this, that Berkoff, deploying the resources of his 'working-class virility', was projecting himself as a guerilla fighter engaged in the struggle for 'space' against the textual and vocal preoccupations of a hegemonic and disciplinary system of drama training.

Upon presenting his physically realised Kafka dramatisation in class, Berkoff found himself disciplined in a most direct manner: Red Beard rejected it – "we want a play not a story", Berkoff was told (Benson 1976/77: 84) – and compelled his deviant student to follow the officially sanctioned script-based path. As a consequence of this, Berkoff recalls, "I sat and read the most dreary bunch of plays and could find little that made any impact on me, since plays are indeed hard to read and must be seen" (*FA*: 214). As he apparently perceived it, the teacher's strategy was also an implicit rejection of his body and its performativity, his supposedly inferior social class, and even, one could say, his 'Jewishness' (through the link to Kafka). In short, it represented a comprehensive rejection of Berkoff as a *person*. Chris Weedon (1987: 121), discussing the ideas formulated by Michel Foucault in *Discipline and Punish* (1979), makes the point that:

> power is shown to take the forms of the surveillance and assessment of individuals, realized in the practices of state institutions, such as

prisons, schools, the army and the workplace. These institutions
discipline the body, mind and emotions, constituting them according
to the needs of hierarchical forms of power such as gender and class.

To these hegemonic institutions one could add mainstream drama schools
(and the whole apparatus of the British theatre Establishment in the
1950s and 1960s) that sought, according to Berkoff, to position him at the
bottom of its pyramid of power.

Characteristically, the feisty Berkoff has claimed the last word in this
discursive power-struggle. In 1972 he dusted off his adaptation of 'The
Bucket Rider' and staged it as a curtain-raiser to *Metamorphosis*, describing
it in a letter to this writer as "one of my small earlier experimental
productions of trying [*sic*] to create the physical life of the written text".[2]
The result, the *benefit* even, of what he has characterised as his lack of
formal schooling, therefore, was that it prompted him to rebel against a
purely script-based approach to dramaturgy and attempt to validate
himself and his acting style by exploring the potential of physical
performance. The *Bucket Rider* adaptation anticipated, at least within the
terms of his 'teleological' career, the strategy that Berkoff would adopt
during the years 1968–70, when he launched his independent career
with his physical dramatisations of Kafka's 'In the Penal Colony',
'Metamorphosis' and *The Trial*.

Berkoff suggests how his need for self-assertion and self-empowerment became particularly acute during his second year as a drama
student. Linked to the educational 'inferiority' noted above, his sense of
dislocation and alienation was exacerbated by what he apparently
perceived to be his social inferiority *vis-à-vis* the predominantly middle-
class teachers and students at the Webber Douglas Academy, a "rather
cosy finishing school" (Berkoff 1989b) situated in affluent Kensington.
He recalls that on his first day there he "wandered in, nervous and
timorous, and sniffed around" (*FA*: 110). This image of him as a defensive
and insecure figure – as a kind of stray dog, a *pariah* almost – is borne out
by fellow-student Terence Stamp, who writes in his autobiography that
"Steven Berkoff was a loner. Dressed in existential black, his big still eyes
missed nothing. He never spoke much" (Stamp 1988: 81). Given the
facility and readiness with 'verbals' that Berkoff has claimed as his
birthright from the mean streets of the East End, it is significant that he
should have apparently lost or suppressed his 'voice' upon entering
Webber Douglas. One explanation for this may be that he was offering
passive resistance to being positioned. Apparently aware of his educational and social 'inferiority' and expecting, following his experience with

Red Beard, as yet unknown disciplinary measures, he deferred in his adoption of a clearly defined subject position and chose instead to remain silently liminal. He appears to have been reluctant to assert himself by 'speaking up' and thus risk being positioned by those he came into contact with, since, as Weedon (1987: 119) argues, "[t]o speak is to assume a subject position within discourse and to become *subjected* to the power and regulation of discourse." Uncharacteristically, therefore, in the light of what is known about Berkoff later in his career, his strategy as a drama student at this time was to remain silent and withdrawn, and thereby make himself unpositionable by his social and educational 'superiors'.

Berkoff's professional stage acting career began immediately upon leaving Webber Douglas with his debut performance in the role of the longshoreman Louis in Arthur Miller's *A View From the Bridge* in August 1959 at the Bradford Alhambra (*FA*: 225). The 1959–60 season continued with small parts in such genteel dramas as *Tea and Sympathy, Hot Summer Night, The Unexpected Guest, The Seventh Veil, Gilt and Gingerbread, Murder at Midnight, The French Mistress, The Stepmother, Not In the Book, How Say You?,* and *Murder on Arrival* (*FA*: 234). A patchy pattern of employment continued during the early 1960s: in 1961 he played the minor roles of Raymundo in Arnold Wesker's *The Kitchen* at the Royal Court Theatre (*FA*: 184–9) and the sixth bellboy in Arthur Kopit's *Oh Dad, Poor Dad, Mama's Hung you in the Closet and I'm Feeling so Sad* (*FA*: 240–1); in 1962 he appeared in Frederick Knott's *Write Me a Murder*, and was cast, somewhat improbably, as Henry VIII in Robert Bolt's *A Man For All Seasons*; in 1963 he performed in *Semi-Detached*; and in 1964 he took the role of Sherwin in *Sir Thomas More*. As Berkoff saw it, these engagements gave him little or no scope for self-expression, since he found himself acting in productions (*The Kitchen* excepted) in which neither theatrical experiment nor self-expression – certainly in terms of physical performance – were possible or even desirable. Not surprisingly, therefore, his recollections of the plays in which he appeared during those years constitute a litany of scathing and dismissive judgements: *The Great Sebastians* by Howard Lindsay and Russell Crouse, for example, was a "bizarre melodrama" (*FA*: 235); Knott's *Write Me a Murder* was "a piece of cod" (*FA*: 250); Hugh Walpole's *The Cathedral* left him feeling "distinctly uncomfortable" (*FA*: 235); Kopit's *Oh Dad, Poor Dad* was a "fiasco" (*FA*: 248); and *The Amorous Prawn* was "a fairly silly play" (*FA*: 227). Clearly, mainstream theatre, at least at the regional rep level, was not the most suitable environment for Berkoff the ambitious, young thespian to stretch his wings in.

In *Theatricality* Elizabeth Burns argues that "the actor, as man or woman *in propria persona*, is first and foremost an interloper. He [*sic*] intervenes between the playwright and the audience so as to make the fictive world, *signified* by the first, a set of *signifiers* for the social reality of the latter [original emphasis]" (Burns 1972: 146). Viewed in this way, Berkoff, the working-class actor most at ease, he tells us, with his own 'natural' street-schooled physicality, found himself called upon to intervene between, on the one hand, middle-class playwrights (and directors) who were locked into traditional text-based practices and, on the other, middle-class audiences that created the demand for such theatre and for whom he lacked empathy. Looking back in one interview at the mainstream theatre in Britain at that time, Berkoff voices the complaint that "[h]ere we were seeing the theatre as a mirror image of society and that was a middle-class society. So success duly depended on how close the image was to the dullards who sat with their chocolates in the stalls" (McAfee 1991). His scope for participation in what was unfolding on the stage in any meaningful way, therefore, was drastically curtailed by the narrow social focus of the plays and of the institution in which he was working.

Berkoff's experience of performing in the role of Aircraftsman 'Taffy' Evans in a production of Terence Rattigan's *Ross* at Leatherhead in 1962 is paradigmatic. He recalls that:

> The week sped past with a few vague memories of a Welshman saying things with an accent as if I had beamed dead thoughts from distant galaxies. Most plays left me like that, with no aftertaste, just a gradually fading impression of something a little bit lifeless posing as some nourishment. You put it in your system and it goes through like polystyrene. (*FA*: 247)

Berkoff characterises his performance in this play, a drama about the Oxford-educated classical scholar, iconic British Army officer and hero T. E. Lawrence ('Lawrence of Arabia') before, in all probability, a well-heeled stockbroker belt audience as an index of his own socio-economic and cultural exclusion. This is particularly so since he played the minor role of a lowly aircraftsman and was required to speak in a regional dialect. In other words, he was playing the part of somebody outside the *English* social elite. His sense of his 'marginalisation' is evident in his statement that "[t]here is a showbiz myth that those who can 'do' accents are not good actors but have a cheap and trivial facility to capture an echo or trait by impersonation. There are even those who think that stooping to impersonate accents is in some way unredeeming for the great classical actor" (*MOM*: 101). The implication here is that the great classical actors are by definition, or at least appear on stage as, members of the upper echelons of English society – of the Establishment, in other words. Such performers have no need of dialects, following Berkoff's line of thought, since they are speaking the only form of English that counts.

Berkoff has frequently voiced his frustration with the mediocrity and inadequacies of the repertory system. In one interview he is character-istically acerbic in his assessment of his fellow-performers (the English performers at least) at that time:

> When I came into this business I was very surprised to find a lot of good and honest and committed people. Sensitive people. I was especially friendly with a group of Irish actors who, like me, felt them-selves to be outside the English system. The Scots and Irish actors were the most articulate and vociferous. In retrospect I think that the English actors of that time were particularly unadventurous and incredibly dull. They were a bunch of stupid dullards. (Cottam 1992)

As far as Berkoff was concerned, therefore, the two parties on either side of the proscenium arch, performers and spectators – middle-class "dullards" alike, in his estimation – were engaged in perpetuating each other's social and aesthetic values, namely those of the English bourgeoisie. His response, as a 'proletarian European Jew', was to align himself with other marginalised groups in British theatre, not only on account of their being non-English but also because they seemed to share his expressiveness and openness to European influences. If the acting style in English mainstream theatre in the 1940s and 1950s was pre-dominantly text-based then 'European' acting was equated (generally dismissively) with *physical* performance. Shellard (1999: 17), discussing the foreign influences upon English postwar drama, observes that:

> This fresh artistic contact introduced new techniques in acting, with Jean-Louis Barrault and the Comédie Française at the Edinburgh Festival in 1948 illustrating how English actors performed primarily with their voices whilst their French counterparts utilised the entire body. Brecht's stress on the "Gestus" of a performer, with body move-ment unlocking textual meaning, was to prove similarly illuminating.[3]

I examine in detail how Berkoff turned to French models for inspiration when he established his independent theatre company in chapter 3.

As we have seen, Berkoff found himself at the outset of his career on what he considered to be the lowest and most mediocre rung of main-

6 Berkoff as Jerry in Edward Albee's *The Zoo Story*

stream theatre; nevertheless, like most beginning actors, his ambition at
that time, he recalls, was to achieve recognition on the West End stage:

> I continued my peregrinations round the country in one crummy rep
> after another. Never mind. I was in the third division, that was true,
> but I was hoping that one day I would hit the first. Birmingham,
> Liverpool, Manchester – these words were like the top division in
> acting as in football and you knew that if only you could get there
> your problems would be over. You would be "discovered". But first
> the weary weekly reps and one-offs. (*FA*: 246)

In the midst of such mediocrity there was only one aspect of British
mainstream theatre at that time which met with Berkoff's unequivocal
approval and with which he has consistently identified himself. That was
the bold charismatic acting of certain stars who succeeded in combining
with virtuosity the vocal and the physical aspects of performance. Berkoff,
usually reticent when it comes to praising his fellow theatre practitioners,
has openly expressed his high regard for the work of such performers as
Peter Wyngarde, Alec McCowen and Christopher Plummer (*FA*: 245–6;
Appleyard 1989). There was a brief moment in 1965 when, as a result of
being inspired directly by Plummer's physical interpretation of Hamlet,[4]
he enjoyed his first taste of success by giving what he considers to have
been a similarly expressive physical performance in the role of Jerry in
Edward Albee's *The Zoo Story*, at the Theatre Royal, Stratford East (see

Figure 6). He recalls that "I had unlocked a way of seeing character and *let it fill my whole body* [my emphasis]" (*IAH*: 63). This key moment in his early career demonstrates how Berkoff's regard for these performers moved beyond passive admiration to become an active strategy with which he set out to justify his own emerging acting style. The clearest indication of Berkoff's respect for this kind of 'big acting' is the admiration that he has frequently expressed for his two greatest actor heroes, Edmund Kean and Sir Laurence Olivier, two individuals with whom he has identified himself most particularly.

Berkoff and 'Edmund Kean'

Berkoff has stated that Edmund Kean (1789?–1833), the legendary English tragedian, was one of his greatest inspirations as a drama student and a beginning actor. A brief recounting of the facts surrounding Kean's life may explain the appeal he held for the frustrated young man. Born out of wedlock, Kean grew up amid considerable hardship. At the age of 15, having enjoyed only a rudimentary education, he joined a company of actors in Kent. For the next ten years he lived the hard life of a strolling player. Kean finally broke through the class prejudices of the theatre establishment at that time when he made his Drury Lane debut as Shylock in Shakespeare's *The Merchant of Venice* in 1814. Following this sensational performance, he specialised in playing Shakespeare's most malign roles, in particular Iago, Richard III and Macbeth. Hartnoll (1989: 178) has described him as "a rough, untutored genius at his best in villainous parts". As a performer he brought wild passion and intense physicality to his characterisations at a time when the acting style in vogue (one associated particularly with John Philip Kemble) was artificial and declamatory. Kean's final years were ignominious, as he squandered his fortune and eventually died from drink and other excesses.

At some point during his year at the City Literary Institute, a fellow-student handed Berkoff a copy of a biography of Kean written by Giles Playfair. This book, Berkoff recalls zealously, "set me aflame" (*FA*: 215). The account of Kean's life that he found in it gave the 'beleaguered' Berkoff access to a cluster of discursive strategies that would give him a blueprint for promoting and justifying his own concerns and ambitions, both theatrical and social, over what he saw as the limited and limiting opportunities for physical self-expression offered by the drama schools. He recalls in his autobiography that "I would carry [Playfair's] book as a symbol of man's awesome achievement over natural handicap. Kean was

61

a small man, perhaps no more than five feet five inches, and really had to fight to overcome opposition to him" (FA: 215). In a letter to this writer, Berkoff stated explicitly that:

> I was fascinated and absorbed and really found [Kean] such an inspiring power, so he became in my mind a mentor. I admired his great physical energy, his courage, his attitude towards the establishment at the time, the way he overcame them all by the sheer force and brute strength of both his physical and mental power and belief in himself.[5]

Berkoff seems to have based his approach to performance both on and off-stage upon what he has characterised in subsequent accounts as substantial similarities between Kean's life and acting style (at least as he gleaned them from Playfair) and his own. In addition, the proximity of the City Literary Institute to Drury Lane, where Kean delivered some of his legendary performances, prompted Berkoff to elaborate a privileged sense of closeness to his hero, whose spirit he "seemed to befriend" (FA: 215) on the streets they had both trod.

A key parallel between the two men that Berkoff seized upon was the tenacious instinct for survival that enabled both of them, as he apparently saw it, to succeed in spite or because of social prejudice and economic hardship. Playfair (1950: 174) writes: "From his earliest days [Kean] had learned to fend for himself, and he had been brought up to the idea of rigorous self-preservation. He had fought hard and painfully for his success. He had hewn his way through years of misery and squalor and frustrated hopes." Similarly, throughout his career, Berkoff has projected himself as someone whose sharp survival instincts have been honed by adversity. This is the subject position he adopted when he found himself surrounded by the more well-heeled students at Webber Douglas and the 'effete', middle-class, English actors in his early years as an actor. Recalling his days as a student, he writes: "Since I had suffered until then six years of unrewarding, frustrating and soulless work, the dreariness of going from job to job from the ages of fifteen to twenty-one, I felt I had had my apprenticeship in the school of hard knocks" (FA: 110). And according to Berkoff's accounts, he adopted a similar subject position during his first years as an actor in the early 1960s:

> When I got [work] I triumphed through my own abilities to find graft, rather than having it all done for me, very much like some of the fortunate but pale creatures who were taken in without flexing much muscle elsewhere and had, so to speak, little combat experience. They came in like pale facsimiles sitting at the toes of the master and

cooing at his every word, never seeing the light of the outside world. And when the time came, sitting in his [sic] master's old chair and wearing his old slippers. I had no master to follow and if this is arrogant then let it be. It is meant only to show that you do not need a master in whose image you create yourself with minor variations. You hew your way out with the bloody axe. (FA: 255–6)

In this passage Berkoff can be seen attempting to justify his hard-won success by means of a constructed parallel between the gruelling early life of Kean and the street Darwinism that, according to him, shaped his own youth. Berkoff's aggressive tenacity is further highlighted here by his conspicuous use, echoing Playfair, of the graphically violent verb *hew*. There is, however, some irony in the fact that Berkoff, despite his dismissal of the "pale facsimiles" with whom he rubbed shoulders, should have reinvented himself so wholeheartedly in the image of a master of his own choosing.

Another recurrent theme in Playfair's account is the sense of educational inferiority that plagued Kean as a result of his impoverished upbringing. Playfair (1950: 30) writes:

After all, if he were destined to be famous, fame would inevitably be a passport to the houses of the rich and distinguished. He would occupy a place in London society. He would meet and be honoured by men and women of every class. And he would have to impress them with his personal qualities. He would not be content to be hailed as a genius on the stage if he were regarded as a dull, stupid, vulgar dolt off it. He wanted to live as a great man as well as a great actor.

To this end, Kean undertook what Playfair characterises as "pathetic" (61) attempts to educate himself that involved the memorisation and subsequent regurgitation in letters and dinner-table conversations of historical, geographical and biographical facts. Despite both these efforts at ingratiation and his prodigious talent as a performer, however, his social 'superiors' looked down on him. Playfair makes the point that "[Kean] complained that they did not treat him as an equal, but as a kind of wild beast on parade" (133). While they grudgingly conceded that he was in possession of some raw gifts as an actor, they could never accept that he met the educational standards expected of a true gentleman. In their eyes, his lack of formal schooling automatically disqualified him from the right to perform the great tragic roles from the Shakespearean canon, that supreme cultural possession of the British elite and marker of education and breeding.

Playfair devotes a good deal of attention to the condescension with which gentle society greeted Kean's intensely physical interpretations of Shakespeare's tragic heroes. He quotes, for example, the diarist Crabb Robinson's contemporary observation that "as Hamlet [see Figure 7], *in spite of his essential lack of nobility,* [Kean] revealed beauties before undreamed of" [my emphasis] (Playfair 1950: 116); and that as Richard III, "His most flagrant defect is want of dignity ... he projects his lower lip ungracefully ... his declamation is very unpleasant. He gratified my eye more than my ear. His speech is not fluent, and his words and syllables are too distinctly separated" (116). And the poet Samuel Taylor Coleridge, seizing upon what he judged to be an erratic acting style, offered the famously ambiguous assessment that Kean revealed Shakespeare "by flashes of lightning" (92), a phrase that could have been taken either to mean strokes of genius or, in the slang of the time, noggins of gin. These two commentators were literary representatives of that upper segment of early nineteenth-century English society that considered its claim to Shakespeare, asserted through what it took to be its social and educational superiority, as natural and unquestioned. By daring to perform Shakespeare's tragic heroes, Kean, base-born, uneducated and, worst of all, *physical*, was adored as a 'popular' star by the denizens of the pit. Whether it was Playfair's intention or not, his treatment of this matter raises the question of the 'ownership' of Shakespeare's works, and of who has the right to interpret them – a class-inflected conflict that continues to this day, as may be seen in the theatre Establishment's response to Berkoff's various interpretations and uses of the Shakespearean canon.

As we have seen, Berkoff, like Kean, has frequently claimed to have been put down in his career by the educational and theatrical powers that be in Britain. On a simple level, I showed how this operated in his early conflict with Red Beard. A typical expression of this feeling of being 'victimised' in his later career is his complaint regarding the reception of his productions of Shakespeare's plays, and his use of Shakespearean allusions in his own plays. He recalls that his subversively physical and 'popular' production of *Hamlet* (Edinburgh 1979), for example, "received the most awful battering from the press" (*IAH*: ix). More recently, Berkoff reaped some of the worst notices of his career for his one-man "master-class in evil" *Shakespeare's Villains* (Theatre Royal Haymarket, 1998).[6] His *The Secret Love-Life of Ophelia* (King's Head, 2001), referred to by one commentator as his "footnote to Hamlet" (Hewison 2001), was also poorly received.[7] Clearly, Berkoff had pressed the buttons of the Bard-

MR KEAN as HAMLET,
—J, say, away—Go on—I'll follow thee.
Pub.d as the Act directs by J.Roach, Russel Court, Drury Lane May.16,1814.

7 Edmund Kean as Hamlet at Theatre Royal, Drury Lane

policing Establishment. As he complained to one interviewer, "I come to [Shakespeare] as an outsider to a certain extent, as a non-academic outsider; self-educated and as a product of a grammar school and a very simple environment, I've been made to feel for years that it's (he affects a Garrick Club accent) 'not reaaahlly for you'" (Kohn 1989). Berkoff's exaggerated description of himself as an underprivileged autodidact is rather undermined, however, by the fact that he received his secondary education at the same grammar school attended by fellow-playwright Harold Pinter. Nevertheless, this strategy highlights his concern with demonstrating how he has prevailed in his struggles solely on account of his own tenacious 'Kean-ness'.

Finally, an important parallel between himself and Kean that Berkoff has elaborated and exploited is what he has characterised as the similarity between his own performance style and that of his "firebrand" (*FA*: 215) hero. Indeed, he has explicitly projected his own acting style through the latter's infamously unpredictable and physical approach to performance, as the following passage from his autobiography shows:

> He was a danger on stage, a wild beast that years of penury and struggle had formed into a dangerously formidable acting force. Does hardship and pain do this? In some instances I believe it does and I would have been fascinated to see Kean act. I am sure it would have taken your breath away by its sheer audacity ... So Kean was another of those symbols I carried in my mind to help me through the long days. I would call on him, feast on him, dwell on his life and see myself reflected [*sic*] in his prism, hoping that in studying him some of it would rub off on me ... He was a wild animal within a civilized art and he gave that art a new form. Even then it was competitive, but he made it into a boxing ring. You went to see blood and he gave it metaphysically [*sic*]. (*FA*: 215–16)

A "wild animal within a civilised art" is very much how Berkoff, despite Terence Stamp's description of him as silent and withdrawn, has opted to portray himself in his recollections of his student days: "Yes, yes, the drama school. I was a highly serious actor. People used to avoid me, backing away and going 'eeeuuugh' when I came in with my eyes blazing" (Appleyard 1989). As his career took off and a recognisable 'Berkovian' style emerged, various commentators have used similarly vivid language, albeit frequently sensationally, to characterise his approach to performance, both on and off-stage. He has been described, for example, as a "full-throttle manic performer" (Irvine 1991), an "arty yob" (Appleyard 1989), a "threat made flesh" (Walsh 1991), and "an awesome *enfant terrible*"(Lambert 1989). The list of hyperbolic epithets that journalists have hung around Berkoff's neck is endless.

Berkoff's befriending of the spirit of 'Kean' did not end with his enactment in real life of the role of Playfair's protagonist. One of the first independent projects that Berkoff sought but failed (for reasons unclear) to undertake in 1965 was a production of Sartre's 1954 play *Kean* (Halton 1965). A staging of this particular drama with Berkoff performing in the role of the eponymous hero would, one imagines, have resulted in a real Berkovian *coup de théâtre*. Significantly, Berkoff has stated that his interest in the play was "not so much because of Sartre but because of Kean."[8] Thus the attraction of it for Berkoff lay less in Sartre's philosophical content or problematic 'Kean' discourse than in what he apparently took to be the substantial presence of his idol in the drama. In other words, Berkoff did not approach the play as a work by Sartre in its own right – Sartre's authorship seems to have been rather an irrelevance for him – but as a blueprint for acting out the 'Kean' he had already encountered and embraced in Playfair's account. In passing, one wonders why Berkoff has never attempted to write his own dramatic account of Edmund Kean's life given the central role it has played in the unfolding of his identity.

Ironically, Sartre has stated, in terms that could justifiably be applied to the whole process of Berkoff's performative construction of his 'self', that "[Kean] was the Myth of the Actor incarnate. The actor who never ceases acting; he acts out his life itself, is no longer able to recognize himself, no longer knows who he is. And finally is no one" (Hill 1992: 205–6). One commentator has asserted that "[Sartre's] Kean is never quite sure when he is acting and when he is not; his two personæ become fused into one impostor" (Masters 1970: 24). Evidently, Berkoff was unaware of this problematic subtext in the play, since he was unable or unwilling to look beyond what was apparently for him the enticing prospect of performing in the role of the man he worshipped. Yet the dispersed quality of Sartre's 'Kean' perhaps offers an explanation for why Berkoff failed to realise his plan to stage the play and why he makes no mention of it at all in his autobiography or, indeed, anywhere else in his writings. Berkoff appears to have felt more at ease with Playfair's monologic 'Kean', which he could pull on as a mask, than with the vertiginous and destabilising textuality that was Sartre's reading of the character. It is perhaps not too much to say that far from 'clothing' Berkoff in an appealing role – a role as attractive to him as Playfair's 'Kean' – Sartre's absent/present protagonist would have drawn troubling attention to the insubstantiality of Berkoff's 'Kean' subject position and thus of his constructed 'self'. Perhaps, as Sartre said of his creation, Berkoff performing as 'Kean' would have deconstructed his 'self' to the extent that he would finally have become no one.

As a final postscript to Berkoff's intertextual relationship with 'Kean' there is his evocation of him in the 'autobiographical' story entitled "Rep" in the *Graft* collection published in 1998. The protagonist and Berkoff-alter ego Harry, a young repertory actor, feeling that he is an undervalued outsider among his mediocre fellow-performers, draws on 'Kean' to comfort himself: "Did they not laugh at Kean, the great nineteenth-century tragedian, but of course Kean had the last laugh as 'they' faded into dusty obscurity. Harry sucked at these venomous little thoughts like they were boiled sweets, filling his mind with comforting flavours" (*G*:

36). Although framed in a fictional mode, this rather desperate and bitter reflection, when taken together with the statements expressed in his autobiography, suggests the emotional commitment that Berkoff, as a young actor, invested in his 'Kean' subject position, and points to the extent to which he drew upon this textuality to compensate for the lack that was and is his 'self'. This tendency, I shall argue, is even more evident in his interpersonal relationship with 'Olivier'.

Berkoff and 'Laurence Olivier'

Laurence Olivier (1907–89) – Sir Laurence after 1947, Lord Laurence after 1970 – was widely lauded as the greatest Shakespearean interpreter of the twentieth century. After making his West End debut, he moved to America in 1930 with the idea of making a name for himself in Hollywood. He failed to make much of an impression on screen, however, and returned to the London stage. He achieved stardom in 1935, when he was cast as Romeo in John Gielgud's production of *Romeo and Juliet*. In 1939 he returned to Hollywood to star as Heathcliff in the multiple Oscar-winning production of *Wuthering Heights*. He followed this with leading roles in such films as *Rebecca*, *Pride and Prejudice* and *That Hamilton Woman*, co-starring in the latter with his second wife, Vivien Leigh. During the Second World War his greatest contribution to the war effort was his jingoistic film production of *Henry V*, which he produced, directed and starred in. In 1947, the year in which he received his knighthood, he also produced, directed and starred in his cinematic adaptation of *Hamlet*. His successes during the 1950s included his film singing debut in *The Beggar's Opera* and his 1955 production of *Richard III*. In 1961 he married actress Joan Plowright and found a degree of stability in his personal life. In 1963 he acted in a notable stage production of *Othello* at Chichester, which was subsequently filmed. During those years he was one of the leading members of the new National Theatre. In 1970, he became Lord Olivier and assumed his seat in the House of Lords the following year. Four years later, suffering from serious illness, he made his last stage appearance. From 1974 until his death in 1989, he seemingly took whatever film job was offered him.

The Czech structuralist Jiri Veltrusky (1964: 84) has argued that the figure of the actor is "the dynamic unity of an entire set of signs" which may include the performer's body, voice and movements. In other words, the actor may be read as a multi-coded 'performance text'. An actor who is a 'star' – a luminary such as Olivier, for example, who has achieved colossal fame and public recognition – is additionally constructed through and by the discourses that his or her celebrity brings into play. The implications of this polysemic process have been explored by Richard Dyer in *Heavenly Bodies*, his study of the social significance of film stars, where he writes:

> The star phenomenon consists of everything that is publicly available about stars. A film star's image is not just his or her films, but the promotion of those films and of the star through pin-ups, public appearances, studio hand-outs and so on, as well as interviews, biographies and coverage in the press of the star's doings and 'private' life. Further, a star's image is also what people say or write about him or her, as critics or commentators, the way the image is used in other contexts such as advertisements, novels, pop songs, and finally the way the star can become part of the coinage of everyday speech. (Dyer 1986: 3)

Viewed in such a light, Sir Laurence Olivier – or rather the multitextual phenomenon that I will signal here as 'Olivier' – is not merely a physical and vocal performance text in Veltrusky's sense but an intertextual discourse, a "media text" (ix). In his construction of 'self', Berkoff, as we shall see, has adopted a subject position that is not only in advantageous proximity to, but intimately conjoined with, the 'Olivier' media text. Such a strategy has enabled him to exploit the general public's familiarity with not only Sir Larry's stage and screen performances but also the well-documented details of his 'private' life in order to co-produce the 'Olivier' text. Implicitly, therefore, Berkoff has encouraged his own public to bring these readings of 'Olivier' to their understanding of the 'Berkoff' construct – to view him and his performance style, as it were, through the discursive prism of 'Olivier'.

The 'Olivier' text, it should be emphasised, is problematic and contested. On the one hand, there is the accepted or orthodox view of his career. The 1993 edition of *The Oxford Companion to the Theatre* proclaims authoritatively that Olivier was "commonly regarded as the supreme actor of his generation" (Hartnoll 1993: 610). Philip Barnes concurs in his *A Companion to Post-War British Theatre*, where he states that in the immediate post-war years "Olivier established himself as the major Shakespearean and classical actor of his generation" (Barnes 1986: 170). The theatre critic Kenneth Tynan, reviewing Olivier's interpretation of Coriolanus at Stratford-upon-Avon in 1959, lists some of the attributes of his acting style:

> This Coriolanus is all-round Olivier. We have the wagging head, the
> soaring index finger, and the sly, roaming eyes of one of the world's
> cleverest comic actors, plus the desperate, exhausted moans of one
> of the masters of pathos. But we also confront the nonpareil of
> heroic tragedians, as athletically lissom as when he played Oedipus a
> dozen years ago. No actor uses *rubato*, stealing a beat from one line
> to give to the next, like Olivier. The voice is soft steel that can chill and
> cut, or melt and scorch ... After letting his voice fly high in the great,
> swingeing line about how he "flutter'd your Volscians in *Cor-i-o-li*," he
> allows a dozen spears to impale him. He is poised, now, on a
> promontory some twelve feet above the stage, from which he topples
> forward, to be caught by the ankles so that he dangles, like the
> slaughtered Mussolini. (Tynan 1975: 263–4)

These are examples of the received perception of Olivier as the *primus inter pares* among English classical actors in the twentieth century. In passing, it is perhaps worth noting that another indication of the extent to which Olivier has come to epitomise the 'star performer' *par excellence* is semiotician Keir Elam's (1991: 86) use of him and his career to exemplify the icon of the 'great actor'. Yet Olivier was of course not only a performer on the stage; he was also a celebrated actor-manager, film actor, director and theatre administrator. Indeed, the general view of him as having embodied the theatre Establishment is supported by his appointment in 1963 as the first Director of the National Theatre, and the naming of one of its auditoria after him (Shellard 1999: 103–11).

On the other hand, alternative viewpoints interrogate this orthodoxy. Denis Salter, in his essay 'Acting Shakespeare in Postcolonial Space', for example, describes how what he calls the "Olivier template" has shaped the received and 'natural' approach to acting in Shakespeare (Salter 1996: 118), and to such an extent, indeed, that it is possible to say that Olivier's style has become the benchmark against which subsequent interpreters, particularly Kenneth Branagh,[9] continue to measure their efforts, whether on the stage or the screen. In his one-man performance/lecture *Shakespeare's Villains* (Theatre Royal Haymarket, 1998) Berkoff spoke intriguingly of the "'hologram' of Laurence Olivier" that haunts any actor's attempt to perform Hamlet.[10] Whilst Olivier's performances have been widely seen as having purveyed "an official Shakespeare" (Anderegg 1999: 65), however, Michael Bogdanov points out that Olivier decimated and distorted Shakespeare's texts in his cinematic adaptations:

> Unfortunately in Britain, we have been influenced by some wonder-
> fully jingoistic productions of *Henry V*, *Richard III* and *Hamlet* by Sir
> Laurence Olivier, which managed to cut out some of the most

essential ingredients of the plays themselves ... We [therefore] inherit a distorted view of these plays, which have been handed down to us through great *tour de force* performances. (Elsom 1992: 19)

Here one might object, of course, that Olivier, with his wealth of experience as a film director, was cognisant of the ways in which cinema as a medium differs from theatre and simply excised those sections of the play that would not have transferred effectively to the screen. Nevertheless it is safe to assume that Olivier was more concerned with his own self-aggrandisement as a director and actor than with any 'faithful' rendering of Shakespeare (assuming that such a thing were possible) and that these films, taken together with his iconic stage performances, were vehicles for the expansion of his career through an implied claim to be the definitive interpreter of Shakespeare .

One of the most troubling moments in Olivier's career – one which Berkoff not only witnessed but also, ironically, singled out for effusive praise – was his implicitly racist interpretation of Othello at Chichester in 1963. Shellard (1999: 108) draws attention to the fact that "[m]any were disconcerted by Olivier's blacking-up (something that would be unacceptable in today's multi-racial Britain) – Tony Richardson, for instance, spoke of the 'degrading image of a NEGRO in capital letters'". To transform himself into this 'stage Negro', another commentator argues, Olivier "cosmetically enhance[d] already instantiated racial and gender aesthetics" (Callaghan 1996: 203) in the manner of, to put it plainly, a Shakespearean Black and White Minstrel (see Figure 8). Worse still, Olivier recalled in his autobiography, without apparent irony, that he "went to the lengths of studying the gait of the barefooted races!" (Olivier 1982: 254) in preparation for the role.

Berkoff, however, has been unworried by his idol's ethnic insensitivity, as is evident from his rapt recollection of witnessing Olivier's performance:

I watched him play Othello at his peak, a night unlike all other nights at Chichester in 1963. He appeared from the shadows, waving his rose gently beneath his nostrils. The house became very still and we braced ourselves for a primal eruption of emotional power. His voice conducted an entire orchestra of emotional stress, from pity to rage, from hysteria to lyricism. He cried and his voice ran up and down those stretched strings of his instrument, spanning more octaves than ever before, touching more memories, smells, secret passages deep down in the hidden vaults of his mind. Panther-like he pounded the stage, breaking down the forts of reason. We [*sic*] watched enchanted and entranced. (Berkoff 1989d)

Far from recognising and deploring the racist and colonialist implications of Olivier's interpretation of the role, then, despite his own
positioning of himself as a Jewish outsider in British society and theatre,
Berkoff was "enchanted" by the erotic charisma of his 'Olivier'. He
followed unquestioningly the received assessment of Olivier's career,
seeing him as "the high priest of acting" (Berkoff 1989d), the epitome of
the virtuoso actor who combined vocal mastery with athletic versatility.
Without wishing to stray into psychoanalytic speculation, Berkoff was
perhaps enchanted by the narcissistic image that he may have had of
himself as 'Olivier', or at least of himself as someone who could have his
talents recognised by the Establishment.

As a beginning actor during the early 1960s, Berkoff recalls that it
was Olivier – or rather his monologic 'Olivier' – whose "light still shone
the brightest" (Berkoff 1989d), that guided him on. 'Olivier', in short,
appears to have represented the very peak of mainstream success to
which Berkoff aspired: "Yes, I deeply believed in him as the most exalted
symbol of the player, and in the profession that I chose to enter, the very
word 'actor' had a new lustre since I was stepping on to the first rung of a
ladder at whose distant crest sat the mighty Olivier" (Berkoff 1989d).
Berkoff's expressions of respect for 'Olivier' appear frequently throughout his interviews, and his non-dramatic and non-fictional writings,
especially the 1989 newspaper article entitled 'Steven Berkoff on Laurence
Olivier', a valedictory piece in memory and honour of the then recently
deceased peer. In his autobiography, Berkoff refers to Olivier variously as
"my great mentor" (23), "the noble one" (23) and "the great Sir" (25), and
he writes, without apparent irony, that "I would have gone down on my
knees and kissed the hem of his jacket and not felt the slightest
diminution of pride" (*FA*: 25).

The language that Berkoff has used to describe his feelings towards
his 'Olivier' frequently exceeds mere expressions of respect to convey
suggestions of obsessive sexual desire. Berkoff characterises him, for
example, as a seducer before whose charismatic charms he was, as a
neophyte actor, seemingly defenceless: "Olivier was a siren tempting you
to the shore where you might be dashed against the rocks of failure,
unemployment and dejection" (Berkoff 1989d). He alludes constantly to
what appears to have been for him the sexual appeal of the physical and
vocal qualities of Olivier's live presence – what Esslin (1996: 60–1) refers
to as the "erotic magnetism" of the actor on the stage. In describing
Olivier's voice, for example, Berkoff hints at sexual ambivalence: "That
instrument of danger or persuasion could ... be so infinitely delicate that

8 Sir Laurence Olivier blacked-up as Othello

he seemed to walk the tightrope between feminine and masculine"
(Berkoff 1989d). Employing a homoerotic metaphor, Berkoff even
suggests the sexual ambivalence of his own feelings towards 'Olivier', as
he fantasises about being mystically conjoined with, and indeed filled by,
his noble 'presence':

> I dreamed Larry; would see him clearly walking down a street by the
> Vic and knew in my heart that if only he knew that my destiny was
> here and with him, he would embrace me and off we'd fly to those
> rarified heights. I became possessed and obsessed and in one brief
> period found his voice coming out of my mouth, which reminded me
> of the dybbuk, where the spirit of another being invades yours.
> (Berkoff 1989d)

A diary entry in Berkoff's travelogue/diary *A Prisoner in Rio* repeats this
theme: "Had strange dreams about Laurence Olivier, whose signature
bears a slight resemblance to mine. Perhaps he is invading my body"
(*PIR*: 177). In these two instances Berkoff presents himself in terms of

emptiness and lack, as a void, a non-presence, a hollow receptacle that achieves full significance or satisfaction only when filled by the spirit of his 'Olivier'. Such an apparently self-negating strategy on Berkoff's part may be seen as a compensatory wish-fulfilment in the face of what he has projected as his own impotence within the theatre hierarchy.

A text that sheds further light on Berkoff's erotic mode of interacting with his 'Olivier' is the short story 'Gross Intrusion', which, along with the other tales in the collection bearing the same name, was written by Berkoff during visits to Brighton in the 1970s (*FA*: 191–5). Brighton, where Berkoff has one of his residences, is a place that is inextricably connected with Olivier, both in the public mind (he became Baron Olivier of Brighton in 1970) and, more importantly, in Berkoff's own consciousness:

> Unbeknown to me at the time, but adding to the general delights of the area, was Olivier's presence in the adjoining crescent. And lo and behold, just as I was parking my motorbike in the Royal Crescent garage amidst the Jags, out comes Sir Larry parking his. Shall I approach and offer my warm greetings and solicitations to someone who has even invaded my dreams? (*FA*: 191)

Thus the stories were written on Sir Larry's baronial 'estate', so to speak, and under the influence of, for Berkoff, his pervasive noble presence.

'Gross Intrusion', which features the Berkoff-alter ego Harry (also referred to, in an echo of Joseph K., as H), is a graphic description of death by anal rape. It may be significant that a homoerotic sex scene should appear in a story written in a location so clearly linked in Berkoff's mind with Olivier. The passage in which Harry is killed parallels, albeit in a violently sexual way, Berkoff's fantasy of being invaded *dybbuk*-fashion by the spirit of his beloved 'Olivier':

> The negro [*sic*] still held Harry by the throat and H was impaled to the hilt … he was thrusting hard now and arched his back once more and as his moment of triumph came, bared his teeth, as if to holler it to the whole world … did not of course see the blood seeping out of Harry's mouth nor feel the slackness when death calmly extinguishes the lights of the body. (*GI*: 97)

Whilst I wish to avoid a psychoanalytic interpretation of this material, it is tempting to speculate in passing whether the "negro" of the tale, Olivier's blackface Othello that so enchanted Berkoff in Chichester, and the 'Olivier' who "invaded" (i.e. penetrated) his dreams are linked. The Negro's penetration of Harry results in the latter's death, in his non-presence, just as the invasion of Berkoff by 'Olivier' necessarily points to the absent/

present quality of Berkoff's 'self'.

Berkoff, I suggest, may be seen to have been indulging in what Fiske has called the "productive pleasure" of 'reading' the physicality of the 'Olivier' text. Fiske is working here with Barthes's (1976) concept of *jouissance*, which, he states, may be translated variously as "bliss, ecstasy, or orgasm". It is, he argues,

> the pleasure of the body that occurs at the moment of the breakdown of culture into nature. It is a loss of self and of the subjectivity that controls and governs the self – the self is socially constructed and therefore controlled, it is the site of subjectivity and therefore the site of ideological production and reproduction. The loss of self is, therefore, the evasion of ideology. (Fiske 1989b: 50)

Jouissance, Fiske continues, "occurs in the body of the reader at the moment of reading when text and reader erotically lose their separate identities and become a new, momentarily produced body that is theirs and theirs alone, that defies meaning or discipline" (51). Berkoff's fantasy of a kind of passive *conjunctio* with his 'Olivier' thus generates pleasure for him since it enables him to evade the hegemonic forces that, as he has apparently seen it, sought to discipline his body. It is a strategy of eluding pain through pleasure, a metaphor for Berkoff's desire that the theatre Establishment would find his body and thus his physical approach to acting irresistibly attractive. For Berkoff, there is moreover the added *frisson* of fancying himself wooed and entered by 'Olivier', the very visible figurehead of the theatre Establishment at that time; of fantasising that the mountain, as it were, comes to *him*. This is one of the many paradoxes of the 'Berkoff phenomenon'; namely, that Berkoff's strategy for the construction and validation of his 'self' is worked through the apogee of the system he simultaneously abhors and desires, a confusion of feelings he has imputed to the British theatre hierarchy: "The Establishment hates me", he informed one interviewer, "but it also loves me" (Brown 1994). It would be nearer the mark, I suggest, if these terms were reversed, viz. Berkoff hates the Establishment but also loves it.

Berkoff exploits the discrepancy that existed between his fantasy of being swept off to glory by a benevolent 'Olivier' and the 'reality' of what he has characterised as his impotent position within mainstream British theatre in one revealing anecdote in his autobiography. Soon after witnessing the Othello performance in 1963, Berkoff succeeded in gaining an audition for a place in the new companies that Olivier was establishing then at the National Theatre and Chichester. This, Berkoff apparently reasoned, was his best opportunity to overcome all the rejections to date and receive the 'official' seal of approval for his physical performance skills. Employing a tongue-in-cheek style to cover his bitterness, he recalls:

> Once the great Zeus had seen his acolyte offering his divine light one great genius would, I thought, recognize the incipient stirrings of another and yes, the great and noble beast would gather me in his arms and say "Come." And so I worked and sweated my balls off in my usual ritual of a week of preparation and duly performed my new piece – not, alas, in front of my idol, but for some poor harassed underlings of Sir. (FA: 23)

As a result, Berkoff was handed what from his perspective was the definitive rejection: Sir Laurence Olivier, his idol, the personification of the British theatre Establishment, denied his body, his physical approach to acting, thus pouring cold water on his fantasy of receiving 'official' recognition.

Berkoff builds upon this rebuff in order to describe and justify how he was thus 'compelled' to search for alternative (that is to say non-mainstream) ways of deploying his physical performance skills (FA: 24). He began to reclaim his body, he recalls, by exploring approaches to physical performance that lay geographically and aesthetically outside Britain. Specifically, he immersed himself in the practices of 'French total theatre' (see chapter 3). Berkoff positions the theatre Establishment and its hegemonic disciplinary strategies in such a way as to show how his style evolved *through* his resistance. In his autobiography he reflects that "water will find an exit no matter how circuitous the route and being rejected so many times may have led me along a more interesting path" (FA: 255). Retrospectively, he has thereby attempted to create a 'teleo-logical' path leading 'naturally' – as natural as the flow of water – and necessarily to his founding in 1968 of the avowedly physical LTG. Paradoxically, for all his stated abhorrence of the theatre Establishment, Berkoff has needed it as a conduit through which he has striven to achieve self-validation and a sense of direction in his creative work.

As a final supernatural postscript to this discussion, it is worth briefly mentioning the tongue-in-cheek claim made by Berkoff in *Coriolanus in Deutschland* that it was Olivier's death that finally facilitated his admittance into the sanctum of the National Theatre. On his demise, Olivier's widow, Joan Plowright, cancelled the production in which she had been due to appear there, with the result that Berkoff was handed his big chance. "I was given a job in death by Laurence Olivier", he muses.

"Olivier seems to have made this possible, since there would have been no other way that the regime would have willingly taken me on" (*CID*: 60). Perhaps the benevolent spirit of 'Olivier' had, after all, 'entered' Berkoff.

Conclusion

In this chapter we have seen that during his time as a drama student and during the early years of his professional acting career, Berkoff became, as a result of both the subject positions he had taken up and the ways in which he had been positioned by the institutions and individuals he encountered, a 'threshold figure'. He had cut himself off from his proletarian Jewish roots, yet seemingly felt out of place among the 'educated' middle-class students and teachers he encountered in his two drama schools and in regional repertory. His deficient knowledge of dramatic literature precluded a convincing text-based approach to performance, and he was rebuffed for his compensatory physical acting style. He thus occupied a liminal position – a situation that may be taken as paradigmatic for the rest of his subsequent career.

Berkoff's identification with 'Kean' was a discursive strategy with which he sought to legitimise his subject position as a working-class physical actor 'performing' his way out of socio-economic and aesthetic impotence. His overt public projection of his 'self' through 'Kean' enabled him to set about authenticating his own physical approach to acting in the face of what he has characterised as a text-obsessed and hostile theatre Establishment. His later 'popular' productions of Shakespeare may be seen to confirm this tendency. His fantasy of being 'penetrated' *dybbuk*-fashion by the erotically charismatic 'Olivier' suggests the paradoxical, Janus-faced nature of his relationship with the theatre Establishment, a relationship founded upon a desire to be adored by an institution that he claims to detest. Both strategies may be seen, therefore, as formative stations along the path of his constructed 'teleology'.

These two interpersonal subject positions, however, explain very little about any 'real' or substantive parallels between Berkoff and the historical figures Edmund Kean and Sir Laurence Olivier and their respective approaches to performance. 'Kean' and 'Olivier' are insubstantial and fleeting phantoms, as Berkoff himself recognised with his use of words such as *spirit*, *dybbuk* and *hologram* to describe them, and as fictional (or spectral) as his own creations. Playfair's monologic 'Kean', as is the case with the signified of any auto/biography, is a subjective and

77

selective construction on the part of an individual author. The palimpsest of Kean's 'life' has necessarily been reinscribed with whatever significance Playfair (and, subsequently, Berkoff) chose to invest it. Sartre's 'Kean', far from an attempt to create a substantial character, is a function of non-signification, which is why, most probably, Berkoff abandoned it. 'Olivier', we have seen, is a contested multimedia text, a profusion of meanings that defy monologic interpretation and appropriation. Thus Berkoff, I suggest, has attempted in vain to construct his 'self' through slippery textualities – 'Kean' and 'Olivier' – that far from achieving closure result only in an infinite deferral of meaning. These discursive strategies do suggest a great deal, however, about how Berkoff has operated within the structure of British theatre and how he has sought to construct and project his 'self' in response to the vicissitudes of his career.

Notes

1 Frost and Yarrow (1990: 37), in their discussion of the non-physical pedagogical approach of British drama schools around that time, note that "RADA, like most other drama schools in Britain in the late 1950s and early 1960s, clung to a traditional view of the stage, largely untouched by the changes being wrought by the 'new wave' of dramatists in the wake of *Look Back in Anger*, and the Berliner Ensemble's visit to London [both in 1956] – or even, at that stage, by the ideas of drama teachers such as Michel Saint-Denis." This observation, as the authors note, may be generalised to include the drama schools that Berkoff attended. For his part, Berkoff is dismissive of the instruction he received at the Webber Douglas Academy: "The terms flew past in a series of play extracts, mime classes, which chiefly consisted of getting into a tableau and us guessing what it was" (*FA*: 114).

2 Steven Berkoff, letter to author, 17 January 1995.

3 As John Willett notes in his *The Theatre of Bertolt Brecht*, there is no single word in English that adequately translates the term *Gestus*. Instead, he offers the following explanation of this key Brechtian idea: "It is at once gesture and gist, attitude and point: one aspect of the relation between two people, studied singly or cut to essentials and physically or verbally expressed. It excludes the psychological, the subconscious, the metaphysical unless they can be conveyed in concrete terms" (Willett 1959: 175). In simple terms, Brecht insisted that the actors, eschewing any emotional identification with their characters, should demonstrate through the physical disposition of their bodies their Gestus or "attitude" towards the stage event.

4 Plummer performed in the BBC Wednesday Play production entitled *Hamlet at Elsinore* (1963), in which Berkoff played the role of the Player King (*FA*: 273).

5 Steven Berkoff, letter to author, 15 November 1996.

6 See, among others, the vitriolic reviews by Charles Spencer in the *Daily*

BERKOFF'S INTERPERSONAL 'SELF'

Telegraph (10 July 1998), Jane Edwards in *Time Out* (15 July 1998), Alastair Macaulay in the *Financial Times* (11 July 1998), Michael Coveney in the *Daily Mail* (10 July 1998), and Nick Curtis in the *Evening Standard* (10 July 1998).

7 See, for example, the reviews of John Nathan in the *Jewish Chronicle* (20 July 2001), Philip Chapman in *What's On* (11 July 2001) and Lyn Gardner in the *Guardian* (10 July 2001).

8 Steven Berkoff, letter to author, 15 November 1996.

9 The film historian Sarah Street (1997: 32) writes that actor-director "Branagh's theatrical background is always in evidence in his films, consciously operating in the footsteps of Laurence Olivier", with his cinematic adaptations of Shakespeare's *Henry V* (1989), *Much Ado About Nothing* (1993) and *Hamlet* (1996).

10 Theatre critic Michael Billington, picking up on this remark, writes in his review of Berkoff's *Shakespeare's Villains* for the *Guardian* (8 July 1998): "Playing Shakespeare's villains, says Berkoff, 'is like being in the ring with invisible ghosts you can't beat'. That is a fascinating remark; and, by his constant invocation of Olivier's shade, you realise Berkoff is a natural romantic haunted and dominated by a demonic genius whose spirit he can never quite exorcise."

79

3

THE LONDON THEATRE GROUP

Once the productions are chosen, I will need a company of actors who can lend themselves to these methods of *mise en scène*, who will interpret *meticulously* the directions I will give them; for, of course, we will only be able to reach the mathematical precision we are attempting in these productions if the actors are prepared to follow scrupulously the directions I will give them. (Antonin Artaud)[1]

In this chapter I turn my attention to Berkoff's relationship and working methods with the LTG during the late 1960s and early 1970s and examine how they relate to the processes and dynamics of his public construction of 'self'. My contention will be that in becoming the *primum mobile* of his own theatre group he was motivated first and foremost by a desire to win power for himself. Following Thompson's formulation in *Ideology and Modern Culture*, I take the term *personal power* in the discussion below to mean specifically

the ability to act in pursuit of one's aims and interests: an individual has the *power to act*, the power to intervene in the sequence of events and to alter their course. In so acting, an individual draws upon and employs the resources available to him or her. Hence the ability to act in pursuit of one's aims and interests is dependent upon one's position within a field or institution. 'Power', analysed at the level of a field or institution, is a capacity which *enables* or *empowers* some individuals to make decisions, pursue ends or realize interests. (original emphasis) (Thompson 1990: 151)

The extent to which individuals enjoy and exercise power in society, therefore, results from their ability to claim or resist through struggle or negotiation the subject positions that are available to them. Moreover, as Burr (1995: 76) observes, "it is when we look at those who appear to be on the margins of mainstream society that we see this struggle writ large." Berkoff has projected himself, as we have seen, as a marginalised individual battling against the power-wielding, hegemonic institution of the theatre Establishment. To this end, he has consistently characterised himself in terms of his *powerlessness*, his *lack* of resources or cultural capital, his *inability* to act in pursuit of his aims or interests as a theatre professional, and of his need, consequently, to assert himself through the empowering subject positions that he has adopted.

Rejection and exclusion at the hands of a supposedly hostile theatre Establishment are constant themes that run through Berkoff's accounts of his career, whether in his autobiography and other writings, or in interviews. Thus the launching and steering of the LTG was, I shall argue, Berkoff's concerted effort – his "struggle writ large" – to intervene in the course of events and become the primary actor, both in the sense of a theatrical performer and of a social agent, in the construction of his 'self' and his career. By claiming multiple new subject positions as the LTG's playwright, director, producer, manager, designer and virtuoso performer, Berkoff was engaged in overcoming what, as we saw in the previous chapter, he has interpreted as the attempts of the theatre Establishment to position him as a minor character actor in repertory or even to deny him employment in the first place. Thus by founding his own group and becoming its creative and administrative driving force, he gave himself the widest possible scope for unencumbered action and control. At the helm of his own company, he could truly perform the 'Berkoff phenomenon' into existence.

The chief weapon that Berkoff used in this struggle, prior to making a name for himself as an original playwright, was the body – his own and those of the other LTG members – deployed spectacularly and sometimes aggressively in physical performance. This strategy fits the self-empowering use of the body by marginalised groups or individuals in Western society. As Fiske (1989b: 100) argues:

> The body is an appropriate medium through which to articulate the social experience of many subordinated and oppressed groups in capitalism whose everyday sense of the social system is not one of fairness and equality: positioned as they are as "losers," the subordinated (whether by class, gender or race) have little sense of being "respected" by the winners, nor do they necessarily feel admiration for the socially successful. They are not "good losers," for society has not given them the "sporting chance" it claims to have given everyone.

In what follows, after considering the question of whether or not Berkoff has been fully justified in presenting himself as subordinated and oppressed, I will investigate the implications for his work with the LTG and for the construction of his 'self' of his choice to adopt these strategies of empowerment.

This chapter is divided into three sections. In the first section, I look at the ways in which Berkoff has attempted to construct a 'teleology' in the creation of his own theatre company and dramaturgical style. Specifically, I examine how Berkoff has attempted to construct his 'self', firstly, through his 'reading' and appropriation of the ideas, working methods and even personality traits (as he has seen them) of certain key practitioners of 'French total theatre', and, secondly, through the ways in which he has characterised the lack of personal control he felt over his career during the first half of the 1960s as a consequence of unemployment and minor engagements. In the second section, I analyse the LTG in terms of its establishment, composition and chronology, and the way Berkoff positioned it (and thereby himself) *vis-à-vis* the alternative theatre scene of the late-1960s. I approach the LTG less as a discrete 'extra-Berkoff' entity than as a macro-subject position adopted by him in his public construction of 'self' and in the creation and development of his own dramaturgical style. In particular, I examine the ways in which the LTG may be seen to reflect the power-related aspects of the 'Berkoff phenomenon'. In the final section, I focus upon Berkoff's methods as the LTG's director, since this is the area of his work in which his wide-ranging preoccupation with self-empowerment can be seen to have been most clearly in operation.

Steps towards independence

According to Berkoff, an aesthetic gulf separates British (specifically English) theatre from what he refers to generally as "European" theatre. In *I Am Hamlet*, he voices the complaint that "when one creates a *mise-en-scène* which is imaginative or recognizes the wandering mind of the spectator, the production is curiously called 'European'. Here in England we are used to a dullness ... a safe representational and 'natural' reading" (*IAH*: 60). And in his autobiography, describing the impact of this aesthetic divide on him personally, he describes how, during the early-1960s, he drifted "further and further away from the obsessively realistic, plausible, social and naturalistic theatre so beloved by the rational-thinking and logical Brits" (*FA*: 108–9). Rejecting the British mainstream theatre that has, as he has consistently characterised it, rejected him, Berkoff projected (and continues to project) himself as an artist who has gravitated 'naturally' across the English Channel towards the liberating ideas and practices associated with the 'French total theatre' tradition.

This strategy may be seen clearly at work in what is most likely the first journalistic piece to be published about Berkoff. The article entitled

'Seven actors in search of character' (Halton 1965), comprising Margaret Halton's profiles and Anthony Armstrong-Jones's full-page colour photographs of Berkoff and six other up-and-coming actors, including Terence Stamp, Ian McKellan and James Fox, appeared on 25 April 1965 in the supplement of the *Sunday Times*. Perhaps the most significant point about this in the present context is how Berkoff, enjoying nationwide publicity for the first time – "suddenly I was news. I became famous for a weekend" (*FA*: 275) – chose to project himself in this piece. The article announced that:

> [Berkoff] is now – for lack of further interesting employment – starting an experimental group with a friend, John Dunhill: they have the performance rights of the Gide/Barrault adaptation of *The Trial*, and hope to put it on next month at one of London's small theatres. They also want to do *Cyrano de Bergerac*, and Sartre's *Kean*. (Halton 1965)

The fact that these plays were ultimately not staged in no way diminishes the significance of Berkoff's bold projection of himself before his audience, the readership of a national Sunday broadsheet, as an "experimental" adherent of French theatre. What is more, one gains from this a sense of how Berkoff in fact worked towards his own exclusion by adopting a position that signalled unequivocally the distance he wished to place between himself and British mainstream theatre. Berkoff's 'marginalisation' may be seen rather as a self-fulfilling prophesy that has shaped and even propelled his whole career. Berkoff has consistently heaped scorn on the whole institution of British mainstream theatre. As I noted at the end of the previous chapter, however, there is a paradox at the heart of this strategy. On the one hand, he has needed the theatre Establishment as something to defy, castigate and push against in order to define and create both his own dramaturgical and performance style and his 'outsider' persona; on the other hand, it is certain that he would have embraced it if the right opportunity for success (in the shape of acceptance into Olivier's National company, for example) had presented itself when he needed the break. One can only speculate how Berkoff's career would have developed as a mainstream 'insider'.

With the LTG Berkoff set up his own company based on 'French total theatre' tenets. Berkoff has sought retroactively to validate this and later strategies by constructing a 'teleological' trajectory for himself in the form of a French theatrical genealogy that goes back further than 1965. He has drawn attention, for example, as did Terence Stamp, to the fact that as a drama student he dressed in the black 'French' existential style (de Jongh 1989), and he notes in his autobiography that he avidly read and discussed the plays of "Europeans such as Sartre and Ionesco" (*FA*: 113). He recalls in one interview that he turned his 'resting' spells in the early 1960s into productive periods of research in which he began to search for alternatives to British mainstream theatre practice: "In those great acres of time an actor spends unemployed I ... used to go to libraries and read and read until I found something I thought might work for me" (Morley 1975). And he emphasises that it was to *French* models of physical theatre that he turned. Specifically, his reading brought him into contact with the ideas and practice of two individuals with whom he has overtly aligned his 'self': the visionary theorist Antonin Artaud,[2] and the actor, director and mime-artist Jean-Louis Barrault.[3] This private research culminated in his taking up the study of mime and physical performance, first in London during 1963–65 with Claude Chagrin (*FA*: 53),[4] then briefly in Paris in the summer of 1965 at the school of her renowned teacher Jacques Lecoq.[5]

Berkoff pinpoints his conversion to 'French total theatre' to the day in 1961 when fellow-actor Peter Brett handed him what he remembers was a "strange book" (*FA*: 182), Artaud's *The Theatre and its Double*.[6] He recalls the impact that this collection of essays had upon him: "I read it quickly and with great enthusiasm. Artaud seemed to be articulating everything I had ever felt about what the theatre could be. I was never to forget that book; for a while it became a kind of bible to me" (*FA*: 182). Yet of equal if not greater importance than Artaud's notions of dramaturgy, which Martin Esslin (1983: 380) describes as having exerted "the most powerful seminal influence on the modern French theatre", was the appeal for Berkoff of the man himself. He recalls that he was "fascinated by the life of this strange, theatrical hermit with his ideas of an explosive theatre full of wild cries and gestures" (*FA*: 182). In this he was far from being alone, since, as Robert Hewison (1987: 89) has observed, "[Artaud's] life as drug addict and mental patient gave him a special place in the mythology of the counter-culture." Among fringe and experimental artists in the early 1960s in Britain and elsewhere, particularly America, Artaud became an icon of theatrical and political liberation. The Living Theatre in New York was foremost among alternative theatre groups that enthusiastically embraced Artaudian ideas. In Britain, Artaud-inspired performance aroused the ire of the theatre Establishment.[7] For Berkoff, therefore, the strategy of positioning himself in proximity to such a rebellious and iconoclastic figure became a convenient and effective means by which he could unfurl his own apparently anti-Establishment colours. Understandably, he recalls being thrilled when a French magazine referred to him as "a new Artaud" (*FA*: 327) following his double bill of *Miss Julie versus Expressionism* (see Figure 9) and *The Zoo Story* at the ICA in 1973. Of greater significance, though, was the fact that his earliest polemical writing about theatre and performance, the piece entitled 'Three Theatre Manifestos' (1978), in which he laid out and expanded upon the 'total theatre' approach he had taken with his early productions of *Metamorphosis* and *The Trial*, evoked Artaud's name and was redolent with Artaudian ideas, phrases and images.[8]

The extremity of Artaud's tortured personality and theories appealed to Berkoff in his desire to shock and draw attention to himself, but it was Barrault who had the greatest practical impact on Berkoff's work. Alongside Artaud's essays, Berkoff also studied Barrault's memoirs, *Reflections on the Theatre* (1951) and *The Theatre of Jean-Louis Barrault* (1961).[9] If, as experimental directors Jerzy Grotowski (1992: 86) and Peter Brook (1968: 60) maintain, Artaud's quasi-mystical ideas about theatre are ultimately unrealisable, then Barrault was by contrast a practical *homme de théâtre*. He is widely regarded as the key figure in the application and transmission of Artaud's vague notions of 'total theatre' (Innes 1993: 95). I examine Barrault's direct influence upon Berkoff's dramaturgy in chapter 5; here, I will concern myself with how Berkoff appears to have applied certain 'power-related' aspects of the work and theories of Barrault and Artaud – specifically, the privileging of the actor's body over the text and, linked to this, the privileging of the director over the ensemble – in the creation and leadership of the LTG.

A primary concern for Artaud had been to put an end to what he saw as theatre's obsession with fossilised texts, which is to say immutable playscripts. He argued that "instead of harking back to texts regarded as sacred and definitive, we must first break theatre's subjugation to the text and rediscover the idea of a kind of unique language somewhere in between gesture and thought" (Artaud 1989: 68). For Artaud, drama based on a written text was, as Fortier (1997: 43) puts it, "the imposition of death and repetition". In the place of words on the page he argued for the centrality of the actor's body on the stage. In the chapter in *The Theatre and Its Double* entitled 'An Affective Athleticism', he writes: "One must grant the actor a kind of affective musculature matching the bodily localisation of our feelings" (Artaud 1989: 88). The actor is "like a physical athlete"; she or he must, he asserts, be a "heart athlete" (88). Barrault echoes these ideas in his recollection that it was "through the study of the Body that I was to approach the technique of the actor"

(Barrault 1951: 21). Berkoff has employed notions such as these to sanction his own physical approach to performance.

With the actor's body taking on more significance in the overall dramaturgical concept, the director/choreographer assumes greater control than the playwright. Both Artaud and Barrault privileged the director over the actors, and bestowed upon the *metteur-en-scène* an autocratic authority. For Artaud, 'total theatre' could result only from a single directorial vision (Knapp 1994: 85). He considered the director to be, as he put it, "a kind of organiser of magic, a master of holy ceremonies" (Artaud 1989: 42). Wiles observes that:

> Artaud devotes ... attention to the role and the almost religious vocation
> of the *metteur-en-scène*, who has a shamanistic function in the creation
> of the theater of cruelty, and who uses actors along with plastic and
> musical elements as vehicles for his creation. (Wiles 1980: 131)

In stark contrast to the freedom he granted himself as director, Artaud saw his actors as "three-dimensional hieroglyphs" which, in a very revealing phrase, must be "rigorously denied any individual initiative" (Artaud 1989: 43). Clearly, then, the athleticism of the actors' bodies was to be placed totally at the disposal of the director, resulting necessarily in a comprehensive loss of artistic freedom on the part of the individual ensemble members.

9 Berkoff and two LTG members rehearsing *Miss Julie Versus Expressionism*

Barrault, though eschewing the extreme and violent language of Artaud, was ultimately no less autocratic in the control he exercised as the *metteur-en-scène* of his own productions. Berkoff read Barrault's recollections of his early experiences as a director ("producer") in *Reflections on the Theatre*, where, in one key passage, he asserts that producing a play

> does not lie only in making others act, nor in agreeing to or turning down the suggestions of the designer or musician. No; we must also be competent to replace others, to make designs for the designer, to set the musician on the right lines; and we do not attain the full liberty of a producer unless we can measure the décor to a nicety, direct the head mechanic, rebut the tortuous answers of the head electrician, the chief upholsterer, the head property-man, the stage manager and the stage director. Even in the best run houses the workmen, nine times out of ten from a sort of qualm of conscience, slip out of our grasp and we have to force them to do what we want. (Barrault 1951: 69)

This is the language of power – the idiom of power over other individuals. Indubitably, Barrault felt the need to have his controlling hand upon every single aspect of his productions. Yet his 'liberty' as producer must be measured against the freedom lost by his fellow theatre workers. The experience of the British actors who worked with Barrault on the 1971 revival at the Round House of his 'total theatre' drama *Rabelais* bear this conclusion out. The actor Bill Wallis, who took part in it, was commissioned by *Theatre Quarterly* to keep a running diary of the production. There he described Barrault's approach to direction:

> It soon became clear that Monsieur Barrault's intention was to recreate as accurately as he could the sight and sound of his original [Paris, 1968] production, provided the actors put themselves completely in his hands and allowed him to steer them through the complex and precise ballet of what was for him an intense theatrical expression of his theatrical philosophy. It was very much his Gargantuan baby. (Wallis 1971: 83)

And he goes on: "Barrault directed the English *Rabelais* mainly by playing every part himself during rehearsals" (93). One actor, he notes, "dropped out of the company, unable to cope" (86). Clearly, as far as Barrault was concerned, total theatre could only be realised through his total control. This, as we shall see, has been the approach taken by Berkoff as director.

As a part-time drama teacher at the Webber Douglas Academy during the years 1967–69, Berkoff found himself in the driving seat as the director of an ensemble for the first time in his career (*FA*: 120–2).

The most significant point about this experience, in terms of the present discussion, is that he unhesitatingly emulated Artaud and Barrault in his adoption of a similarly autocratic approach to his work. Teaching some of the physical and ensemble skills that he had learned at the École Jacques Lecoq (*FA*: 96), he describes his class as "a Berkoff workshop" (*FA*: 122). Already, then, he had proudly and possessively attached his own name to what he was projecting as a distinct style of performance. In a telling phrase, suggesting the power that he was asserting over his students, he refers to his "Meyerholdian vision" (*FA*: 121) as a director.[10] Looking back at his experience of forming the LTG, Berkoff has stated that "one of the best ways to find actors is to give a class to them if you can" (*FA*: 314). He thus wasted no time in perpetuating a traditional teacher-student hierarchy of power by teaching his students exactly what he wanted them to do. Even before the actual formation of the LTG, therefore, Berkoff's key power strategy, the total control of a physical theatre ensemble by an autocratic director, was firmly in place. In the process, he projected himself as an Artaud/Barrault/Lecoq/Meyerhold-inflected *metteur-en-scène* to justify and validate his own power-driven approach to directing.

The marginalisation through unemployment that Berkoff has characterised as having thwarted his professional ambitions during the early 1960s continued, according to him, to hinder his career after his return from Paris in the autumn of 1965 (Kohn 1989). His claim to have been singled out for rejection, though, must be seen in the context, first, of a profession in which unemployment is endemic, and, second, of what actually appears to have been his own success in finding engagements. Berkoff reports that in 1966 he secured work in, among other plays, Shaw's *Misalliance* and Albee's *Who's Afraid of Virginia Woolf?* at the Belgrade Theatre, Coventry, and Albee's *The Zoo Story*, Strindberg's *The Creditors*, and Doris Lessing's *Play With a Tiger* at the Glasgow Citizens' Theatre (*FA*: 284–6). In addition, he appeared in minor roles in the BBC television play *The Pistol* (1965), in the film *Prehistoric Women* (1966), and in an episode of the TV series *The Champions* (1968). Although these engagements were interspersed with periods of 'resting', it does appear that Berkoff was still more successful than the vast majority of his colleagues in keeping himself gainfully employed as an actor. His complaints about being passed over, therefore, suggest more about how Berkoff has positioned *himself* as a victim rather than any actual strategy of marginalisation on the part of a hostile theatre Establishment.

From Berkoff's perspective the 'lack' of employment coming his way was less problematic than his inability to secure the kind of work that would showcase his talent and propel him towards the mainstream success he really craved (*FA*: 387). In a 1989 interview, he laments: "I never got any good parts. Maybe I'm not good at working for other people: I believe in really big acting, like Olivier in *Coriolanus*, those great naked leaps of animalistic daring. You try doing that in Rep in Dundee when you're unknown and see how far it gets you" (Morley 1975). Berkoff's best opportunity to unleash his "big acting" came in 1967, when he auditioned for Peter Brook's Artaud-influenced production of Seneca's *Oedipus* (Old Vic, 1968) (*FA*: 116–19). As Kohn has put it, acceptance by Brook at this moment in his career would have offered Berkoff the chance "to [gain] the patronage of the Establishment and [remain] true to his beliefs" (Kohn 1989). In other words, here was a golden opportunity for Berkoff to achieve the success he desired without having to compromise his subject position as a performer in the 'French total theatre' tradition, and to create (as he imagined it) a unique niche for himself *within* British mainstream theatre.

Peter Brook, along with Peter Hall and Michel Saint-Denis, had been appointed co-director of the RSC in 1962. Despite being so closely associated with the theatre Establishment, however, his work in the 1960s, both theatrical and theoretical, did a great deal to create a bridge between mainstream theatre and the incipient alternative theatre scene. His landmark 'Theatre of Cruelty' season (LAMDA, 1963–64) is widely considered, to use Sandy Craig's (1980a: 20) metaphor, as one of the early harbingers of the alternative theatre storm. John Elsom, for his part, has asserted that "[i]f 'mainstream' theatre was influenced by the season, 'fringe' theatres were transformed by it" (Elsom 1979: 146). The experiment, undertaken with actors from the RSC, and culminating in an Artaudian (and Brechtian) production of Peter Weiss's *Marat/Sade* (Aldwych, 1964), was indicative of an incipient shift in dramaturgical practice away from traditional text-based and Stanislavskian character-based acting towards a search for "a universal theatre language" (Innes 1993: 125) expressed through physical performance. A primary effect of the season, according to Elsom, was "to free the actor from his [*sic*] dependence on spoken dialogue, with all those other related pressures of imitation and character development, so that he could develop his expressiveness by other means – athleticism, mime, contacts with the audience" (Elsom 1979: 145). Brook's work, inspired by the 'French total theatre' tradition, particularly the ideas and practices of Artaud and Barrault, anticipated some of the key ways in which Berkoff was seeking to position himself during the second half of the 1960s. Berkoff, looking back at that time, warmly praises the 'Theatre of Cruelty' season as "Peter Brook's summit of creativity" (*TSB*: 10), and asks rhetorically in his autobiography: "Who could not be stunned at the *Marat/Sade, The Dream* or *The Physicists?*" (*FA*: 116). Thus it seems fair to say that Brook's groundbreaking work represented all that Berkoff was setting out to achieve in terms of using 'French total theatre' as a tool to gain *mainstream* success. From Berkoff's perspective, Brook would have been the perfect patron. Yet it was not to be.

Berkoff, echoing the disappointment and bitterness he felt after his failure to be taken on board by Olivier, describes in elaborate and ironic detail the whole experience of auditioning without success for another "Sir" (*FA*: 116–20). He concludes, in a perceptive moment of introspection, that "[p]ossibly [Brook] didn't see in me what he was looking for. Maybe he saw too much. Maybe he thought, 'Here comes trouble'" (Kohn 1989). Even Brook, then, so well-disposed towards the French tradition of physical performance with which Berkoff was identifying himself more and more, rejected him as a maverick who would never fit into his concept of an ensemble. Berkoff recalls the whole incident bitterly as "the end of one particular dream" (*FA*: 119). In his autobiography he makes much of this stinging rejection in order to signal that this was his last chance to be accepted into the mainstream; that he had no choice, as it were, but to go it alone with an independent company of his own. It also served to reinforce Berkoff's positioning of himself as a misunderstood and undervalued artist who was outside the pale of the mainstream – a further 'teleological' step in the retro-evolution of his career.

Establishment and composition of the LTG

Just as the socio-political status quo in Britain and in other Western and industrial societies from New York to Tokyo was shaken by the libertarian and egalitarian tremors of the counter-culture during the 1960s, so too in the theatrical world people broke away from and disrupted the rigidly organised and hierarchical companies of the established commercial theatre and formed independent groups in order to stage productions on their own terms. As Elsom (1979: 17) observes, it was

> now the era of instant theatre, on any issue, created by anyone, in any style, performed anywhere. A radical, flamboyant, egalitarian edge to the work permeated the whole process: workshops and collectives replaced traditionally atomized ways of working; old hierarchies and divisions were broken down.

Leading British alternative theatre director Roland Rees, looking back at that time of turbulent growth and change, recalls that there "was a strong sense of being with a group. Instead of hiring actors, many companies based their work on the composition of the group members. People stayed together, to work together" (Rees 1992: 206). It was in the context but not, I suggest, in the *spirit* of these developments that Berkoff gathered together a small group of actors, including some of his former-students from the Webber Douglas Academy, in the summer of 1967 and began holding workshops above an Islington pub in order to train them in mime and ensemble skills. Abandoning his original plan to perform Eugene O'Neill's *The Hairy Ape*, he set about preparing to stage his own short adaptation (shorter than the more fully developed version staged at the Round House in 1969) of Franz Kafka's 'Metamorphosis' (*FA*: 290–3). This was the genesis of the loosely formed company that would subsequently become known as the London Theatre Group. By positioning himself as the group's teacher, director, writer and leading performer, Berkoff established the chain of command from the very outset (see Figure 10).

The 'fluidity' of the LTG's existence, as seen in the conflicting accounts offered by Berkoff of its chronology and the amorphous nature of its membership, parallels the 'fluidity' of the 'Berkoff phenomenon'. The confusion surrounding the life span of the LTG has arisen from the contradictory accounts of the group's formation that he has put forward. The programme notes for *Agamemnon* (Greenwich, 1976), for example,

10 Berkoff at the front of his London Theatre Group

state that the "London Theatre Group was founded in 1968. They gave their first performance at the Arts Laboratory with Berkoff's adaptation from Kafka's 'In the Penal Colony'". The programme notes to *East* (Greenwich, 1976), however, declare that the group was formed in 1972. Finally, to add to the jumble of dates, Berkoff informed one interviewer that the company did not come into being until 1973 (Elder 1978: 39). There has been nothing to indicate that the LTG has ever been formally disbanded, thus its present status is unclear.

The membership of the LTG has been similarly amorphous. The actress Petra Markham, who played Greta Samsa in the first production of *Metamorphosis* at the Round House in 1969, has remarked that "Steven himself was the basis of the group – actors came and went".[11] The same situation evidently obtained six years later, since the programme notes for *East* (Kings Head Theatre Club, 1975) describe the LTG as "a collection of artists who continually return to work under the direction of Steven Berkoff". Performers such as Linda Marlowe, Matthew Scurfield, Barry Philips, Wolf Kahler, Hilton McRae, Terry McGinity, and others, appeared sporadically in the group's productions during those years. It is not possible, however, to identify a stable ensemble with any identity beyond that which Berkoff's teaching, writing, directing, designing and star performances gave to it. The programme for the tryout of *Metamorphosis* at the LAMDA Theatre Club in 1969, prior to its move to the Round House, makes no mention of the LTG, indeed of any ensemble. The sparse notes indicate merely that the curtain-raiser 'The Penal Colony' [*sic*] and 'Metamorphosis' were adapted and directed by "STEVEN BERKOFF", the only name on the cast roster to appear in capital letters. The implication of this was that Berkoff was evidently more concerned with kick-starting his own independent career than with group success.

As I have already noted, a number of writers have been content to locate Berkoff and his LTG within the broad sweep of alternative theatre in the 1960s. Yet if Berkoff and the LTG were indeed alternative, I suggest that this was strictly in a theatrical rather than any macro-political sense, and then only in terms of the final product on the stage and not the rehearsal process. We have seen that Berkoff's political consciousness (at least as he has given public expression to it), far from being in any way ideologically oppositional, was and continues to be limited to a romantic notion of the individual proletarian's Darwinian struggle for personal survival and success. Berkoff states, for example, that he set up his own company "out of a desperate need to work" (*FA*: 292). The paradox of

Berkoff's apparently alternative theatre practice, it should be emphasised, is that it was a strategy designed to secure *mainstream* success. In other words, although Berkoff was not actually a card-carrying member of the alternative community, he positioned himself in close proximity to it, presumably in order to validate his mime-based approach to performance and catch the attention of prominent mainstream directors and producers who would often drop by at fringe venues. Peter Brook had come to the Arts Lab to see *In the Penal Colony*, and Berkoff recalls seeing Jean-Louis Barrault and Arnold Wesker visit the venue together on another occasion (*FA*: 110). It was clearly possible, therefore, for an unknown actor or director with at least one foot in the alternative sector to be discovered and propelled towards mainstream success.

As with his constructed French pedigree, Berkoff has also been at pains retroactively to signal his proximity to the alternative theatre scene as part of his 'teleological' career path. He notes, for example, his appreciation of the two events during 1963–64 identified by Elsom (1979: 141) as having inaugurated the new 1960s theatre: the ex-patriot American Jim Haynes's establishment of the Traverse Theatre in a former brothel in Edinburgh, and the Brook/Marowitz 'Theatre of Cruelty' season. Berkoff's warm response to the latter has already been noted; and he recalls that at the Traverse "you saw the best theatre you could hope to see anywhere" (*FA*: 268). Berkoff's identification with Artaud and Barrault, together with his mime studies, particularly at the École Jacques Lecoq, a school described by Clive Barker (1978: 54) as "a seedbed of alternative talent", may be read as strategies designed to display further his own 'non-mainstream' credentials. Elsewhere, Berkoff has been keen to demonstrate his openness to the influence of such Artaud-influenced off-off-Broadway companies and artists as the Living Theatre, Joseph Chaikin and the Open Theater, and the La Mama Experimental Theatre Club.[12] These groups exerted a tremendous impact upon the development of alternative theatre in Britain in the 1960s, particularly as a result of their visits to London during the summer of 1967, precisely the time when Berkoff was forming the LTG. Yet it was undoubtedly Berkoff's choice of the Arts Lab as the venue at which to present his very first production in 1968 that has contributed most of all to the general perception of him as an alternative theatre artist.

The Arts Lab, described as "the mecca of the underground society and a centre for cultural – and chemical – experiment" (Craig 1980a: 16), was set up in a disused building in Drury Lane in 1967 by Jim Haynes.[13] In his autobiography, *Thanks for Coming!*, Haynes (1984: 151) observes that "London in 1967 was the capital of the world and the Arts Lab was very definitely one of its centres". Berkoff states that he was a regular visitor to the Lab (*OV*: 179), and it was to Haynes that he turned in early 1968 when he was seeking a venue for his first production. Recalling the initial encounter with Berkoff, Haynes noted in a letter to this writer that

> Berkoff approached me out of the blue to ask if I would let him mount Kafka's IN THE PENAL COLONY in the Drury Lane Arts Lab. And since my "Artistic policy was to try never to say no," I said yes, why not. Let's do it! I knew nothing about him before he approached me. I had never heard of him before he knocked on my door.[14]

Prior to staging the Kafka adaptation, then, Berkoff had not been a visible member of the alternative scene, at least from Haynes's well-focused perspective. By using the Arts Lab "out of the blue", however, it would seem that he set out to position himself both chronologically and geographically at the very hub of the 1960s counter-culture and the new theatre, where he could more effectively showcase his talent. It was a strategy that enabled Berkoff to gain exposure by positioning himself alongside such notable alternative companies as Portable Theatre, the Freehold, and the People Show, all of which had launched themselves at the Lab. The very name of the LTG itself was telling. Compared with the avowedly democratic names of the companies just mentioned and of other contemporary alternative groups such as Red Ladder and Welfare State, the LTG's title may be read as a power-statement, as Berkoff's claim, at a time when London was a key locus of 1960s counter-culture, to be seen as the premier alternative theatre company in the Metropolis: the *London* Theatre Group or, perhaps, *the* London Theatre Group.

Despite (or even because of) the success of his first production, Berkoff remained emotionally, philosophically and politically separate from the emergent alternative scene. This is evident in his recollection of the success of *In the Penal Colony*, in which he draws attention not to any alternative or counter-cultural impact of the production but to the money he earned for himself:

> The money left at the box office and the sheer unadulterated pleasure of thinking that I had done this myself. Nobody had handed it to me on a plate. I had ripped it out of the frustration of unemployment and when I took my share of the takings I felt just great. (*FA*: 110)

He was thus a threshold figure lurking on the fringe of the fringe, as it were; contemporaneous with the new 1960s theatre, yet standing aloof from it except on those occasions when it served his purpose to draw closer to the fire and benefit from a warmer relationship. This ambivalence is manifest in his revealing statement that:

> We at the Lab were, without trying to sound too precious, into classes and group exercises. So I was becoming divided, half-drawn to the passivity and gentleness of the hippy culture while still being part of the fortnightly rep and Play of the Week on TV, and now my occasional branch out on my own. That was of course the very best, but I suffered under a strange delusion. I thought, Oh, how lovely it would be to join some turgid large company and be the 'great' actor I still yearned to become, rather than see my fate deliberately pushing me to investigate my own creativity. (*FA*: 108)

Thus he can write of "we at the Lab" whilst simultaneously relating the 'real' dream he continued to harbour of being recognised as the "great actor". It is paradoxical that Berkoff, concealing himself within a Trojan Horse of 'alternativeness', should have launched himself at the Arts Lab in order to secure the recognition of *mainstream* directors. Haynes, his door generously open to all-comers, was not blind to Berkoff's tactic: "I don't think that Berkoff considered himself part of any group ever, certainly not counter-culture London. He was fortunate that spaces were available to him when he needed to do something."[15]

Characteristically, in later years, having used the Arts Lab to achieve the public profile he sought, Berkoff showed his true colours, so to speak, by lowering his 'alternative' banner and raising the pirate flag of his mainstream ambitions for all to see. In a 1975 interview with Sheridan Morley, he declared with brutal frankness that:

> I hate the concept of the 'fringe' as a place full of non-Equity members having a go and gratifying their own egos. I'm not into street theatre or any of that rubbish, and I don't want to work in attics or flea pits ... What I want now is a regular West End home and then maybe we'll [*sic*] get the acceptance here that we get abroad. (Morley 1975)

His contempt for the alternative scene he exploited is made unambiguously clear in this bilious outpouring. For Berkoff, the only success worth achieving – acceptance on the stages of the West End – is equated with gaining the recognition of a theatre Establishment he has professed to hate. It is evident from this how Berkoff has contributed to his own marginalisation in both the mainstream and alternative sectors of the theatre, and to the perception of him as a self-serving "odd man out".

The philosophical and political gulf that separated Berkoff from the alternative theatre scene becomes clearer if one compares his working methods with those of Nancy Meckler's group the Freehold, a company with which Berkoff's LTG – aesthetically if not politically – appeared to share some points of similarity. Both groups had started out at the Arts Lab and both were committed to physical performance along Artaudian lines. Around that time, it was Meckler's company arguably that went the farthest and succeeded most in creating the disciplined 'total theatre' of the kind closest to Berkoff's own ideal. There is some evidence, indeed, to suggest that Freehold directly influenced the work of the LTG.[16] Many of the most significant impulses of that time found their way into the work of this group, as Roland Rees has suggested in his description of the Freehold's approach and objectives: "Freehold had a particular style evolved by Meckler through exercises, popular with American companies, originating from the Polish director Grotowski. It was not language based, but deployed physical and non-naturalistic methods of exploring texts" (Rees 1992: 19). Yet John Elsom is one commentator who has pointed out the crucial difference in the working styles adopted by Meckler and Berkoff:

> Most of the Freehold's basic ideas were developed through group improvisation, but Stephen [sic] Berkoff's London Theatre Group (1969) ... developed along more authoritarian lines. Berkoff ... was particularly concerned with carefully organised movement patterns, performed by the group in a style which was not quite dance, not quite army drill and involved some mime. Improvisation would have been out of place in his theatre, and probably out of step as well. (Elsom 1979: 149)

Most telling here is Elsom's suggestion that Berkoff denied artistic freedom to his collaborators. In almost defiant contrast to the democratic and cooperative spirit of the 1960s counter-culture, and despite his statements to the contrary, Berkoff, like his idol Barrault, placed himself in full control of practically every aspect of the LTG's productions, from writing to designing, and directing to performing. This exertion of total personal control was a primary strategy adopted by Berkoff, and a very ironic one given his 'proximity' to the alternative scene. It is in his approach as the director of the LTG that his concern and even obsession with power may be seen to have been most nakedly in operation.

To a limited degree, Berkoff's concern with control was typical of a certain tendency observable among actor-based companies at that time. Sandy Craig, describing the alternative physical theatre companies active then, notes that "nearly all these [actor-based] companies have been dominated by a single personality, usually the director, e.g. Nancy

Meckler with The Freehold, Steven Berkoff with the London Theatre Group, Mike Bradwell with Hull Truck" (Craig 1980a: 25). This is explicable perhaps in terms of the need at least partially to replace the logocentric authority of the playwright with the logocentric authority of the director/choreographer. In the case of the LTG, however, Berkoff carried this tendency to an unequalled extreme of autocratic control. Following the lead of his mentors Artaud and Barrault, Berkoff adopted an approach to directing that was, one could say, antithetical to a fully participating ensemble. This may be partly attributable to Berkoff's ambiguously self-serving understanding of the concept of *ensemble*.

First and foremost, Berkoff conceives of *ensemble*, as he does of his own theatre practice, as something fundamentally un-English. This has enabled him to construct a rather clear-cut binary opposition between British and European practices in order to align himself with 'non-Brit' theatre and justify his (self-imposed) 'isolation' and 'exile':

> Ensemble work is a tricky concept for the Brits since it really comes from countries where people like and love each other and are free and liberal with each other. You have to be fond of experimenting since it means you desire to merge with your group. An ensemble is really a big family that does not feel uncomfortable, but in class-ridden British society many directors feel a little awkward with the idea of ensemble work. (*FA*: 53)

By making the use of an ensemble a key point of difference in his European/British duality he moves beyond aesthetics to invest the distinction with a certain 'political' significance. He states, for example, that:

> Any idea of form or concept or desire to utilize the valuable energies of the actor was considered [in Britain] to be 'European'. European meant you tried to impart some sense of 'method' and psychology into the proceedings ... But British theatre tended to represent our old politics. We were an imperialist nation and worshipped and doffed our forelock to the guv'nor. Our ideas were based on a sort of economic supremacy and the quasi-religious belief in the colonial empire with its hierarchy and bosses ... what could the theatre resemble but the country's social structure? The actor with the most lines was the richest and the rest just scumbags hanging around the dressing rooms, getting pissed and waiting to go on for their 'My Liege ...' (*FA*: 97)

To judge from these two extracts, then, ensemble, for Berkoff, carries implications of collectivity, democracy and un-English or 'European' approaches to performance and dramaturgy.

97

In some of his statements Berkoff certainly appears to take ensemble to refer to a group of theatre workers who value and draw upon communal effort and energy. He notes in *Coriolanus in Deutschland*, for example, that in an ensemble

> each link is vital to the whole, unlike your average Shakespeare where it doesn't matter a fart whether you're alive or dead as long as the principals are there. For British groups the idea of ensemble and collecting the energy of the mass is as foreign as the Aztec language. Ensemble is also about brotherhood and unity. It carries the power of the play and invigorates the audience. (*CID*: 106)

Key words here are *brotherhood* and *unity*, which point to a spirit of democracy and equality in operation. These 'communal' and 'anti-Establishment' notions are problematised, however, by Berkoff's own contradictory pronouncements and, more tellingly, by the recollections of various collaborators concerning Berkoff's own autocratic working methods as a director.

In a letter published in the *Sunday Times* (26 July 1981), Berkoff leaves behind all notions of communal effort and seeks to justify his own one-man-band efforts by comparing himself to, among others, his hero Jean-Louis Barrault:

> I direct my own works since there is no-one who can stage them as I do, and I have a belief that the artist must govern his own work from the germination of the idea to its final flowering on film or stage.
>
> I have not been alone in this thought, since Chaplin, Keaton, Welles, Woody Allen, and Barrault have made their contribution unique from following their single vision.

Despite what he has projected as his democratic proclivities, then, Berkoff's concept of an ensemble is evidently a company of actors who express his purpose and vision by delivering themselves up, like Craig's *Übermarionetten*,[17] to his absolute directorial control. Indeed, in his preface to the published version of *Metamorphosis*, Berkoff describes the ensemble as "animated marionettes" (*TT*: 72). Just as the alternative physical theatre of the late-1960s sought to liberate performance from its "degrading subservience to the pre-existing script" (Connor 1997: 143), so there was a similar movement away from the repressive director who, in the words of Bernard Dort (1982: 62), "has not only gained authority over all the other workers in the theatre, but left them helpless and impotent, and in some cases reduced them to slavery." It is ironic that Berkoff's apparently liberationist theatre practice has revolved so tightly around his own logocentric and enslaving practices.

Berkoff's dictatorial approach with the LTG was at its most manifest in rehearsals (see Figures 11 and 12). Petra Markham recalls that:

> I don't think our rehearsal time was particularly democratic – Steven was in control and one just tried to please him. Rehearsals were very long – very wearing and precise. He would demonstrate what he wanted, and I would try and copy him. He was rather like a ringmaster in a circus. He wasn't tolerant of other ideas – he alone understood what he was trying to achieve.[18]

The fact that Markham had previously been one of Berkoff's students may perhaps explain the power that she claims he exerted over her and the other group members. Yet Berkoff has been equally dictatorial when directing established artists not generally known for their wilting egos such as Roman Polanski and Mikhail Baryshnikov, both of whom played the role of Gregor Samsa in the 1988 Paris and the 1989 Broadway revivals respectively of *Metamorphosis*. Polanksi, recalls that Berkoff

> doesn't have a simple way of sharing his ideas with the cast or with any of his collaborators. As you know, probably, he's got abrasive manners which make it double [*sic*] difficult to follow him, and there was always a lot of tension on stage. It was to some, I'm sure, a permanent mystery, you know, what it's going to be like. He's got his concept of the theatre and his ideas are very, very strong, and, as I told you, he knows what he's doing. He knows what he wants and he gets there. It's difficult on his colleagues, or rather collaborators, and every actor, but who cares?[19]

Baryshnikov, for his part, recalls more damningly that Berkoff "never allows you to think during the rehearsal. He pushes you into the direction and then he kind of mimics you in front of you."[20] One unnamed LTG collaborator even claimed that Berkoff 'burned out' some actors: "Nobody can work with Steven for very long; he is just too demanding" (Brown 1986). This is a view supported by the late Joseph Papp in his recollection of the rehearsals for *Coriolanus* at the 1989 New York Shakespeare Festival:

> [Berkoff's] confrontations with society, with people were explosive. There were criticisms from within the company. People came to me: the designer came to me and resigned ... the lighting designer ... the costume designer. They both came to me and told me that it was impossible to work with him, that he insulted them in front of the company, which he probably did ... I had [the actor] Christopher Walken walk out one day and he said he was going to go away.[21]

Steve Dixon, who acted in the original production of *West* in 1983, recalls that rehearsals with Berkoff could be "stressful because he also seemed to thrive on conflict between members of the ensemble, he stirred that up, wanted a cauldron atmosphere to get the raw aggression out of us."[22]

Given the consistency of these judgements by his various collaborators and ensemble members, it is remarkable that Berkoff has insisted upon projecting himself as an even-handed democrat: "In the theatre I work with actors in a collaboration, seeking their inspiration and ideas which I then try to fuse" (*PIR*: 159). In answer to Craig Rosen's question whether actors in his various ensembles enjoyed individual freedom to create within the Berkovian aesthetic, his reply was as follows: "Oh, a tremendous amount of freedom. The more ideas, the more diversity, the more community to kind of experiment with a different character every day, every hour. To keep changing, finding, and then gradually honing it down. An enormous amount of freedom."[23] Clearly, Berkoff's perspective of his artistic freedom as director has been at odds with the expectations of a good number of the members of his various companies.

It is evident from this discussion that Berkoff's primary concern as the director of the LTG and later groups that he has gathered together has

11 Berkoff the director at work in a rehearsal for *The Trial*

been with the creation of theatre through the exercise of his own will-to-power. The journalist Brian Appleyard has observed that:

> During the rehearsals he is ferocious, cruel and tyrannical with the cast. Once the show is up and running he becomes one of the boys. It is a style that has made him many enemies and inspired the almost knee-jerk description of Berkoff as a megalomaniac. He is unquestionably obsessed by the issue of his own freedom. (Appleyard 1989)

And another commentator who witnessed a rehearsal at the National Theatre for the 1991 revival of *The Trial* offers the following vivid picture of Berkoff at work as a director:

> As his actors run through scene after scene, Berkoff surveys them like a drill-sergeant, softly prowling the margin of the rehearsal floor, sometimes turning, like a player of Grandmother's Footsteps, to address the production manager behind him. But mostly he stands like one of Kafka's own "wrathful judges," poised and spring-heeled, his grey-stubbled Prussian head hunched, his blue eyes frighteningly watchful, his hands joined behind his back, Napoleonically, a baton-sized pencil shared among fat fingers. (Walsh 1991)

12 Berkoff (back to camera) leading a rehearsal for *Macbeth*

Why, one may ask, has Berkoff felt it necessary to have recourse to such autocratic methods?

With regard to such extreme manifestations of control, it is useful to consider Sawicki's (1991) notion that repression and the need to resort to force – and Berkoff's directing in a "ferocious, cruel and tyrannical" manner can certainly be regarded as force – is rather to be taken as evidence of a *lack* of power; repression is used when the limits of power have been reached. In his biography of Kean, to return once again to Berkoff's great idol, Giles Playfair makes the following observation, equally applicable to Berkoff in this context, that "[Kean] never for one instant felt secure. He was continually in the same state of mind as a dictator who rules uncomfortably by force and who fears a revolution or a sudden calamitous fall from power" (Playfair 1950: 174). Despite his 'control freak' subject positions, Berkoff, a liminal figure shifting uneasily back and forth between the mainstream and alternative sectors, emerges as a figure that has always felt insecure about his constructed 'self' and his position in British theatre. Berkoff's obsession with full personal control over the LTG suggests that the 'Berkoff' and 'LTG' constructs, composed of contradictory and fleeting discourses, can only be held together by main force.

Conclusion

In this chapter I have argued that far from belonging to the democratically organised alternative theatre scene that emerged in the 1960s, Berkoff replicated (with compound interest) the hierarchical power structure of the mainstream that he claimed to despise. Indeed, Berkoff's *modus operandi* as director of the LTG (and later ensembles) locates him in a tradition of autocratic direction that goes back over a century. In his article entitled 'Celebrity and the Semiotics of Acting', Michael Quinn (1990: 156–7) observes that:

> The dream of an artistic ensemble of actors is really a director's dream, and the idealization of the repertory company, accomplished by despots like Georg II of Saxe-Meiningen, was really the achievement of a directorial authority in the theatre that allowed actors to become more or less interchangeable.

Characteristically, it is the "despots" – Artaud, Barrault, Meyerhold and others – that Berkoff has most admired and emulated. Indeed, the manner in which Berkoff formed the LTG and exerted control over virtually every aspect of its activity may be taken as emblematic of the tendency towards autocratism that has informed his whole career. As a company the LTG enjoyed no existence independent of Berkoff himself, but was rather a creation of Berkoff deployed in his public construction and projection of 'self'. Far from being an egalitarian ensemble, the LTG was a constantly shifting constellation of individuals who orbited around their heliocentric leader.

Some commentators dealing with the British theatre scene of the late 1960s have been tempted to see Berkoff as an alternative artist. Yet Berkoff's 'alternativeness' at the time when he embarked on his independent career is best seen as an opportunist act of *bricolage*, as he appropriated and resignifed certain discourses to suit his purposes: 'French total theatre', for example, became the means to signal his separateness from British theatre and society; the Arts Lab and the alternative theatre scene became springboards for *mainstream* success; a 'democratic' ensemble became a locus of Berkoff's self-empowerment, and so on. Berkoff's formation of the LTG appears to have been motivated primarily by his desire to win and centralise power in his own hands. As evidence of Berkoff's lack of alternative political 'credentials', there is his frequently expressed desire for total personal control. The following passage from his autobiography is a typical example:

> Be your own master is a lesson I learned and had to relearn. When working for a large organization one naturally has to fit into the existing structure and that can be very comforting, for all the organizing and planning tours, casting, finding the dough and even deciding on the ads can be very tiring, but the down side is that you have no control over your product. (*FA*: 95)

Far from embracing the egalitarian working methods that were the practical expression of the 1960s *Zeitgeist*, Berkoff, as the founder, trainer and leader, as well as the playwright, director, designer and virtuoso actor of the LTG was, I suggest, ahead of his time in so far as he can be seen to have anticipated the aggressive, meritocratic individualism of Thatcherism (see chapter 6).

Notes

1 From a letter to Marcel Dalio dated 27 June 1932, quoted in Artaud (1989: 63).
2 Antonin Artaud (1896–1948) was originally a member of the Surrealists but was expelled from the group in 1926. After that he followed a solitary path with few allies and channelled his energy into various fields, including poetry

and essay writing. He envisioned a new form of theatre, which he called the "Theatre of Cruelty", in which naturalism would be shattered and spoken language set aside in a convulsive though carefully orchestrated act. His visions of a total spectacle with lights, violent gestures and noise in place of music were set out in the essay collection *The Theatre and Its Double* (1938). All his efforts to implement his projects met with utter failure, however. After a series of journeys in 1936 and 1937 to Mexico, Brussels and Ireland, his disillusionment with the restrictions of society and the pursuit of his creative limits had been aggravated to a critical point leading to an apparent physical and mental breakdown. He underwent asylum internment from 1937 to 1946, during which time his health deteriorated due to starvation and electroshock treatment. Yet the final two years of his life were extremely productive. He sought to establish a physical language without transcendental references, directing his fury against society in a state of constant confrontation. See Martin Esslin, *Antonin Artaud* (London: Calder, 1990), Stephen Barber, *Antonin Artaud: Blows and Bombs* (London: Faber & Faber, 1993) and Bettina Knapp, *Antonin Artaud* (Chicago: Swallow Press, 1994).

3 Jean-Louis Barrault (1910–94) began his theatrical career as a pupil of Charles Dullin. In 1940 he was admitted as a member of the prestigious Comédie Française. After the Second World War he organised his own company at the Théâtre Marigny with his wife, actress Madeleine Renaud. Barrault's precise, imaginative physical style was influenced by his study of mime. He is perhaps best remembered for his portrayal of Hamlet and as the mime in Marcel Carné's film *Children of Paradise* (1944). See his autobiography *Memories for Tomorrow* (London: Thames & Hudson, 1974) and his memoirs *Reflections on the Theatre* (London: Rockliff, 1951) and *The Theatre of Jean-Louis Barrault* (London: Barrie & Rockliff, 1961).

4 Claude Chagrin was chosen by Laurence Olivier to be his movement and choreography specialist at the National Theatre. Chagrin's work greatly enhanced the original London productions of Peter Shaffer's *Royal Hunt of the Sun* (1964) and *Equus* (1973), and Stoppard's *Rosencrantz and Guildenstern Are Dead* (1967).

5 Jacques Lecoq started his career in movement by teaching physical education, sport, and helping disabled people to walk. In 1945, he was an actor in the company 'Comédiens de Grenoble', where he discovered acting under masks and created body training adapted to the needs of the actors. In 1948, he left France for Italy where he stayed for eight years. At the invitation of the University Theater in Padou, he taught movement to the troupe and created his first mime shows. While there, he discovered the origins of the *Commedia dell'arte* in the markets of the town. In Milan, he created his school of the Piccolo Theater. His experience of choreographing Greek tragedies at Syracusa in Sicily enabled him to discover and experiment with the dynamics of the chorus. In 1969, he became a teacher at the Architectural School in Paris and created his International School of Mime and Movement, the École Jacques Lecoq. See Jacques Lecoq, *The Moving Body* (London: Methuen, 2002) for Lecoq's own account of his pedagogical philosophy and methods.

6 Although first published in French in 1938, the full impact of this work upon

the English-speaking theatre world dates from the appearance in 1958 of the first English translation (New York: Grove Press; translated by Mary Caroline Richards).

7 The impassioned tirade of conservative theatre writer Laurence Kitchin may be taken as representative of the Establishment attitude in the mid-1960s towards Artaudian ideas. He denounced *Le Théâtre et Son Double* as the "bible of sick theatre" which, following its publication in English in 1958, "had an immediate appeal, not only to addicts of the macabre, but to enthusiasts eager to make a new start in the drama and get rid of existing traditions, root and branch" (Kitchin 1966: 23).

8 The following extract from the 'Three Theatre Manifestos' is a typical example of how Berkoff evoked Artaudian principles in the early development of his dramaturgy: "Artaud suggests that the actor should look for texts, not written expressly for the recruiting of actors to bring them to life, but works that already exist in the public consciousness ... ancient works and myths, the Bible and the Cabala, novels and historical events ... works that contain their own narrative truth, historical perspective and power: these are the best subjects for actors" (*TTM*: 11–12). And again: "Only by harnessing the resources of energy and inspiration, by bringing back the super-actor, by ridding the theatre of the poseurs and by taking a leaf from Brecht, Artaud, Meyerhold, La Mama, Ronconi, Olivier, or anyone who in his [sic] time has made theatre breath-taking" (12).

9 *Reflections on the Theatre* was originally published as *Réflexions sur le Théâtre* (Paris: Jacques Vautrain, 1949), and *The Theatre of Jean-Louis Barrault* as *Nouvelles Réflexions sur le Théâtre* (Paris: Flammarion, 1959).

10 The Russian actor and director Vsevolod Emilievich Meyerhold (1874–1940) is famous for developing 'Biomechanics', a theatrical method in which actors were completely controlled by the director. Meyerhold manoeuvred his players like puppets, and ordered them to suppress their personal emotions in order to concentrate on gesture and movement.

11 Petra Markham, letter to author, 2 November 1994.

12 In New York, in the early 1950s, 'off-Broadway' theatre arose as an alternative to the commercial tradition of Broadway and became associated with low-budget productions of plays by contemporary dramatists such as Edward Albee and Tennessee Williams. By far the most radical off-Broadway company was the Living Theatre, set up by Julian Beck and Judith Malina in 1948. In the early 1960s, as off-Broadway became more commercial and professional in its approach, a more radical alternative theatre scene referred to as 'off-off-Broadway' emerged in small venues in Greenwich Village and the Lower East Side. The engaged politics and Artaudian experiments of the Living Theatre were inspirational for this new generation of counter-cultural artists. The most important off-off-Broadway groups included the Bread and Puppet Theatre (founded by Peter Schumann in 1961), the La Mama Experimental Theatre Club (founded by Ellen Stewart in 1961), the Open Theater (founded by Joseph Chaikin in 1963), and the Performance Group (founded by Richard Schechner in 1967). See Theodore Shank, *American Alternative Theatre* (Basingstoke: Macmillan, 1982) for a detailed account of these developments.

13 Jim Haynes was one of the most influential figures on the alternative scene in Britain during the late 1960s. While studying at the University of Fdjnburgh he started a bookshop and gallery (The Paperback) and the Traverse Theatre, and helped to create the Edinburgh Festival Fringe. After moving to London in 1966, he co-created the London Traverse Theatre Company, co-launched the underground newspaper "IT", and set up the Arts Lab.

14 Jim Haynes, letter to author, 3 February 1995.

15 *Ibid.*

16 That Berkoff was influenced by the work of the Freehold may be inferred from comparing the photographs of the latter's production of *Antigone* (1970) (see Craig 1980b: 107) and the LTG's production of *Agamemnon* (1973) (see *TSB*: 78–83). The similarities in choice of play genre (Greek tragedy), and in the use of stylised physical performance, of ensemble choreography, and of knitted 'chain-mail' costumes are striking. A key figure in the transmission of this influence was the German actor Wolf Kahler, an ex-member of the Freehold who later joined the LTG and worked closely with Berkoff on the development of *Agamemnon* (*FA*: 368; *AFHU*: 7).

17 Gordon Edward Craig (1872–1966), the English scene designer, producer, and actor, began acting with Henry Irving's Lyceum company. Feeling that the realism in vogue at that time was too limiting, he turned to scene design and developed new dramaturgical theories. He strove for the poetic and suggestive in his designs in order to capture the essential spirit of the play. His ideas, though often impractical, gave a new freedom and impetus to scene design. He envisioned the ideal actor as a 'super-puppet' or *Übermarionette*, devoid of ego and emotion, that delivered itself up wholly to the will of the director.

18 Petra Markham, letter to author, 2 November 1994.

19 Quoted from the South Bank Show, Channel 4, 1989. Berkoff offered his own gloss on their troubled working relationship: Polanski, he recalls, "seemed to have little to say to me after rehearsals and found it a little difficult to take direction" (*MOM*: 85).

20 *Ibid.*

21 *Ibid.*

22 Steve Dixon, letter to author, 23 November 1999.

23 Quoted from Craig Rosen's interview with Berkoff.

4

CONFINEMENT AND ESCAPOLOGY

A kick at the Establishment is not necessarily aimed to demolish it. In the case of John Braine's hero, Joe Lampton, it was more a matter of kicking at the door in order to be let in. Joe does not lacerate himself about good causes. (Peter Lewis, *The Fifties*)

Despite the fact that Berkoff's 'self-made-man' neo-Conservatism placed him philosophically, politically and emotionally at a distance from the counter-cultural scene in London, his work with the LTG during the years 1968–74 located him close to that current of 1960s alternative theatre in Britain, influenced variously by Grotowski, Artaud, off-off-Broadway, and the pedagogy of Jacques Lecoq, that experimented with physical perform- ance. The theatrical practices of such companies as Beth Porter's Wherehouse La Mama and its offshoot the Freehold, Steve Rumbelow's Triple Action, Paddy Fletcher's Incubus, and Berkoff's London Theatre Group, were predicated upon a 'politics of the body' that challenged the conventional text-based and naturalistic approaches of mainstream theatre. In varying degrees and styles, the purpose of these different groups was to destabilise the 'literary' structures of dialogue, character, plot, and unified theme associated with mainstream theatre (Vanden Heuvel 1993: 36–7). This is not to say, however, that the privileging of the actor's body led necessarily to a complete abandonment of the written text. The Freehold, for example, worked in a "productive relationship" (Chambers 1980: 106) with writer Peter Hulton on such classic texts as *Antigone* (1969–70) and *The Duchess of Malfi* (1970), and Berkoff, of course, used his own scripts, which he subsequently fixed in published form, as the basis for his own productions. The key point is that the texts were *physically* realised in the productions.

All the LTG productions staged during 1968–74, apart from the revivals of Shakespeare's *Macbeth* (The Place, 1970) and Albee's *The Zoo Story* (Newcastle University, 1973), were Berkoff-penned adaptations of classic literary or dramatic works. Chronologically, they are as follows: *In the Penal Colony* (Arts Lab, 1968), *Metamorphosis* (Round House, 1969), *The Trial* (Oval House, 1970), *Agamemnon* (RADA, 1971), *Knock at the*

107

Manor Gate (Sussex University, 1972), *Miss Julie Versus Expressionism* (ICA, 1973), and *The Fall of the House of Usher* (Edinburgh Festival, 1974). These productions, however, cannot be considered of equal value or significance within Berkoff's *œuvre*. *Knock at the Manor Gate*, *Miss Julie Versus Expressionism* and *The Zoo Story* were staged hurriedly as works-in-progress in order to fulfil the obligations of Arts Council grants rather than as fully realised dramatic statements (*FA*: 313–4; 326). Furthermore, these three plays, together with *Macbeth* and *In the Penal Colony*, have never been revived by Berkoff, and photographs of the productions are conspicuously absent from *The Theatre of Steven Berkoff* (1992), his otherwise comprehensive photographic retrospective of his stage work, which suggests that they were viewed by him as inferior works that did not adequately represent his aesthetic aims.

The remaining plays, *Metamorphosis, The Trial, Agamemnon,* and *The Fall of the House of Usher,* I take as the major early productions with which Berkoff projected himself and his evolving actor-based dramaturgy. Out of these four plays I focus my attention in this chapter on *Metamorphosis* as a case study, not only because, as his first major independent production, it was the one in which he unveiled his brand of 'total theatre', but also because for more than two decades he has emphatically signalled in his non-dramatic writings the central position that this play has occupied in his career and work. Berkoff's earliest polemical piece, 'Three Theatre Manifestos' (1978), prefaces the first published version of *Metamorphosis,* making it clear that he was placing the playscript in a dialogic relationship to the manifestos in order to exemplify his reflections on mime-based 'total theatre'. He has also written a piece entitled 'Twenty Years of *Metamorphosis*' (1989), in which he looks back on the longevity and success of this adaptation, and a book-length memoir, *Meditations on Metamorphosis* (1995), dealing with his experiences of directing ten productions of the play in various languages around the world during the years 1969–92. There he writes: "What [*Metamorphosis*] did for me was to allow me the scope to explore, experiment and extend my vision and, finally, to be responsible for my own creation" (*MOM*: xvi). In what follows I particularly want to examine the theatrical and metatheatrical qualities of the play and, more particularly, of Berkoff's performance as the protagonist Gregor Samsa in the original production in order to examine how he has used the role to project himself and his relationship with the theatre Establishment.

The structure of this chapter is as follows. In the first section, I describe the key theatrical characteristics of the *mise-en-scène* for *Metamorphosis* and examine how Berkoff sought to validate it by positioning himself and his dramaturgy in close proximity to the iconic 'name' and early mime-based work of Jean-Louis Barrault. I focus in particular upon the key defining element in the *mise-en-scène*, namely Berkoff's solo acrobatic performance as the man/beetle hero. In this context it is useful to consider theatre semiotician Jean Alter's notion that there are two primary functions of performance, namely "performant" (related to virtuoso display) and "referential" (related to content) (Alter 1990: 38). In the case of Berkoff's performance as Gregor these two functions, I shall argue, became indistinguishable. In other words, Berkoff's dexterous display *was* the content, or, to borrow Marshall McLuhan's famous dictum, the medium was the message. In the second section, I turn to the meta-theatrical significance of the play, and examine in particular Berkoff's performance in the original production, as a dramatisation on stage of the 'drama' (as he projected it) of his career. I focus upon Berkoff's enactment of his 'confinement' by and 'escape' from the disciplinary strategies and conventional performance practices of mainstream theatre. A primary concern will be to interrogate the apparently resistant quality of *Metamorphosis* and demonstrate how Berkoff used his performance in it, paradoxically, to showcase his physical acting skills in order to achieve mainstream recognition.

Theatricality: 'French total theatre'

Kafka's novella 'Metamorphosis' provided Berkoff as a developing writer and director with very suitable raw material for his first major independent production. As Beck (1971), Rolleston (1974), Klinger (1983) and Kiefer (1989) among others have amply demonstrated, Kafka's fiction is highly dramatic and theatrical in character. Beck (1971: 143), describing Kafka's adoption of stage techniques in 'Metamorphosis', has observed that:

> Each section of the story is limited to a small, clearly defined area (Gregor's room and the living room); props are placed and accounted for as if they were to be made concrete on a stage. With the exception of Gregor, the characters are minimally developed and resemble type characters of the drama, who fulfill one function or embody only a single trait. The movements of the characters are recorded with the precision of stage directions, and the exaggerated action often culminates in a grouping of characters that recalls the tableaux of the Yiddish theater.

Structurally too, Beck argues, the story "progresses like a drama, building through a series of crises (Gregor's three confrontations with the outside world) to a final denouement (Gregor's death and removal)" (143).

This theatrical quality of Kafka's fiction has made it an attractive source of material for scores of dramatic and cinematic reworkings (Wunderlich 1979: 825–41). As Martin Esslin (1983: 355) points out:

> even if Kafka's own modest attempt to write a play ['The Guardian of the Crypt'] came to nothing, the directness of his narrative prose, the concrete clarity of its images and its mystery and tensions, have proved a constant temptation to adapters who felt that it was ideal material for the stage.

We have seen that Berkoff had already succumbed to this temptation as a drama student with his ill-received version of 'The Bucket Rider'. The strategy of launching his independent career with his three major Kafka adaptations not only enabled him to exploit this latent theatricality more fully, it served his purposes in three other key respects.

Firstly, as I discussed in chapter 1, it enabled Berkoff to elaborate a Kafka-inflected 'Jewish victim' subject position through a close identification with the Czech writer and his fictional alter egos. In his preface to the published text of his adaptation of *The Trial*, for example, Berkoff states that:

> Kafka expressed me as I expressed Kafka. His words stung and hung on my brain, infused themselves into my art and were regurgitated in my work ... Joseph K's mediocrity was mine and his ordinariness and fears were mine too: the 'under-hero' struggling to find the ego that would lead him to salvation. (*TT*: 5)

Similarly, looking back to the time in 1955 in Wiesbaden when he first read the novella 'Metamorphosis', Berkoff recalls, "I could at last really identify with something. The Beetle" (*FA*: 168). Even though Kafka's story does not deal with any specifically *Jewish* themes, Berkoff reinscribed the man/insect protagonist with qualities of collective Jewish victimhood:

> The historic Jew, excluded by law from most arts and crafts, from a thousand possibilities of expressing himself [*sic*], from landowner-ship to farming, was allowed only a handful of despised professions, which of course included dealing in old clothes, tailoring and usury. So the modern Jew inherits the legacy of the past and Willy Loman and Gregor Samsa return home, exhausted by the system that feeds on them and sucks away at their lives. (*MOM*: 103)

Berkoff's projection of himself through such an iconic victim was a means to enact his own 'victimisation' by the British theatre Establishment. Yet, as I will show, simultaneously and paradoxically this strategy was designed also with the objective of achieving mainstream recognition.

Secondly, it enabled Berkoff to exploit the undoubted selling power of Kafka's iconicity. When this writer asked Jim Haynes why, in his opinion, Berkoff had chosen to start off at the Arts Lab with *In the Penal Colony*, his reply was simple and to the point: "One always has to have a 'hook' to get people into the theatre, and Kafka is an excellent hook."[1] Berkoff's awareness of the Czech novelist's power of attraction is evident in his statement that the novelist was "the magnet that drew the audience" (*MOM*: xv) to his double-bill of *In the Penal Colony* and *Metamorphosis* at the Round House in 1969. Moreover, it is safe to assume that he had noted the success of David Hare's Kafka adaptation *Inside Out*, the first production by Portable Theatre, which was staged at the Arts Lab prior to his own debut there (Elsom 1979: 157). Kafka, then, was an extremely pragmatic choice.

Finally, his strategy of dramatising works by Kafka enabled him to lend 'legitimacy' to the new Berkovian style by claiming a direct genealogical link to his "great hero" (*FA*: 110) Jean-Louis Barrault, who had collaborated with André Gide on *Le Procès* (The Trial) (Théâtre du Marigny, 1947), the first ever documented stage adaptation of a work by Kafka (Wunderlich 1979: 826). Emphasising this 'French connection', Berkoff declared in a 1975 interview that "I'd turned to Kafka for the adaptations because, like Welles and Barrault,[2] I was fascinated by the sheer theatricality of his imagination" (Morley 1975). Berkoff's accounts of his efforts to stage *The Trial* and, more especially, *Metamorphosis* are shadowed throughout by Barrault. We have seen that he had planned to stage the Barrault/Gide adaptation of *The Trial* as early as 1965. He studied the English translation of that version together with Barrault's own account of the *mise-en-scène* (Barrault 1961: 123–30) before beginning work on his own adaptation in 1970 (*FA*: 308). As a result, Barrault's dramaturgy left its imprint upon the flowing 'cinematic' style and mime-based choral approach of Berkoff's version.[3] It is in the 'French total theatre' conception of *Metamorphosis*, however, and in Berkoff's own performance in the premiere and early revivals of that play, that Barrault's 'presence' is most evident. I turn now to the Frenchman's influence in three key areas: the initial conception of the play, the *mise-en-scène*, and Berkoff's solo performance as Gregor Samsa.

Berkoff, recalling another epiphanic moment in his career, states that it was reading Barrault's detailed description (Barrault 1951: 30–45) of his struggle as a young unknown actor to create a centaur-like figure in *Autour d'une mère* (As I Lay Dying) (Théâtre de l'Atelier, 1935) that gave him, another young unknown who was eager to test the waters, the confidence to "plunge in" to the whirlpool of 'total theatre' with *Metamorphosis* (*TT*: 71). Faulkner's novel, with its man/horse protagonist, had provided Barrault with the germ of an idea to create his first independent venture, a mime-drama that would serve "as a manifesto for the rehabilitation of the art of gesture" (Barrault 1951: 177). He recalls: "This book was to engross me throughout the whole year ... That was a real 'encounter', and I am quite sure that it was the only book I read that year ... [it] absorbed me, and in my turn I put all my energies into absorbing it" (30). Regarding the approach he took to performing the 'centaur', he writes: "In *As I Lay Dying* a certain wild young man tames a horse wilder even than himself. Now this horse appealed to me from the miming point of view. So it was from the point of view of the horse that I worked at *As I Lay Dying*" (30–1). This anecdote unlocked the dramatic potential of Kafka's story for Berkoff, with the result that he, too, built his adaptation around his own solo performance as the literally grotesque half-human/half-animal figure of Gregor Samsa. Even if Berkoff himself had not acknowledged Barrault's powerful influence, it is evident from the parallels between the latter's recollection just quoted and Berkoff's description in the 'Three Theatre Manifestos' of his own encounter with Kafka's story and his subsequent desire to stage it and mime its man/ beetle protagonist:

> I had read the story many years ago ... and its first impression on me was overwhelming, the identification so strong that it became imperative for me to play the beetle. I played it as a human-being locked within the carapace of the beetle, and I physically attempted to enact the rhythms of an insect and its frenetic scurrying move-ments. The use of mime made this possible. (*TTM*: 7)

At the outset of his independent career Berkoff, hungry to make his mark, had much to gain from aligning himself closely with the "French Laurence Olivier" (Shellard 1999: 20) who, since his first visit to the Edinburgh Festival in 1948 with *Hamlet* had been widely admired in Britain. In 1951 Olivier invited Barrault and his company to perform at the St James Theatre in London. The "World Theatre" impresario Peter Daubeny likewise brought him to London on several occasions during the

1950s. He was thus highly respected in mainstream/Establishment circles within British theatre. Yet in the following decade Barrault also found favour with the alternative theatre sector and the broader constituency of the counter-culture as a result of his intervention in the student-led rebellion in Paris in May, 1968, the "crucial year for fringe theatre" (Hammond 1973: 38). In a gesture that cost him his position as the director of the Théâtre National de l'Odéon, he voiced his support for the protesting students and workers. Later that year his *Rabelais* (Élysées-Montmartre, 1968) provided an anti-authoritarian gloss upon *les événements de Mai* (Barrault 1974: 311–33). This high-profile exercise in 'total theatre' was brought to London, where Barrault directed revivals of it at the Old Vic (1969) and the Round House (1971). The actor Bill Wallis, who participated in it and compiled a "production casebook" for *Theatre Quarterly*, drew attention to Barrault's status at that time, noting that his "name and reputation as a man of the theatre were our incentives to seek to take part in the production rather than a love of Rabelais, or a personal commitment to a particular area of theatre or political or social principles" (Wallis 1971: 83). Berkoff has written that he witnessed certain works by Barrault during the 1960s (*TSB*: 10). Regardless of whether or not he personally saw, or was familiar with, *Rabelais*, it remains beyond doubt that Berkoff was able to count upon the theatre-going public's familiarity with Barrault and his work in order to 'co-produce' his own public persona and dramaturgy. As we have seen in the case of 'Olivier', Berkoff refracted his 'self' and his dramaturgy through the prism of the Frenchman's iconic figure and work, both of which, as in the case of Berkoff, straddled the mainstream and alternative sectors of the theatre, in order to validate his 'self' and his work.

Both *Autour d'une mère* and *Metamorphosis* were experiments in 'total theatre' that were designed to launch the independent careers and show-case the mime-based dramaturgies and performance styles of two young artists disillusioned with the naturalism that dominated mainstream theatre practice in 1930s France and 1960s Britain. Barrault's production, and particularly his solo performance, marked his first practical application of the explorations he had undertaken with Étienne Decroux in the early-1930s into the potential of mime as a theatrical tool (Barrault 1951: 21–9; Weiss 1979). Barrault's experiments locate him in the French tradition of mime and physical performance that extends back to Copeau's Vieux Colombier (Leabhart 1989: 60–74).[4] We have already seen how Berkoff linked himself to this tradition through his study of the writings of Artaud and Barrault and through his brief period of study at

the École Jacques Lecoq. With *Metamorphosis* he created his own 'manifesto for the rehabilitation of the art of gesture' by emulating Barrault and
making his mime-based performance in the lead role the key component
of the *mise-en-scène*.

At this point it is worth considering how exactly Barrault and Berkoff
conceived of 'total theatre'. In his memoirs, Barrault (1951: 83–4)
described it as:

> life transmitted to the stage by means of the *total* utilisation of all the
> means of expression at the disposal of a Human Being and the *total*
> utilisation of his [*sic*] whole range of musical and plastic expression
> (song, lyrical diction, prose diction, cries, breathing, sighs, silences,
> prosaic bodily expression, the art of gesture, symbolic gesture, lyrical
> gesture and dance).

The following description by Christopher Innes (1993: 98) of Barrault's
mise-en-scène for *Autour d'une mère* shows how he set about realising this
concept on the stage:

> In the two hours of stage time there were only thirty minutes of
> dialogue; and much of this was in the form of choral songs or
> religious chants. There were no sets, and both costumes and props
> were minimal. The actors were practically naked, their only 'costumes'
> being belts, to which were attached symbolic objects, each repre-
> senting the character's dominant passion. The performers created
> the environment for the different scenes by vocal sound effects and
> rhythmic gestures, producing unaided the rasp of a saw for building
> the coffin or bird calls for the forest. It was solely their movements as
> an ensemble that evoked the dominating context of the natural
> world: flowing and tumbling for the river in flood, a light and leaping
> dance for flames in the fire, or heavy mechanical bending movements
> for cotton-pickers in the fields. There were no atmospheric lighting
> effects and no external emotional tone from music, the only accom-
> paniment being a tomtom.

Berkoff echoed Barrault's description of 'total theatre' in his statement of
the dramaturgical creed of the LTG. The common purpose shared by the
group members was, he wrote, "[t]o express drama in the most vital way
imaginable; to perform at the height of one's power with all available
means. That is, through the spoken word, gesture, mime and music"
(*AFHU*: 7). Many of these performance elements found their way into the
mise-en-scène of *Metamorphosis*, and the majority of Berkoff's subsequent
productions, notably his 'total theatre' versions of *The Trial*, *Agamemnon*
and *The Fall of the House of Usher*. I now give a brief overview of Berkoff's

use of stage setting, script, ensemble, and solo virtuoso mime-based performance in *Metamorphosis* in order to demonstrate how closely he was following in the footsteps of his French mentor and thereby positioning himself outside mainstream British theatre practice.

The stage in *In the Penal Colony* had been dominated by the monolithic 'Heath Robinson' torture machine (*FA*: 294). A key lesson that Berkoff had learnt from this early theatrical experiment was that the use of such realistic and ponderous properties would be inimical to the creation of 'total theatre'. In his 'Three Theatre Manifestos', reflecting on the two productions that followed *Penal Colony*, he declared that "a set that is solid seems a dead weight on a stage whose message should lie in what is imaginative and ephemeral. It cannot be moved and seems an absurd piece of evidence to remind an audience of time and space" (*TTM*: 15). With *Metamorphosis*, Berkoff followed the example of Barrault by employing a minimal stage setting as the foundation of his style. This he describes in his introduction to the published playscript:

> A skeletal framework of steel scaffolding suggesting an abstract sculpture of a giant insect is stretched across the stage – this serves as the home of the family or as the carapace. The stage is void of all props – everything is mimed – apart from three black stools (metal) situated equidistant downstage for the family to use. (*TT*: 77)

The stools, Berkoff notes, served as "miniature stages" (*MOM*: 108) on which the family members could twist and turn as they create the environment of the play through mime.

The script, like the lean setting, served to minimalise and physicalise the story. As in the case of *Autour d'une mère*, the greater part of the stage time in *Metamorphosis* was taken up by mimed and choreographed action. Berkoff's replacement of Kafka's third-person narrator by the voices and gesturing bodies of the chorus permitted him to *enact* the streamlined text. A comparison between the openings of Kafka's story (in the Muir translation published by Penguin) and Berkoff's playscript illustrates this point. The story begins thus:

> As Gregor Samsa awoke one morning from uneasy dreams he found himself transformed in his bed into a gigantic insect. He was lying on his hard, as it were armour-plated, back and when he lifted his head a little he could see his dome-like brown belly divided into stiff arched segments on top of which the bed-quilt could hardly keep in position and was about to slide off completely. His numerous legs, which were pitifully thin compared to the rest of his bulk, waved helplessly before his eyes.

> What has happened to me? he thought. It was no dream. (Kafka 1961: 9)

The corresponding scene in Berkoff's adaptation is as follows:

> MR S: [*enters*] As Gregor Samsa awoke one morning from uneasy dreams …
> MRS S: [*enters*] He found himself transformed in his bed into a gigantic insect …
> GRETA: [*enters*] His numerous legs, which were pitifully thin compared to the rest of his bulk, waved helplessly before him.
> [*Movement starts.* GREGOR *is in front. Suddenly the movement stops –* FAMILY *dissolve the beetle image by moving away – leaving* GREGOR *still moving as part of the insect image.*]
> GREGOR: What has happened to me?
> FAMILY: He thought.
> GREGOR: It was no dream. (*TT*: 79)

From this, one can see how Berkoff did very little to change the language of the original. This shows that his focus, as creator of this adaptation, was less on altering the language of the dialogue in an original way than on creating a 'score' for the physical performance of the actors.

One of Barrault's primary concerns in staging his Faulkner adaptation was to demonstrate how every detail of the narrated story could be conveyed through choreographed choral movement, stylised gesture and mime. Recalling the ensemble's performance in *Autour d'une mère*, Barrault wrote: "We brought life to the elements. The torrid quivering Sun, Rain, a River, a Flood, Water, Drowning, Fire, a Conflagration, Birds (buzzards), Fish, a City, the Circulation of Traffic" (Barrault 1951: 36). Likewise, the actors in *Metamorphosis* mimed everything, from such quotidian actions as eating breakfast (*TT* 83) and doffing an "imaginary hat" (85) to more stylised representations of psychological states such as "anguish" (84) and "horror" (91). Throughout the play they froze in tableaux that convey, for example, their "outrage and opposition" (88) or the images in family snapshots (101). The following statement made by Berkoff in his 'Three Theatre Manifestos' with regard to *The Trial* holds good for the dramaturgy of *Metamorphosis*: "The actors could easily be the environment as well as playing the protagonists, and perhaps they were meant to be the environment, since man [*sic*] created and built his environment, and it was made naturally in his image to fit his own body" (*TTM*: 15). Similarly, with regard to *Agamemnon*, Berkoff writes that "I made it an oratorio, plus a physical enactment of the events: the actors became the horses, re-enacted the battles, and we were the sea. Becoming the environment releases in the actor the total possibilities of his [sic] human potential" (AFHU: 8).

Apart from creating the physical and psychological environment of the drama, the other main purpose of the ensemble in the original production of Metamorphosis was to offset Berkoff's solo performance. He writes: "The family were placed so as to be able to function without masking Gregor from the audience" (MOM: 108). Moreover, in the stage directions he seems to echo Gordon Craig by referring to the other characters as "marionettes" and "automatic figures in wax-works" (TT: 81). Gregor's father is even described as a "two-dimensional creation" (MOM: 26). In other words, Berkoff approached the other dramatis personae, and the actors performing the roles, as something akin to 'living stage properties' to be manipulated within the framework of the total production. Michael Quinn (1990: 103) has argued that ensemble-based performance is a style that "[resists] the celebrity syndrome and performer-role identification". This may well have been true with regard to the practice of the other more democratically organised alternative theatre companies mentioned above; in the case of Berkoff's LTG, how-ever, particularly in the context of Metamorphosis, the opposite was the case, namely that he used the ensemble as a tool to highlight his own role and performance in a bid, I suggest, to create celebrity status for himself. Following Barrault's example, Berkoff fronted the LTG ensemble in Metamorphosis and showcased his physical performance skills as the "gymnastic bug" (TSB: 14). It was the flourish of his self-reflexive virtuoso performance more than anything else that inscribed the unique Berko-vian signature upon this production, as well as upon subsequent works,[5] and most stridently separated his dramaturgy from that of more demo-cratically organised physical theatre groups at that time.

The location of the room/cage elevated Gregor/Berkoff to a position that was literally and figuratively over and above the ensemble. Looking back after more than twenty years at his performance high up on this gymnast's frame he characterises himself as an 'acrobat' who dazzled his audiences with displays of what Barba (1991: 10), in a very different context, has termed "virtuosic techniques" that seek "amazement and transformation of the body". His display was the enactment of just such a transformation, a metamorphosis, from human to insect. Berkoff recreates the 'danger' and 'impossibility' of his 'high-wire' act as a "trapeze artist" (FA: 105) (see Figure 13) in that original production for his present audience, the readers of his autobiography:

I, at one stage, had to climb out and hang from the ceiling like an insect ... So I practised in a gym and learnt how to climb and drop my body, hanging just by my legs and ankles, afraid nightly of being killed, but willing it, in my fanatic desire to outdo everyone else, my own self and my fears. (*TT*: 72)

With all the hyperbole of a circus barker shouting out to prospective punters he has also retrospectively commodified himself as a 'master illusionist':

Berkoff, on reading ['Metamorphosis'], could see in it the Theatre of the Impossible, as Kafka's stories are the legends of the impossible. Who in the world has the resources, the higher flights of the absurdist imagination but the surreal magician, Berkoff – actor/writer/director/ novelist [*sic*] and ex-menswear salesman from Stepney? He sets himself the task of keeping an audience awake by the brilliant attempts to plunge into the unconscious areas of the imagination. (*TT*: 71)

13 Berkoff as the acrobatic man-beetle Gregor Samsa

It is evident from a statement such as this, however tongue-in-cheek, that Berkoff's primary motivation for creating and staging this play/production was the showcasing of his 'self' through his solo physical performance skills. The *raison d'être* of the ensemble, I suggest, was to serve this goal of creating celebrity for the star performer.

Berkoff has characterised his non-naturalistic performance style as a 'circus acrobat' and a 'popular' actor *à la* Edmund Kean as somehow harking back to the 'truer' theatricality of Shakespeare's day and the street life of the East End:

> Theatre used to be a tremendous world of soloists, acrobats, harlequins – every actor had to sing, dance, mime; every man to be a Shakespearian actor had to do juggling, sword fighting, lots of things. Now suddenly, in this age of realism, that's all gone. The last stylization you had in England was in the Elizabethan era. (Elder 1978: 40)

Or the Berkovian era. As we shall see, Berkoff's physical performance in *Metamorphosis* was less a subversive act than a strategy of *enablement* that would allow him, so he apparently thought, to catch the attention of the theatre Establishment. His assertion that "the animal *is* the *mise-en-scène*, the production" (*TT*: 72) might be reformulated, therefore, as "*Berkoff* is the *mise-en-scène*, the production." The objectification and commodification of his 'self' in this 'alternative' production further shows that Berkoff was concerned with achieving *mainstream* success for himself.

Metatheatricality: confinement and escapology

Punishment, in the form of exclusion, confinement, beatings or execution, is a central theme running through much of Kafka's writing. The story 'In the Penal Colony', the novella 'Metamorphosis' and the novel *The Trial*, the three works dramatised by Berkoff, are concerned very much with 'staging' scenes in which the bodies of the protagonists and other characters are punished.[6] These three works are, I believe, sufficiently familiar for me to be able to dispense with lengthy descriptions of the plots and characters. What I wish to do, instead, is briefly to highlight the different ways in which they foreground physical punishment. I will then suggest why this subject matter provided such suitable raw material for Berkoff, the young physical actor whose body was being, as he characterised it, singled out for disciplinary treatment by the theatre Establishment.

The victims of the torture machine in 'In the Penal Colony' are put to death literally – or *literarily* – by having the judgement and sentence of the court written, or rather engraved, upon their naked bodies with the needles of the Zeichner (writer). The first victim has "HONOUR THY SUPERIORS" (Kafka 1961: 174) inscribed on his body until he finally expires. This terrifying and cruel mode of execution brings together writing and absolute disciplinary control in a single discourse of power. Fiske almost certainly had this story in the back of his mind when he observed that "[p]ain is an important means by which social control is written on the body: it is inflicted juridically as punishment for those who deviate" (Fiske 1989b: 95). This metaphorical 'death-by-text' suggests the punative discourse of a logocentric patriarchy of which, for Berkoff, the theatre Establishment was a part. His performance in the premiere as the officer, the second victim, was, I suggest, his metatheatrical thematisation and enactment of his own 'death' as a 'deviant', namely what he has characterised as his 'victim-isation' by the agents and institutions of a bourgeois, Gentile, Anglo-Saxon, text-obsessed and, therefore, implicitly *anti-Berkoff* theatre Establishment.

In the case of *The Trial*, as we have seen, Berkoff identified himself with the persecuted hero Joseph K., who is arrested by representatives of higher yet unknown authorities and accused of unspecified crimes. The novel charts his vain attempts to uncover the nature both of the accusations against him and of the court that is supposedly trying him. Finally, having failed to prove his innocence, he is executed. The form of punishment inflicted upon Joseph K. that evidently preoccupied Berkoff most in his creation of this adaptation was *exclusion*. For Berkoff, *The Trial*, particularly the crucial section of the novel entitled 'Before the Law', was a metaphor for what he has characterised as his own futile wait to be admitted through the portal of the mainstream. In his autobiography he writes:

> In Kafka's *The Trial* there is the parable of the man who waits at the door of the law: he sits outside the door for years, waiting for what he believes will be his moment to be called and he never is called, and then one day he asks the doorkeeper why he has seen no one else enter the door of the law and the doorkeeper, seeing that the man is near his end and very old, says, "The door was meant only for you. I am now going to shut it." The story of our lives ... Suddenly its meaning became clear to me: we tend to wait for years for that golden opportunity when we will enter the door and find salvation, but we wait and put it off with all sorts of excuses ... Why don't we enter that door that we claim is ours? Because we don't know what is lurking on the other side and so we stay with what is safe. (FA: 76–7)

Kafka's novella 'Metamorphosis' is another fictional treatment of physical punishment that Berkoff has interpreted and resignified in order to project certain things about himself and his relationship with the theatre Establishment. Patriarchal control in this story is embodied by the protagonist's father. Gregor is first "disabled" (Kafka 1961: 44) and finally dies as a direct result of his father's violence. The language used by Kafka to describe Mr Samsa and his actions indicates that he is the very embodiment of power and violence. At the beginning of the story, we are told that Mr Samsa hammers on the door of Gregor's bedroom "with his fist" in contrast to the "cautious tap" of his kinder-hearted mother (11). He is described as "fierce" (21), and drives Gregor back into his room with a stick "like a savage" (24). Furthermore, Kafka uses quasi-militaristic imagery to describe Mr Samsa's tyrannical control over Gregor and the family. He dresses in "a smart blue uniform with gold buttons" (43), and fatally "bombards" (44) Gregor with apples.

Berkoff's strategy of identifying himself with Kafka and his victimised alter egos is seen most clearly in the link that he sought to manufacture between himself and Gregor. Berkoff emphasised this connection with the explicit parallels he constructed between the relationship he recounts having had with his own parents and the relationship that Gregor Samsa had with his family, particularly his father, in the novella. Berkoff has characterised his unhappy relationship with his father, Abraham (Al), as a mirror of Gregor's relationship with his father. Berkoff recalls having been constantly criticised by his father just like Kafka and his creation Gregor (FA: 58). At best, it appears that Al Berkoff was indifferent to his son (FA: 139). Berkoff recalls that "[m]y own father reminded me of Mr Samsa. He was the archetype of the East End dad ... who appeared not to have the slightest taste for music or for books" (MOM: 80). Berkoff recalls (FA: 28) that for his father, as for Gregor's bourgeois patriarch (Kafka 1974: 16), work was paramount. Berkoff emphasises Mr Samsa's (and thus perhaps Berkoff Senior's) domineering nature in one telling vignette interpolated into his stage directions: "[Image – FATHER wrestles with his son – the age-old desire of the father wishing to kill his male offspring. GREGOR is thrown into his cage]" (TT: 103). Berkoff used Gregor's imprisonment by his father as a metatheatrical dramatisation of his own 'entrapment' by (as he saw it) the patriarchal theatre Establishment.

In staging his adaptations of these three 'parables of punishment', Berkoff was apparently swimming with one particular current of modern theatre. In Bodied Spaces Stanton B. Garner (1994: 161) argues that:

> Of all the forms that the body has assumed on the post-Brechtian political stage, the most pervasive and urgent is the body in its deepest extremity, the suffering, violated entity that Elaine Scarry has termed "the body in pain". Described through dramatic speech and represented onstage, the body in contemporary political theater is often a body tortured, disciplined, confined, penetrated, maimed, extinguished.[7]

The effect of such plays as Edward Bond's *Saved* (1965), Dario Fo's *Accidental Death of an Anarchist* (1970), Caryl Churchill's *Vinegar Tom* (1976) and Howard Brenton's *The Romans in Britain* (1980), Garner continues, has been the creation of a "landscape-spectacle of atrocity" (161). What differentiates Berkoff from these politically motivated playwrights, however, was his self-referential concern with the metatheatrical enactment of his own 'punishment'.

Resisting 'confinement' by means of virtuoso physical performance – escapology, in a word – is a dominant theme running through Berkoff's work, career and public self-construction. Indeed, he has overtly identified himself with and has felt 'invaded' *dybbuk*-like by the spirit of the most iconic escapologist of them all, the illusionist Harry Houdini.[8] Looking back on a career in which he has attempted to solve the "difficulties of life" through his plays, he told one interviewer that:

> it became a challenge, just like Harry Houdini. Every challenge was to escape and create a new escape. It takes some people weeks to put on a play. But it takes me years because I must find the kernel, I must find the key. And that was what Houdini was trying to find, the mysteries of the key. He had hundreds of keys ... When I first took to the theatre I took to the audience something that was beyond reality. I wanted to create magic. I wanted to find the key. As my grandparents were Russian and I am second-generation English I feel that Houdini is part of my inheritance. He and I work in this neutral area of movement, like boxing. It's a great equaliser. Houdini put on what was unstageable and unthinkable, and that's what I did. And because Houdini is a medium, I feel he has invaded me, he's somewhere inside, and all my life has been, how can I escape? (Iley 1993)

Thus Harry Houdini, the Jewish creator of spectacle and magic, was yet another individual with whom Berkoff created a close link in his construction and projection of 'self'. Nowhere has Berkoff adopted the subject position of 'escapologist' more thoroughly and overtly than in his performance as Gregor Samsa – an act, he recalls, that enabled him to "show off a bit by hanging upside down like Houdini" (*FA*: 123).

In Kafka's story Gregor, having awoken to the 'straitjacket' of his beetledom, becomes less and less capable of movement. He finds himself doubly confined by the armour-plated body that "literally imprisons him" (Beck 1971: 142) and by the walls of his own room in which he is penned by his family. In an interesting semantic observation Anthony Thorlby (1972: 38) has suggested that Kafka may have seen these internal and external forms of confinement as two sides of the same coin of incapacitation:

> The words Kafka uses to describe Gregor's state (*Ungeziefer, Insekt, Käfer* [vermin, insect, beetle]) doubtless had connotations and associations for him that are less evident in English: a dirty little monster, a creature divided into sections, a being imprisoned – the word *Käfig*, a cage, has alliterative similarity to *Käfer*, and it was through hints of other meanings hidden in words, which in this case again resembled his own name, that Kafka transformed the world.

The orthographic similarity of the key words *Kafka, Käfer* and *Käfig*, Thorlby continues, suggests that, in creating Gregor, Kafka was describing *himself*, and was metaphorically dramatising the sense he had of his own inner (psychological, artistic) and outer (social) incarceration. The Czech writer was interested in the ambiguity of this "closed-in state" and whether it implied a "stronghold and security, or imprisonment and deprivation" (38). Similar oppositional dynamics (inner/outer confinement, imprisonment/release) are made manifest in Berkoff's adaptation through the dual role of the scaffolding that simultaneously serves, on the one hand, as "Gregor's room or cage" (*TT*: 77) and, on the other, as the gymnastic apparatus upon which he demonstrates his liberating physical performance as the man/insect.

Berkoff's solo performance shared Kafka's ambiguity in its Janus-faced dramatisation of self-denigration and self-empowerment. In the 'Three Theatre Manifestos' Berkoff writes that, as the beetle, "I made myself feel trapped, bound to the floor on my belly" (*TTM*: 7). He has retrospectively projected himself as an individual in a debased position (in which, it should be emphasised, he had placed himself) who had no choice but to 'come out swinging' both on the stage and in society. In his autobiography this shift to self-empowerment is evident in the following reflection:

> *Metamorphosis* was to me the supreme analogy for human beings locked in the worst conditions imaginable. Imprisoned in the over-whelming sense of worthlessness so that if heat turns carbon into diamonds, then by a reverse process self-disgust turns you into a

> verminous insect. That suited me just fine. A bug. Loathsome, inferior, outsider, yet also magnificent, a fighting bug that, once transformed, can sink no further into obloquy. Once in the pit of self-abasement you know where you are. (ΓΛ: 103)

The implication here is that the 'heat' of his virtuoso physical performance transformed him from 'carbon' (a lowly and often unemployed repertory actor) into a 'diamond' (an independent creator of original and sparkling 'total theatre').

Berkoff set out in *Metamorphosis*, I suggest, to demonstrate how he could acrobatically perform his way out of the 'confining' practices of mainstream theatre, particularly text-based naturalism, to which, according to him, he had been literally sub-jected as an actor in repertory. He recalls that:

> I was younger then and still living off the soup of frustration deep in my craw. I had created the whole production, but the motive behind it all, the driving force, had been my desire to show this monster/creature/human and express the versatility that conventional theatre could never accommodate. I wanted to demonstrate the ideas that are open to us when we eschew the plaintive whine of naturalism. (*MOM*: 55)

The unyielding presence of a single stage property – Gregor's cage-like room in *Metamorphosis* or, to take a example from a later work, the sofa in *Decadence* (see below in this section) – may be understood as a metonymic representation of a traditional naturalistic stage setting around which or despite which he was 'forced' to perform as a virtuoso. In *Metamorphosis*, the chorus, too, may be viewed as a metonymic representation of the confining values and aesthetics of bourgeois society and the naturalistic theatre practice it has perpetuated. The two-dimensional members of Gregor's family with their marionette-like movements are, Berkoff suggests, more restricted and incapacitated than the seemingly disabled yet actually gymnastic Gregor/Berkoff:

> The family, living in fear of time and money, sometimes became animated marionettes that moved, reflecting the insect's movements, so that they as a group, more than Gregor, were the dung beetle in reality. They were the creature, with their obsessive collecting of their balls of dung – their small, paltry, bourgeois achievements. (*TT*: 72)

The implication of this is that Gregor/Berkoff, alone among the figures on the stage, can act with dexterity and freedom. The man/beetle alone is liberated through performance.

Further enactments by Berkoff of the subversion of or escape from 'confinement' may be found in various other plays. In *The Trial*, for example, the ensemble's use of hand-held screens graphically dramatise the claustrophobic sense of confinement felt by Joseph K. As Berkoff explains, "[o]ur set of ten screens became the story and as the story could move from moment to moment so could our set ... A room could become a trap, a prison, expand and contract and even spin around the protagonist" (*TT*: 6). Berkoff's performance as Titorelli in the original production of that play revolved around the mimed sequence of his entrapment in and escape from the picture frame that imprisoned him (*TT*: 58). *The Fall of the House of Usher* begins with Madeleine Usher lying "in a rigor mortis position" after her live burial in a coffin that is demarcated by a square of light (*AFHU*: 42–3). Later, she is "mummified" in a winding sheet by her brother (68). As Berkoff's stage directions suggest, however, this very 'incapacitation' serves to foreground her liberation-through-performance: "*When she is cocooned she begins to dance with the* FRIEND ... *The* FRIEND *begins to pull the cloth away and she spins out of it to* USHER" (69). Moreover, the physical house is presented as Usher's "prison and ... snail shell" (64), a confined space within which Usher/ Berkoff must create the environment of the play through mime alone. Finally, recalling the minimal setting of his play *Decadence* (1981), he reflects: "Since we were mainly fixed to the sofa our moves had to be *creative within a confined environment* (a phrase which could symbolize my life)" (original emphasis) (*FA*: 346). This final observation by Berkoff is indeed significant, since it shows his awareness of what has been one of the chief factors motivating the development of his dramaturgy.

These may all be seen as examples of what Jencks (1977), in the different context of architecture, has termed "double-coding", whereby an artist ironically and self-consciously "uses and abuses, installs and then subverts, the very concepts [he or she] challenges" (Hutcheon 1988: 92). It is in such a way, I suggest, that Berkoff set out to dramatise meta-theatrically what was apparently for him the constricting naturalism of mainstream theatre in order to subvert it and to demonstrate what the performing body – specifically *his* performing body – was capable of within and in spite of such confinement. In short, if Gregor was *dis*abled then Berkoff, in the role of the beetle, became *en*abled through his virtuosic performance. In so doing he may be seen to have dramatised what Martin (1990: 175–6) has called the "overflowing" quality of the moving, acting and desiring body that resists the attempt of authority in art or in politics to enforce a unified and monolithic structure.

In Kafka's story the meek and self-denying Gregor Samsa is unquestionably a victim. After sacrificing himself to the soul-destroying routine of a salesman in order to support not only himself but also his sister and parents, he finds himself trapped inside an insect's body and finally dies a wretched death as a result of his father's violence. The tragedy (or tragicomedy) of the story arises from his inability to manifest his humanity, since to the others he becomes nothing more than a bug. At no point in the story, though, does he offer resistance to his fate or the individuals around him, particularly Mr Samsa. Through his passivity he may even be said to have acquiesced in his own annihilation. As the Kafka scholar Heinz Politzer (1962: 79) puts it, "[h]e agrees to his own demise as he once had submitted to the yoke of his job".

Berkoff's interpretation of Kafka's protagonist is markedly different. In the playwright's hands, Gregor the bug becomes "a hero of huge proportions: he snarls, he spits, leaps out of the family" (TT: 71). This statement of defiance demonstrates clearly how Berkoff reinscribed his 'Jewish' man/beetle – and, by association, his own 'self' – with a pugnacious and fearless heroism. This is underlined by his description not only of Gregor but also of Kafka's other protagonists, not as victims but as "contestants for the obvious overwhelming battles that they face" (TT: 71). Berkoff has been consistent in this view, as may be seen from his comments about the 1986 revival of the play at the Mermaid Theatre, London. He writes that the actor Tim Roth "perfectly caught the agony of Gregor's flight *without falling into the trap of portraying him as a victim*" (my emphasis) (MOM: 48). This heroic Berkovian 'Gregor' evokes the tough, militaristic Jew, the *sabra*, who secured Israel's victory in what Berkoff has called the "David and Goliath battle of 1967" (FA: 127). In his recollections of a visit to Israel, when he took his production of *Hamlet* there in 1980, he writes about this 'new' type of Jew:

> [Israel] was the most polyglot society on earth and the genetic pool was so varied that it managed to get rid of, in a few generations, the signs of inbreeding and the unhealthy restrictions of ghetto life. I saw few exaggerated noses, few sunken, staring eyes, but I did see healthy, fit and strong Israelis, called *sabras* after the very prickly cactus. Sabras were a new race of Jews, a very powerful and healthy race. (FA: 131)

Here is further evidence of Berkoff's belief in Darwinism. By ascribing heroic qualities to his 'Gregor', I suggest, the role became for Berkoff, the 'theatrical sabra', a vehicle for his own liberating display of virtuosity and his own public projection of himself as an individual artist engaged in a discursive power struggle in which only the fittest would survive.

Berkoff's reading of and performance as Gregor located the dramatic tension inside a single grotesque and tragicomical body that is half-beetle (victim) and half-man (hero). In this context it is useful to consider Orr's (1991: 40) assertion that:

> The tragicomic hero may be culturally and mentally impoverished but it is a poverty enriched by performance. Character is defined by expression, by play, by the supercharged role adopted in a particular game. It depends crucially on performance. The hyperactive performer atones for the poverty of culture and the poverty of self.

Performance thus becomes a means of self-empowerment, and Berkoff the 'hyperactive' performer in the role of the physically impoverished man/beetle may be seen to have been enacting his attempt to overcome his "poverty of culture and the poverty of self".

Gregor dies a physical death in the adaptation as in the story, yet a final transcendent victory, as it were, goes to Berkoff as the actor metatheatrically performing his 'victimised' yet ultimately 'victorious' social 'self' through the role of the man/beetle. A comparison of the scene in which Gregor dies in the story and in the play highlights this point. In Kafka's tale Gregor simply expires alone and without any final reflection upon his fate. His corpse is discovered by the charwoman, who then reports his death to the parents (Kafka 1961: 58–9). In the play, by contrast, Berkoff's invented scene unfolds as follows:

> MRS. S.: He looked at me – just as we closed the door – he turned his head – his eyes – Gregor's eyes, full of agony, looked at me in such a way as only a child looks at his mother as if to say – no more – no more pain – I sensed his spirit creeping out of him, reluctant to inhabit such a painful dwelling, releasing him, go Gregor, go – bear no hatred for me – forgive – be free, be free my little boy ... free ... free.
> GREGOR: [intones with her] Free ... free.
> MRS. S.: [as the last faint whisper is expelled from GREGOR] Dead ... (TT: 120)

Evidently, Berkoff's purpose in this final dialogue is to stress Gregor's (and his own) 'escape' from the straitjacket of mainstream theatre practice, particularly text-based naturalism, and the twin confines of unemployment and minor roles in repertory. The title of the play thus takes on a further dimension, suggesting a second 'reverse' metamorphosis: Gregor's posthumous liberation and 'rehumanisation' through the escape of his spirit from the imprisoning and lifeless body of the insect. The 'return' of his humanity may be seen in his mother's recognition of him as "my little boy" and in the restoration of his speech.

Bakhtin's interpretation of the grotesque as an image of rebirth is of relevance here. In *Rabelais and His World* he asserts: "The grotesque image reflects a phenomenon in transformation, an as yet unfinished metamorphosis, of death and birth, growth and becoming" (Bakhtin 1984: 24). He argues further that:

> The essence of the grotesque is precisely to present a contradictory and double-faced fullness of life. Negation and destruction (death of the old) are included as an essential phase, inseparable from affirmation, from the birth of something new and better ... This principle is victorious, for the final result is always abundance, increase. (62)

Grotesque images, he maintains, "remain ambivalent and contradictory; they are ugly, monstrous, hideous from the point of view of 'classic' aesthetics, that is, the aesthetics of the ready-made and the completed" (25). This accords well with Berkoff's interpretation of and performance as Gregor. He appears to have identified himself with the latter's victimisation but not with his final death and defeat as it is described in the story. The metatheatrical significance of Berkoff's appropriation and performance of the role of Gregor is that the crushed bug fights back. Berkoff thus set out, I maintain, to snatch a personal final victory by asserting his artistic freedom and integrity through a phoenix-like resurrection from Gregor's death. This is a full-scale reinscription upon the palimpsest of Kafka's story and protagonist, rather than mere interpretation. Again, Bakhtin is useful here: "Even the struggle of life and death in the individual body is conceived by grotesque imagery as the struggle of the old life stubbornly resisting the new life about to be born, as the crisis of change" (50). The defiant shout of Berkoff's performance as the grotesque Gregor suggests his championing of 'working-class', 'popular' and thus 'ugly' aesthetics over the 'balanced' and 'beautiful' aesthetics of the bourgeoisie. John Fiske (1989b: 97) has argued that:

> A defiantly grotesque, excessively strong body bears the values of class consciousness, for it is the political meanings of the body that matter. The individual body becomes the class body as the site of the subjection of the proletariat in capitalism: it is therefore appropriate that the physical body, particularly in its grotesque, offensive, dirty aspects, should become the means of evading, resisting and scandalizing that social power. The body that refuses to be aestheticized (for aesthetics is merely class disciplinary power displaced into metaphors of beauty, symmetry, and perfection), works culturally as both the language of the subordinate (though not of subordination) and the means of participation in subordinate cultural forms.

Whatever 'class consciousness' Berkoff brought to his physical interpretation of this character, it was not enlisted in any class struggle. The paradox here is that Berkoff apparently wanted to appeal to the very bourgeoisie that he was 'scandalising' with his 'ugly' aesthetics. What he desired above all else, as I have already suggested, was acceptance into the mainstream. This is made abundantly clear in his satisfied recollection that "*Metamorphosis* had placed me smack in the forefront of theatrical attention" (*FA*: 299).

Conclusion

In this chapter I have been concerned with examining the paradoxical quality of Berkoff's *Metamorphosis*, and, more particularly, of his performance in the original production. We have seen that he projected himself as an individual who had been marginalised by a patriarchal and hostile theatre Establishment. It was this ill-treatment, as he painted it, that resulted in his establishment of the LTG and his 'fighting back' with physical performance. In *Meditations on Metamorphosis* he writes that the play – more exactly the original production – was "*my metamorphosis* from common under-employed actor to entrepreneur, director, actor, writer, mime, all rolled into one fist – one giant ball that would shatter the plate-glass window of British theatre" (*MOM*: 55). My contention is that the apparent violence and vehemence of Berkoff's 'attack' on the *status quo* disguised a far more conciliatory strategy of negotiation by means of which he hoped to gain the 'official' acceptance of the theatre Establishment. Far from setting out to shatter the Establishment's window with *Metamorphosis*, Berkoff was actually putting on a spectacular display of acrobatics in front of that same window with the intention of gaining admittance through the door next to it – a door that he, like the man from the country in the 'Before the Law' parable in *The Trial*, evidently hoped would now be opened to him. Having been rejected by Olivier and Brook, the production may thus be seen as a high-profile 'audition' of his own devising in which, for once, he landed the plum role. This conclusion is supported by Berkoff's own admission that:

> the dreadfully stupid, ridiculous and insane thing was that while I was creating my own theatre and style and drawing the audience, I was asking for work elsewhere. I even, at the time, wrote to the RSC, hoping that they might be able to see what I had achieved ... I still harboured the old chimera of wanting to be the great classical actor. (*FA*: 123)

The first production of the play was greeted with considerable critical acclaim (*FA*: 106–7). With this adaptation he succeeded in showcasing the Berkovian dramaturgical style and his multifaceted skills as playwright, director and, above all else, virtuoso actor. Ironically, though, his approach was so obviously 'Berkocentric' that this very success, as he himself concedes, was ultimately counter-productive in terms of gaining the mainstream recognition he craved:

> My first production of *Met* was a triumphant success, but I had no invitation, no expression of curiosity, or desire from any quarter to go anywhere. No matter, I had done this myself and what it did for my ego was colossal. I knew that I would have to do it myself and rely on no one, since I had discovered that everyone was out for himself. (*MOM*: 73)

Thus he singlehandedly manufactured his own subsequent unemployability – *re-confined* himself, as it were – on account of the comprehensive control he had proudly exerted over every facet of this LTG production, and the vehemence and stridency with which he had proclaimed his independence. He did 'escape' in one crucial sense, however, in so far as *Metamorphosis* can be seen as the first major step in the evolution of his dramaturgy. Yet Berkoff's grand public gesture of apparently turning his back on the theatre Establishment – of demonstrating perhaps all too well that he was "out for himself" – certainly undermines his claim to have been excluded by it. It is more correct to conclude, I believe, that Berkoff elaborated his own 'marginalisation' in order to have something against which to kick and against which to shape his dramaturgy and his own public persona at the outset of his independent career.

Notes

1 Jim Haynes, letter to author, 3 February 1995.
2 The American director Orson Welles produced a film version of *The Trial* entitled *Le Procès* in 1961.
3 A full examination of Barrault's influence upon Berkoff's adaptation of *The Trial* is beyond the scope of the present discussion. A comparison of Bentley's (1950) detailed description of Barrault's *mise-en-scène* and Berkoff's accounts of his own dramaturgical approach (*TTM*: 19–20; *TT*: 5–6; *FA*: 376–9) reveals palpable similarities, particularly in the use of a highly disciplined choral ensemble, stylised mime, and 'cinematic' dissolves between scenes.
4 Jacques Copeau (1879–1949), the leading French theatrical producer and critic, established the experimental Théâtre du Vieux Colombier in Paris in

130

1913. Ever in search of a more truthful and direct performance style, Copeau was an influential figure in the modern theatre with his use of improvisation and masks. He encouraged and taught many young dramatists and actors, including Étienne Decroux, Barrault's mime teacher. See John Rudlin, *Jacques Copeau* (Cambridge: Cambridge University Press, 1986).

5 In the case of *The Trial*, for example, despite having 'democratically' allotted himself the minor role of Titorelli, Berkoff's solo performance still managed to overwhelm the ensemble effort. One critic, reviewing the 1973 revival, observed that: "Berkoff's actors are not allowed to do their talents justice or even, in some cases, to suggest what talent is there to be done justice to. The exception, predictably, is Steven Berkoff, who gives himself one extended high-speed workout as Titorelli the court-painter ... Like much of the production, his 10–minute outburst is admirably done, but inappropriate – doubly so, in fact, for the speed and delivery shows up the sluggishness of some of the ensemble work" (Davies 1973). Another critic, witnessing the 1991 revival at the National Theatre, in which Berkoff reprised his performance as Titorelli, makes a similar observation, noting that Berkoff "joins the cast near the end, like a star attraction at the Palladium" (Peter 1991).

6 At one time Kafka had indeed considered publishing the three works 'In the Penal Colony', 'The Judgement' and 'Metamorphosis' together under the collective title *Punishments* (Gray 1973: 186).

7 See Elaine Scarry, *The Body in Pain: The Making and Unmaking of the World* (New York: Oxford University Press, 1985).

8 Harry Houdini (1874–1926), whose real name was Erik Weiz, was born in Budapest of Jewish parents (his father was a rabbi). The family emigrated to New York when he was 13. His worldwide fame rested upon his ability to escape from handcuffs, ropes, safes, packing cases, straitjackets, underwater coffins and his famous 'Chinese Water Torture Cell'. The self-styled 'King of Handcuffs' died from a ruptured appendix after he was punched in the stomach by an admirer wishing to test his physical prowess.

5

BERKOFF'S COCKNEY CARNIVAL

... the characters themselves from Shakespeare's play, as a result of being around for almost four hundred years, have now detached themselves from their original context, so they're in a sense roaming free in a kind of cultural terrain, and therefore can be appropriated and put into a new context. (Charles Marowitz, *The Act of Being*)

In his review of the LTG's production of *Agamemnon* at the Round House in December, 1973, the theatre critic Jonathan Hammond (1974: 54) pointed to the contrast between the considerable mime skills of the ensemble and "the sorry mess of the adaptation of Aeschylus's original it is required to perform". Seizing upon this discrepancy to signal a crucial moment for Berkoff and his group, he noted that:

there is no doubt that the company has a style, discipline and skills all of its own. All it needs now is the courage to break away from classical adaptations and mould and create its own material out of its own individual and collective preoccupations and fantasies. Perhaps Berkoff can find a good young writer (there are plenty of them about) to help the company do this. If this can happen, it will continue to flourish; if not, it may well disappear up a creative cul-de-sac. (54)

Hammond's observation almost certainly alerted Berkoff, if he was unaware of it already, to this aesthetic imbalance, and the "good young writer" was found, namely Berkoff himself. Characteristically, it was his individual preoccupations rather than the group's collective fantasies that he would draw upon for material. In *East* (Traverse Theatre, 1975), his next production after *Agamemnon*, and in its sequel, *West* (Donmar Warehouse, 1983), he used highly stylised language and material that drew equally on his proletarian background and on the iconic power of Shakespeare's language to create a dramaturgy that would propel him into the public eye in a spectacular and notorious fashion.

Both plays are set nominally in working-class districts of London (the East End in *East*, and Stamford Hill in *West*) and both share the same primary characters: the two teenage tearaways Mike and Les, Mike's

Mum and Dad, and his girlfriend Sylv. In terms of language, plot structure and overall character development, however, the two plays are dissimilar. *East* is a loose arrangement of nineteen vignettes that include a gang war, and the graphic sexual fantasies of various characters delivered in soliloquies. There is no coherent plot as such, and none of the characters can be said to undergo any moral or psychological development. This is underlined by the fact that the play ends with the same exchange of dialogue between Mike and Les with which it opens, implying that the characters are locked in a circle of violence, lust and dull routine punctuated by leisure activities that offer only temporary diversion. The structure of *West*, by contrast, is more clearly defined. The fragmented story of *East* gives way to a linear plot and a drama divided into two distinct acts. Berkoff loosely transposed the storyline of *Beowulf* to the streets of North London, with Mike facing his own 'Grendel', Curly, the leader of the Hoxton Mob, in single combat. The play, Berkoff writes, is also "a cross between *High Noon* and *Henry V*" (*FA*: 65). Like Will Kane, the marshal in the Western, and Shakespeare's King Harry, Mike goes through an initial period of doubt and introspection before overcoming his fears and the misgivings of those around him to vanquish his enemy and vindicate himself. With regard to language, the dramatic dialogue and soliloquies in *East* are composed of Cockney profanity mixed with pseudo-Shakespearean archaisms, whereas the shock effect of the language in *West* relies less upon obscenities than upon deliberate misquotations from Shakespeare's plays, most notably *Hamlet*.

There are two principal Berkoff-alter egos in these plays. This is suggested by Berkoff's description of the role of Mike as "a part I was tailor-made to play" (*FA*: 18), and of the role of Les (Berkoff's first name in real life is Lesley) as a part that is "more autobiographical" (*FA*: 48). In *West*, they are joined by three members of Mike's gang, Ken, Steve and Ralph, who, Berkoff notes, "bore only a fleeting resemblance to real people, but were more an amalgam of types and splinters of Mike" (*FA*: 68). Thus it is fair to conclude that all the young male characters in these plays are, to a greater or lesser extent, kaleidoscopic reflections of 'Berkoff'.

The key influence on Berkoff in his post-*Agamemnon* search for material on which to base an original play was Anthony Burgess's novel *A Clockwork Orange* (1962) or, more precisely, Stanley Kubrick's 1971 cinematic adaptation of the novel, in which Berkoff appeared in the minor role of a brutal policeman. In his autobiography, he acknowledges that "*East* was dressed as if we were some strange yobbos crossed with ... *A Clockwork Orange*, which I don't mind saying must have had some effect on me" (*FA*: 68). Actually, the novel and film had a considerable impact upon Berkoff's conception of *East* in three key ways. First, it provided him with a model for the play's characters and milieu. As Bawden (1976: 145) notes of the film, employing a description that almost exactly fits Berkoff's play, "[i]n an unnamed city of the future, [the protagonist] Alex leads a teenage quartet indulging in rape, robbery, destruction, and gang warfare." Second, Burgess's stylised language, with its bathetic juxtapositions of archaic words, inflated rhetorical flourishes and slang, influenced the synthesised language of *East*. And last, the film, which, as Bawden points out, "acquired a notoriety which polarized audiences, undoubtedly contributing to its enormous commercial success" (145), provided Berkoff with a strategy for creating a *succès de scandale* and thus highly saleable infamy for himself at an important juncture in his career. In this chapter I examine how in *East* and *West* Berkoff employed carnivalesque and ludic strategies to create 'cultural space' for himself as a dramatist, as a physical performer and as a budding celebrity. Before proceeding, I need to clarify what I understand here by the terms *carnivalesque* and *ludic*.

The concept of the carnivalesque derives from Mikhail Bakhtin's *Rabelais and His World*. In that work Bakhtin (1984: 10) argues that:

> As opposed to the official feast, one might say that [medieval and Renaissance] carnival celebrated temporary liberation from prevailing truth and from the established order; it marked the suspension of all hierarchical rank, privileges, norms and prohibitions. Carnival was the true feast of time, the feast of becoming, change, and renewal.

Seen in this way carnival is not merely celebration but political and social subversion. In this discussion I suggest that there is an analogy between, on the one hand, the 'official' feast and mainstream theatre, and, on the other hand, between carnival and Berkoff's 'unofficial' theatre as represented by the two plays under consideration here. As Fiske (1989b: 82) argues, the carnivalesque is the result of the collision at the unofficial medieval and Renaissance festival between two languages, "the high, validated language of classical learning enshrined in political and religious power, and the low, vernacular language of the folk." The bristling, multi-coded language synthesised by Berkoff in *East* and *West* is such a carnivalesque collision between the 'high' register of Shakespeare and the 'low' register of Cockney.

Turning now to the term *ludic*, this word describes a concept that is closely associated with Johan Huitzinga's classic study of human play *Homo Ludens*, where he defines play as:

a free activity standing quite consciously outside "ordinary" life as being "not serious," but at the same time absorbing the player intensely and utterly. It is an activity connected with no material interest, and no profit can be gained by it. It proceeds within its own proper boundaries of time and space according to fixed rules and in an orderly manner. It promotes the formation of social groupings that tend to surround themselves with secrecy and to stress their difference from the common world by disguise or other means. (Huitzinga 1955: 13)

Whilst I accept this conception of play as an activity standing outside the productive realm of work, I follow Roger Callois, who built his own theory of play in *Man, Play and Games* (1961) upon Huitzinga's work, in his refutation of the latter's notion of play as something that is secret and mysterious. Callois's notion of play as an activity that is "nearly always spectacular or ostentatious" (Callois 1961: 4), as we shall see, more fittingly describes the ludic endeavours of the delinquents in *East* and *West*. Moreover, Callois's four-fold typology of forms of play provides a useful analytical tool for approaching the 'leisure' activities of the characters in these plays.

This chapter is divided into two main parts. In the first section, I examine Berkoff's creation and use of spectacular language in these two Cockney plays. I focus in particular on two main areas, the polyphonic and performative qualities of this synthesised speech. In the second section, I look at how Berkoff apparently sought simultaneously to free himself from the working-class culture of the End East by excavating and 'destroying' it in *East*, and to elevate himself through subversive textual raids on the Shakespearean canon in *West*. My purpose will be to demonstrate that Berkoff's apparently counterhegemonic strategy with these two plays can be seen as a personal rather than a collective carnival by means of which he sought to 'lose' his working-class past and construct a middle-class future by gaining mainstream recognition.

Language and spectacle

Berkoff's primary concern in his early productions with the LTG had been the creation of a spectacular dramaturgy centred on *physical* performance, with the dialogue taking, as it were, a back seat. As we saw in the case of *Metamorphosis*, Berkoff did not stray far from the original published English translation when he distributed dialogue to his characters. The turning point in Berkoff's development as a writer, I suggest, was *Agamemnon*, a work in which, as Hammond correctly observed, there were signs that Berkoff had begun to experiment with a style of dramatic dialogue that would shock and dazzle his audiences, and also serve as a choreographic 'score' for heightened physical performance. Two examples from that play may demonstrate this. First, there is the shock effect of the comic strip onomatopoeia used in the herald's speech to convey the sounds of modern warfare in Troy/Vietnam: "mortar / shrapnel / tommy gun / and blow pipe / RAT TAT TAT TAT / RAT TAT TAT TAT / KA BOOM / KA BLAST / KA BLAM / SPLAT!" (*AFHU*: 20–1). Second, there is the performative stichomythia in the "Battle One" scene, in which two actors 'dance' a slow-motion ballet of death that is determined by the words of the chanted dialogue: "I am fighting for Troy / I am fighting for Greece / Your blood soaks me / Your sword is my pain / Your skin tears like silk" (14). In this section I examine how Berkoff pursued this two-fold aesthetic experimentation with the polyphonic and performative language of *East* and *West*.

The non-unitary language in these two plays exemplifies Bakhtin's (1981) notion of *heteroglossia* as a "plurality of experiences and meanings [in language] which are determined dialogically" (Birch 1991: 65). The multiple 'voices' in *East* and *West* consist of Cockney dialect and slang, classical allusions and Shakespearean parody. The closest parallel to this in modern theatre is perhaps the Italian playwright Dario Fo's *grammelot*, the jesting language that he developed from dialect and onomatopoeia, which Birch describes as "an invented, theatrical language, which draws, carnival-like, from a wide number of language sources in order to create a praxis which demands that privileging high culture (and associated standard languages) be changed" (85). Similarly, Birch argues, Berkoff's synthesised idiolect "foreground[s] a very distinctive non-standard variety of language in order to deconstruct and, in some cases, overthrow control" (88). In what follows, however, I shall question Birch's conclusion that Berkoff had a counterhegemonic purpose in mind.

Berkoff grounded the language of *East* and *West* in the colourful speech patterns of Cockney. This is most evident in two features: first, in his use of rhyming slang, for example, "boat" (*CP*, 1: 9) for face (boat race=face) and "china" (9) for mate (china plate=mate); and second, in his use of slang words, for example, "kikes" (14) and "abes" (33) for Jews, and "copped" (37) for saw. Yet his aim was not to present the dialect with naturalistic precision, "to reproduce slavishly", as he puts it, "the speech patterns of Joe Bloggs in Barnet" (*FA*: 158). This may be seen by the fact that he made no attempt in his written text to represent the everyday sound of Cockney. This is in marked contrast to the nostalgic Sam Weller-type speech of the "'loveable' Cockney low-life" (Chambers and Prior 1987: 39) in such dramas as Norman and Bart's *Fings Ain't Wot They Used T'be* (1959) and Stephen Lewis's *Sparrers Can't Sing* (1960), with their dropped t's, glottal stops and 'cor blimeys'. Rather, Berkoff's concern was with rendering what I shall term the *colour* of Cockney speech, namely the expressive power of its violent and ribald imagery. His characters are articulate, but in the sense that they, like the Teddy Boys of his youth, play and fight skilfully with 'verbals'. Indeed, he has called the profane Cockney speech in *East* a "frontal assault"[1] upon his audience's sensibilities. This 'in-yer-face' facility with spoken language is very different from the 'educated' articulateness of the East Enders in such plays as Wesker's *Chicken Soup with Barley* (1958) and Kops's *The Hamlet of Stepney Green* (1958) who discuss politics and art in a sanitised 'Cockney' unlikely to be heard in Whitechapel Road.

A useful perspective on Berkoff's evocative rather than descriptive use of Cockney dialect is offered by Bakhtin in his discussion of the vernacular language used in the streets and marketplaces of the Middle Ages and Renaissance as they appeared in Rabelais's *Gargantua*. Abuses, curses, profanities, and improprieties, he argues, were (and still are) seen "as a breach of the established norms of verbal address; they refuse to conform to conventions, to etiquette, civility, respectability" (Bakhtin 1984: 187–8). Bakhtin's translator uses the term 'billingsgate' to describe in English this 'unofficial' language.[2] This is a felicitous term in the present context, since it designates a location not far from where Berkoff was born as well as the profane Cockney slang not only of the fish porters there but also of the characters in his plays. With *East*, therefore, Berkoff may be seen to have positioned himself 'close' to the source of the original billingsgate. I should emphasise here that I confine any observations concerning Berkoff's use of billingsgate to *East*, since profane language only appears in a single phrase in *West*.[3]

Curses appear frequently in *East*. Mike provokes Les, for example, with "fuck off thou discharge from thy mother's womb" (8) and Sylv repels Mike's lustful advances with "Piss off thou lump" (16). Obscene oaths, too, appear often. Les expresses surprise and disgust, for example, with "Oh fuck, Harry's farted again" (23). There are also speeches in the play that fit what Bakhtin categorised in Rabelais's work as the "most ancient hyperboles of belly, mouth and phallus" (Bakhtin 1984: 184). The most striking example of this is "Mike's Cunt Speech", a monologue which catalogues the wide variety of female pudenda subdued by the all-conquering hero. A similar instance is the following extract from a one-page soliloquy in which the priapic Mike waxes lyrical about his peerless member:

> The length of an ass, the stamina of a Greek, the form of Michelangelo's David, the strength of Westminster oak, as solid as a rock, as tricky as a fox, as lithe as a snake, as delicate as a rose, the speed of a panther, reflexes match the piston power of the Flying Scotsman, as hot as hell – as the forge whereby the shoes are beaten for the horses that drag the sun round the earth each day, as pretty as Paris, its helmet matches the battering ram that felled the walls of Troy, its shape like the crest of Achilles, *balls* like the great cannon that Pompeii used to subdue the barbarian. (17)

In passing, it should be noted that this extract also offers the clearest illustration in both plays of Berkoff's parodic use of classical allusion.

Any consideration of the 'demotic' language of *East* needs to take account of its severely gendered quality. Given that the main characters are testosterone-driven male thugs, it is hardly surprising that the language of the play is aggressively sexist. Women are only referred to pejoratively as the objects of male lust, as "scrubbers" (28) and "slags" (29) fit only for "some bunk-up or gang bang" (29). Furthermore, Berkoff compels his female characters to use the same male-speak, thereby depriving them of their sexuality and gender. Sylv's "Longing Speech", for instance, becomes a *male* sexual fantasy but from a supposedly female point of view: "Wish I could cruise around and pull those tarts and slags" (18), she muses. She also fantasies about participating in their gang wars. In short, as Chambers and Prior (1987: 52) point out, "Sylv, typically, dreams a macho dream", yet not because, as Currant (1991: 180) suggests, she is a "willing adherent of misogynistic logic", but because that is the way Berkoff as writer has compelled her to speak. Whilst Berkoff undoubtedly had a comic intent with this role-reversal, he offered no final liberation or redemption for Sylv, or indeed for numerous other female characters in his plays such as Donna in *Kvetch*, the Waitress/Wife in *Greek* or the Woman in *Lunch*, all of whom acquiesce in and desire their own rapes. This suggests that Berkoff's self-empowerment through his alter egos has been gained at the expense of weaker individuals, in this case women. This problematises Birch's claim that one of Berkoff's motivations in creating the language of *East* was the overthrow of control, since, as we can see here and as I showed in the context of his working methods with the LTG, he has tended to challenge external control in order to replace it with his own.

In *East* and *West* Berkoff constructed a cod-Shakespearean language. His initial model for this, as mentioned, was *A Clockwork Orange*. In his novel Burgess makes frequent use of the archaic *thou* and of obsolete phrasing and lexical choices, shifts in register from familiar insults to rhetorical vocatives, and juxtapositions of futuristic slang with elevated speech, as in the following two examples: "If fear thou hast in thy heart, O brother, pray banish it forthwith" (Burgess 1984: 20); and "For being a bastard with no manners and not the dook of an idea how to comport yourself publicwise, O my brother" (25). Berkoff created a similar pseudo-archaic linguistic base through his use of such words as *thou, doth* and *lest*. Yet he went further by evoking and resignifying the kind of language associated with Shakespeare. He did this by inserting three main elements into the dramatic speechs: short 'Bardic' echoes, consisting of inverted phrases, as in "delights fleshy" (17); 'sound bites' taken from Shakespeare's plays, such as Mike's declaration that "I am that merry wanderer of the night" (25), which is quoted verbatim from *A Midsummer Night's Dream* (i, 2, 43);[4] and distorted quotations of famous lines from various Shakespearean dramas. Thus when Mike declares that "they'd tell sad stories of the death of kids who lived not wisely but too well" (10), he misquotes "Then must you speak / Of one that loved not wisely but too well" (*Othello*, v, 2, 352–3), and when Dad spurts to Mum: "thou lump of foul deformity – untimely ripped from thy mother's womb" (14), he parodies "Macduff was from his mother's womb / Untimely ripped" (*Macbeth*, v, 10, 15–16).

These raids upon Shakespeare's plays become all the more effective or shocking when they are juxtaposed with Cockney profanities. An example of this is when Les says of Sylv: "I told her to get to a nunnery, in other words piss off" (27), a phrase that both echoes "Get thee to a nunnery" (*Hamlet*, iii, 1, 123) and translates it into contemporary street-talk. Here, and in many other instances, Berkoff achieves his comic effect through anticlimax, in the strict rhetorical sense of a deliberately ironic descent in register. In his chapter 'Shakespeare in quotations', John Drakakis (1997: 165) argues, though not in the specific case of Berkoff, that the general effect of such raids is "to prise [the] cultural icon [of Shakespeare] free from the cultural energy with which it is cathected, and to dissolve the 'essence' of its mythology in a carnivalesque laughter."

Such misquotations have allowed Berkoff to create notoriety for himself by challenging the Establishment's hegemonic claim to ownership or guardianship of the cultural icon 'Shakespeare'. Yet it was an un-focused challenge, since his burlesquing of the Bard in *East* involved no thoroughgoing engagement with any of the plays raided but seemed rather to exemplify Frederic Jameson's description of postmodernism as a "pure and random play of signifiers" which

> no longer produces monumental works of the modernist type, but ceaselessly reshuffles the fragments of preexistent texts, the building blocks of older cultural and social production, in some new and heightened bricolage: metabooks which cannibalize other books, metatexts which collate bits of other texts. (Connor 1997: 47)

One intriguing explanation for this eclectic borrowing from Shakespeare may be that Berkoff, who had acted in no major Shakespearean productions, came to the Bard's language through speeches he had memorised as audition pieces: "I got to know Shakespeare more for the 'numbers' that I could pluck out" (*FA*: 64). For Berkoff, therefore, the canon appeared to have represented a compendium of famous lines or 'numbers' waiting to be relocated and resignified in *East* through acts of *bricolage*.

The more thoroughgoing interaction with 'Shakespeare' in *West* is expressed less through archaic words and 'Bardic' fragments than through a much larger number of distorted versions of quotations, particularly from *Hamlet*. Indeed, the very opening of *West* is an extended parody of the scene in which the Prince is told of his father's nocturnal wanderings:

> LES: Breathless, I was aghast when I saw / standing between the full moon and the blinking lamplight, this geezer / all armed, a certain aim he took / and felled the swarthy git from Hoxton with a deft and subtle chop / I never witnessed Mike I swear such venom and gross form in leather stacked / his coat stitched and embellished with fine lattice work of studs (to be more deadly when swung) no other weapon being handy like.
> MIKE: Armed you say?
> RALPH: From top to toe.
> STEVE: From head to foot.
> MIKE: Then saw you his face?
> KEN: He wore his titfer up.
> MIKE: By Christ, would I had been there.
> LES: He would have much amazed you.
> MIKE: Very like, very like. (49)

It is clear from this that Berkoff was consciously aligning the character of Mike with the character of Hamlet. And in order to see how Berkoff resignified Shakespeare's prince, it is necessary to establish precisely what kind of speeches he raided from the original text and how he altered them.

The main quotations from Shakespeare in *West*, all of which are declaimed by Mike, are mostly distorted in order to proclaim his personal qualities as a streetfighter and gang leader. The phrase "Unhand me / by heaven I'll make a corpse of him that lets me" (62), for example, echoes "By heav'n, I'll make ghost of him that lets me" in *Hamlet* (i, 4, 62). Berkoff's substitution of *corpse* for Shakespeare's *ghost* is more in keeping with the violent street-gang milieu of *West*. Similarly, Berkoff's "My fate cries out and makes each petty artery in this body as hardy as the hardest villain's nerve" (62) is a distortion of "My fate cries out, / And makes each petty artere in this body / As hardy as the Nemean lion's nerve" in *Hamlet* (i, 4, 82–5). Again, Berkoff replaces Shakespeare's "Nemean lion's nerve" with an image more appropriate to his characters. Berkoff's heroic and muscular 'Hamlet', as glimpsed through his alter ego Mike (played by Rory Edwards in the original production) and through his own 'hard-man' performance as the prince in *Hamlet* a year after writing *West*, was in stark contrast to such earlier mainstream interpretations as Peter O'Toole's fey Prince in 1963, David Warner's "ganglingly unheroic Hamlet" in 1965, and Ben Kingsley's "thinking Hamlet" in 1975 (Bate Jackson 1996: 169–71). It also elided into the 'East End villain' persona he was constructing for himself following the success of *East*. Underscoring this, Berkoff has described Shakespeare's language as the "last vestige of the frontal verbal assault" (*TTM*: 12), which is remarkably close to his description of Cockney speech noted on p. 137 above.

Berkoff's strategy of projecting himself through Mike through Hamlet amounted to a carnivalesque inversion of rank. Marek Kohn argues that in "bestowing this mantle of myth and royal language upon his characters, Berkoff asserted that the working class deserves the trappings of nobility" (Kohn 1989). As we have seen, however, Berkoff betrays no political commitment to his social class. Thus his monologic reading of the character of Hamlet through the muscular and proletarian Mike, I suggest, was an attempt to say something about *himself* by employing the classic carnivalesque 'Festival of Fools' strategy of simultaneously bringing the Prince down to 'street level' whilst elevating himself to the 'aristocracy'. As such, Berkoff was perhaps indicating that *he* deserved the trappings of nobility.

As we have seen, Berkoff has projected himself in the mould of his idol Edmund Kean as a person who, as a consequence of his social class, dialect and lack of formal education, has been put down and marginalised by an Establishment elite that has long exploited and policed Shakespeare's iconicity to tighten its grip on cultural power. His complaint that he has been excluded from performing in major Shakespearean productions is a recurrent theme throughout his career. Looking back in one interview he declares:

> Shakespeare is my mentor but they are denying me my heritage. I don't want to see the same old crud performed as Shakespeare. It's like looking through the window, there's a fire burning in the hearth and you're watching a lot of rich kids playing with those big toys and they're not playing very well. It's very elitist and Oxbridge. (McAfee 1996)

This 'exclusion' has led him to become the independent producer and director of, and lead actor in, his own productions,[5] allowing him to declare: "I've done Shakespeare: he's as much my territory as anyone else's" (Kohn 1989).

Berkoff has not been concerned merely with contesting the Establishment's supposed ownership of the canon but also with challenging what he has characterised as mainstream theatre's castration of Shakespeare's language. Arguably, one of the benefits of Berkoff's lack of formal education is that he has been liberated from the orthodox perception of Shakespeare as the avatar of Great Literature. For Berkoff, routinely seen as the "scourge of the Shakespeare industry" (Kohn 1989), the work of Shakespeare does not belong in the realm of 'official' culture at all but with the 'people':

> Theatre came from the street, as Shakespeare would quickly acknowledge, as would the Commedia del Arte and Dario Fo. You ignore the rumblings of the thoroughfare at your peril, and the current, stultified theatre is like a plant that has been cut off from its roots, or, worse, like a plastic flower ineptly impersonating life. (Berkoff 1992d)

He recounts how in his first year as a drama student he was made aware of the 'popular' quality of Shakespeare's language by one instructor who revealed to him "the real and often sexual intent" (*FA*: 221) of Shakespeare's speeches. Berkoff recalls, for example, how this teacher glossed the phrase "love's majesty" uttered by Richard III as "the flowering of an erection" (*FA*: 221). As a result of this, Berkoff began to approach the work of Shakespeare, to borrow Bakhtin's (1984: 18) phrase, as a "rehabilitation of the flesh". In one interview he complains that "Maybe the Establishment have misinterpreted Shakespeare all these years. I suspect that they have it wrong. I suspect that they have not only misinterpreted it, they have castrated it" (Kohn 1989). In 1963, in Lincoln, in his first professional engagement in a Shakespearean drama, playing

Orlando in *As You Like It*, Berkoff witnessed such 'emasculation' first-hand, as the director cut "all reference to just about anything that vaguely symbolized 'horniness'" (*FA*: 251).

Orthodox critics, predictably, have been appalled by Berkoff's juxtaposition of Cockney profanity and Shakespearean grandeur. Ruby Cohn (1991: 94), for instance, has opined: "It is ironic that English verse drama, idealized after World War II for its spirituality, should belch forth in Berkoff's indiscriminate demotic energy." Yet it is not ironic at all, I suggest, when one considers the social and cultural whirlwind of the 1960s counter-culture, driven as it was by sexual liberation and an iconoclastic popular culture that gleefully attacked all sacred cows. Such a dismissive perspective, of course, is dependent upon an acceptance of a 'natural' hierarchy of registers in the English language that sets Shakespeare at the apex and lodges Cockney billingsgate somewhere near the bottom. An alternative view is offered by Clive Barker (1969: 105), who argues that "[o]nly in the working-class vernacular does the range of metaphor and simile and the specific and articulate power of expression in any way match the toughness and richness of Shakespeare's language." Berkoff's achievement in *East* was to demonstrate this equivalence between the two registers and to position them, to borrow Drakakis's metaphor, in "an arabesque of mutual validation" (Drakakis 1997: 162).

I turn now to the performative quality of the language in these two plays. The vast majority of the speeches in *East* and *West* consist of long soliloquies. In Scene 9 of *East*, for example, Les delivers a monologue about being imprisoned for underage sex that runs to three and a half pages (21–5). Even when the characters engage in what appears to be dialogue they often speak 'past' each other in monologues that implicitly involve the audience as addressee. These extended speeches enabled Berkoff to push into new aesthetic territory by creating a dramaturgy in which linguistic spectacle translated into physical spectacle in two key ways. First, the language of the soliloquies served as a choreographic score that determined the actions and movements of the actors. An example of this is the two-page speech delivered by Mike as he acts out the fight scene in *West*:

> (*The* CHORUS *leaves the stage.* MIKE *is alone. He acts the battle.*)
> MIKE: He hits me with a hook / I'm down / a bolt to fell an ox / crumbles slow / then smashes me with a right / and now / I sway / a drunk looking for a hold / a volley a hard straight comes whipping out / smashing home / I go down slow like the *Titanic* / but grab hold on the way. (88)

Such language blurs the conventionally clear-cut distinction between dramatic speech and stage directions. With regard to the latter, Aston and Savona's (1991: 76) distinction between "extra-dialogic" and "intra-dialogic" stage directions is a very useful way of approaching the performative language in the above extract. The extra-dialogic stage direction here, "He acts the battle", gives the performer no precise clue as to how the scene might be enacted, whereas the intra-dialogic directions embedded within the monologue, such as "He hits me with a hook" and "I'm down", clearly prescribe his movements.

There is a direct link here to older dramatic conventions. Aston and Savona point out that in classical, medieval and Renaissance dramas there is a "significant absence of a register of stage directions operating in parallel to the dialogue" (75). Berkoff's almost exclusive use of intra-dialogic stage directions in *East* and *West* positions him in close proximity to these older traditions, particularly, as he has been keen to point out, to Shakespearean dramaturgy. In his autobiography he complains that:

> the idea of Shakespeare as a word power is totally misunderstood. Shakespeare requires and stipulates that there are no sets in his production and that the words do the action. He stripped his stages down to the minimum and his actors were given high-definition text with which to accomplish the task. (*FA*: 295)

He thus draws upon Shakespeare's irreproachable example to create his own "high-definition text" and to justify his anti-naturalistic mime-based style.

The fight scene considered above, with its intra-dialogic directions to smash, sway, hit and so forth, remains more or less within the realm of realistic action. The more figurative phrases such as "a bolt to fell an ox" and "I go down slow like the *Titanic*", however, point to how Berkoff's language serves as a gestural score and to how his language *becomes* action. It follows that hyperbolic and figurative language will result in a mimed performance that is spectacular and fantastic. The two scenes in *East* in which Mike acts out the male and the female genitals demonstrate this. The pseudo-classical bombast with which he describes his penis was discussed in the previous section. Here it is sufficient to note that phrases in that monologue such as "piston power of the Flying Scotsman" and "*balls* like the great cannon that Pompeii used" (17) are intra-dialogic directions to render the dimensions and attributes of his member gesturally. In the case of "Mike's Cunt Speech", the performer in the 1999 revival at the Vaudeville Theatre mimed climbing into a gigantic vagina in a manner fit, as one squeamish critic expressed it, "to make maiden aunts blench" (Usher 1999).

From this, it can be seen that the performative language in such scenes enabled Berkoff to stage a carnivalesque spectacle centred on what Bakhtin terms, in relation to Rabelais, "the material bodily principle, that is, images of the human body with its food, drink, defecation, and sexual life" (Bakhtin 1984: 18). In the medieval and Renaissance carnival, these images of the body were offered, Bakhtin argues, "in an extremely exaggerated form". As Fiske (1989b: 81–2) expresses it:

> The physical excesses of Rabelais's world and their offensiveness to the established order echoed elements of the medieval carnival: both were concerned with bodily pleasure in opposition to morality, discipline, and social control ... The carnival, according to Bakhtin, was characterized by laughter, by excessiveness (particularly of the body and the bodily functions), by bad taste and offensiveness, and by degradation.

Just as the 'in-yer-face' language of *East* is a carnivalesque subversion of the hierarchy of registers, so, too, the "grotesque realism", to use Bakhtin's (1984: 18) phrase, of the mimed performance was intended as an assault upon the sensibilities of the audience.

The second main point about the language of the monologues is that it enables the performer as actor-narrator to demonstrate her or his character and actions and thereby involve the audience in some way in the drama that is unfolding on stage. The following scene from *West* demonstrates this:

> MIKE: Do you wanna dance / we slid on to the floor like two seals in a pool / wearing an ashen look about her face / smelling like a perfume counter at Boots / she had that look about her / like I couldn't care if you dropped dead look / her eyes scanning other talent / searching out the form / of course we do not get too close / just enough to give a hint of things to come / a lasso of lust waves encircles her.
> SYLV: He ... he looks like any other / with easy grin / street-corner patter / so we dance a bit and then he asks me.
> MIKE: Do you fancy a drink?
> SYLV: With him / as if he bought me / for a dance / whereas I stand or sit with or without mates / watching lines of faceless trousers stomping up and down.
> MIKE: She looks nice.
> SYLV: He looks OK / nice eyes / love crumbled grey / and smoking already for me / he says he don't half fancy taking me home / back to my gaff. (66–7)

As the actors playing Mike and Sylv perform the actions, they simultaneously describe them and each other to an implied addressee, the
audience. The spectators in the auditorium are thus privy to the characters'
assessments of each other, which they are implicitly invited to agree or
disagree with. On occasions, the performers in *East* and *West* demolish
the division between stage and auditorium by addressing the audience
directly. Mike's 'threat' to the audience in the epilogue of *West* is an
example of this:

> ... tell me what you do and how you do it / never mind I'll find out / I'll
> get the wind on you / I'll break out of this maze and sniff around your
> pen / I'll be the beast you fear / until I get an answer / straight up I
> will / you had me do your dirt / and stood around to gape / while I
> put down the fears that kept you sleepless in your beds. (93)

In such instances there is a superficial parallel to Brecht's notion of 'epic
theatre'. The crucial difference between the work of the two men, however, was the perlocutionary effect that each sought to produce on his
audience.[6]

The primary purpose of Brecht's "epic theatre" was to bring about
changes in his audience's understanding in order to initiate political
change. As he wrote in 1927, "[t]he essential point of the epic theatre is
perhaps that it appeals less to the feelings than to the spectator's reason.
Instead of sharing an experience the spectator must come to grips with
things" (quoted in Willett 1959: 170). Berkoff, by contrast, evinced no
such engaged political motivation. The perlocutionary effect of the
language in *East* and *West* varies according to the speech and the context,
but it is never didactic, and never presents a political programme. Berkoff
was not 'aiming' these plays at proletarian audiences who needed to be
shown how they were being exploited by the capitalist system. This is
clear from the fact that the programmes of all the productions (including
the 1999 revival), as well as the published text of the play, include a
glossary of the Cockney slang used by the characters, indicating that
Berkoff was spitting his expletives at audiences he suspected were
unfamiliar with Cockney billingsgate yet were educationally and culturally
equipped to recognise the misquotations from Shakespeare. Far from
asking his audiences, like Brecht, to consider how best to effect social or
political change, therefore, Berkoff was setting out to create notoriety for
himself by shocking, exciting, amusing and disgusting his middle-class
patrons that he also hoped to impress.

Back to the future

With *East,* and later with *West,* Berkoff turned away from adaptations of literary works to revisit in a semi-autobiographical fashion his working-class past. In his preface to *East* he writes:

> This play was written to exorcize certain demons struggling within me to escape. *East* takes place within my personal memory and experience and is less a biographical text than an outburst or revolt against the sloth of my youth and a desire to turn a welter of undirected passion into a positive form. I wanted to liberate that time squandered and sometimes enjoyed into a testament to youth and energy. It is revolt. (3)

I now examine the double-edged quality of this 'return home' and attempt to show how the authenticating conventions that he employed were used against themselves ironically to deconstruct or, to use Berkoff's word, exorcise this past.

Unlike the earnest socialist proletarians in Wesker's *Trilogy,* for example, the working-class East Enders in these two plays are neither defined by nor do they identify themselves with their work. They neither experience pride in honest labour nor are they involved in any political struggle to improve working conditions for themselves or, still less, their fellows. They despise both the employment they are engaged in and the bosses who provide it, yet they refuse to enter into any political process that might lead to the amelioration of their lives. In *East,* for example, Sylv declares in her "Speech of Resolution":

> We will not end our days
> In grey born blight – and stomp
> Our hours away in fag end waste.
> And kiss the minutes till they budge
> While we toil in some stinking
> factory. (40–1)

And in *West,* Mike asks rhetorically:

> Why should I yoke myself to nine to five / stand shoulder to shoulder with the dreary gang who sway together in the tube / or get acquainted with parking meters / be a good citizen of this vile state / so I can buy an ultra-smart hi-fi and squander fortunes on pop singles. (79)

There is only one scene in both plays where we witness a character in what can loosely be described as a work-related situation. This is Scene 9 in *East,* in which Les describes a day of 'work' in a menswear shop that involves shirking his duties, 'absenting' himself through extended sexual fantasies and stealing from the cash register. Apart from this both plays present their characters 'at play'.

The first act of Arnold Wesker's *Chicken Soup with Barley* is located in a naturalistically and factually real East End that is evoked through the action on-stage and the characters' accounts of what has occurred off-stage. The mention of place names like Gardiner's Corner and historical events such as the Battle of Cable Street ground the drama in its environment, the Jewish East End of the 1930s. The possible world of Berkoff's *East* and *West*, by contrast, is a 'ludic East End' that may be equated with Bakhtin's marketplace festival, a fantasy world where *hoi polloi* cock a snook at officially sanctioned culture and institutions. Bakhtin (1984: 153–4) writes that:

> The marketplace of the Middle Ages and the Renaissance was a world in itself, a world which was one; all "performances" in this area, from loud cursing to the organized show, had something in common and were imbued with the same atmosphere of freedom, frankness and familiarity. Such elements of familiar speech as profanities, oaths and curses were fully legalized in the marketplace and were easily adopted by all the festive genres, even by the Church drama. The marketplace was the center of all that is unofficial; it enjoyed a certain extraterritoriality in a world of official order, it always remained "with the people."

Berkoff's 'East End' is a similarly extraterritorial world. It has no substantial geographical or historical existence but is rather the site where the characters engage in their self-destructive leisure activities. I now examine the ludic performances that are enacted on this carnivalesque stage-cum-arena-cum-marketplace according to Callois's four-fold typology of play, namely contests (*agôn*); mimicry; vertigo-inducing games and activities (*ilinx*); and games of chance (*alea*). My purpose is to show how these playful activities, far from liberating the characters, serve to suck them down further in a spiral of self-entrapment whilst Berkoff implicitly elevates himself out of a class and an environment he has forsaken and attempts now to "exorcize".

The characters in both plays are driven by two types of *agôn*, namely combat and courtship. Although these contests fulfil one of the main conditions of play set forth by Huitzinga, namely that they are unproductive in so far as they create neither goods nor wealth, they are none-theless serious in that the self-worth of the characters involved hangs upon the outcome. In *West*, Mike views the combat between himself and the Hoxton King as a direct threat to his self-esteem. When his friends urge him to recognise the superiority of his enemy, he retorts hotly with:

> Swallow it, you mean! And wear a hideous yellow on my back / to strut before a wanton ambling nymph / that's what you see for me / Mike the King of N16 / I'll drown more villains than a mermaid could / deceive more slyly than old Shylock would / and set the murderous Hoxton King to school / can I do this and cannot get his crown / balls, were he Al Capone I'd pluck it down. (52)

So seriously does Mike view the impending fight that he trains for it as if for a boxing championship: "I do a thousand press-ups every day and forearm curls / a score of chin-ups on the bar / have made my arms a vice to crush a bear / bench-press 300 pounds" (52).

As he sets off to meet his foe on the appointed day, his mother asks him where he is going. His reply, a statement of purposeful intent, is as follows:

> For a fight to the death / a battle of honour / destruction of a monster / to kill the plague / to slay the dragon / to defend the weak / to prove my worth / to destroy the mighty / to avenge the dead / to annihilate the oppressor / to be a mensch / to have a punch-up. (76)

He goes on to prove his self-worth by slaying the dragon. The victory, which provides him with more self-esteem than a regular job, is an end in itself, even though it leaves him disfigured and wounded. He annihilates his "oppressor" not, like Beowulf, in the collective cause of improving the lot of his community but "to be a mensch"; in other words, to find satisfaction and meaning in his own personal human existence. This, I suggest, is a metatheatrical treatment by Berkoff of his struggle for individual success.

The other kind of *agôn* in these plays is the courtship struggle between the male and female characters. In Scene 6 of *East*, for example, Mike and Sylv spar verbally with each other:

> SYLV: ... I am the vision in your head ... tight box, plumbing perfect – switches on and off to the right touch ... not thy thick-fingered labourer's paws thou slob and street-corner embellishment ... thou pin-table musician ... thy flesh would ne'er move – would shrink under my glare – so try.
>
> MIKE: Tasty verily – so thou, bitch, seeks [*sic*] to distress my johnny tool with psychological war, humiliating it into surrender-shrink. (16)

It is evident that Mike's self-worth depends as much upon his success in bedding Sylv as upon besting the Hoxton King. In *West*, Mike's victory in the love-war is achieved with the capitulation of Sylv: "And he asked me out the next day / and from then on all I wanted was to be a sacrifice / like an offering" (68). Once again, we see that Mike's (Berkoff's) self-empowerment is gained at the expense of weaker and submissive individuals. Just as the male characters have no interest in undertaking any action that might benefit society or their class collectively, so, too, they betray no interest in the 'greater good' of a positive relationship with their female partners. The sexual micro-politics mirror the social macro-politics in that they reflect back only the appetite of hungry males prowling in the urban jungle.

Turning now to mimicry, Callois (1961: 19) defines this category of play in the following way:

> All play presupposes the temporary acceptance, if not of an illusion (indeed this last word means nothing less than beginning a game: *in-lusio*), then at least of a closed, conventional, and in certain respects, imaginary universe. Play can consist not only of deploying actions or submitting to one's fate in an imaginary milieu, but of becoming an illusory character oneself, and of so behaving.

At the risk of stating the obvious, the very act of performing on a stage is generally (but not always) a form of mimicry. Callois argues: "[Mimicry] consists in deliberate impersonation, which may readily become a work of art, contrivance, or cunning. The actor must work out his [sic] role and create a dramatic illusion" (78). In another sense, however, this formulation is too simplistic, since Callois bases it upon an absolute separation between the possible world of a theatrical event and the real world outside the walls of the playhouse:

> For the actor ... a theatrical performance is mere simulation. He [sic] puts on make-up and costume, plays and recites. But when the curtain falls, and the lights go on, he returns to reality. The separation of the two universes remains absolute. (45)

Yet such a simple binary opposition between 'real' and 'theatrical' is inadequate, I would argue, particularly when one approaches meta-theatrical performance as in *East* and *West*, and, as we saw in the last chapter, in *Metamorphosis*.

As the following exchange between Mike and Les in *East* shows, Berkoff exploits this slippery division/non-division between worlds or orders of reality:

LES: Do you mean we're in a play?
MIKE: Something of that kind.
LES: I am not, even if you may be. (25)

This exchange raises interesting ontological questions. Are Les and Mike characters in a play or real life figures? Or are they both or neither? When one adds to this the fact that both Mike and Les are Berkoff-alter egos, one enters a vertiginous world of constantly shifting and mutually reflecting and distorting mirror images. In the original production of *East*, Berkoff the actor impersonated the character Mike, who in turn was one of Berkoff's alter egos. In a circular pattern of signification, therefore, Berkoff mimicked someone mimicking his 'self'. In *West*, the character of Mike is refracted through the illusory character of Hamlet, the role-player who (in Shakespeare's tragedy) cannot decide whether to be, that is *exist*, or not. In his autobiography, Berkoff writes: "The plays, particularly *East*, were a game, a charade or masquerade" (*FA*: 46). These bewildering games of mimicry exist in the realm of carnival which, as Bakhtin argues, "belongs to the borderline between art and life. In reality, it is life itself, but shaped according to a certain pattern of play" (Bakhtin 1984: 7). Berkoff may be seen, therefore, to have been playing with aspects of his adolescent 'self' that he wished to exorcise and be rid of.

With regard to the third category of play, *ilinx*, the characters in the plays engage in escapist games or activities that bring about temporary excitement and pleasure through vertigo or thrill-inducing movement. The dancing of the characters is a case in point. Callois (1961: 25) argues that "men [*sic*] surrender to the intoxication of many kinds of dance, from the insidious giddiness of the waltz to the many mad, tremendous, and convulsive movements of other dances." In *West*, Mike narrates his jive with Sylv :

I took her on the floor / the crystal ball smashed the light into a million pieces / a shattered lake at sunrise / the music welled up / and the lead guitarist / plugged into ten thousand watts zonging in our ears / callused thumb whipping chords / down the floor we skate / I push her thigh with mine / and backwards she goes to the gentle signal / no horse moved better / and I move my left leg which for a second leaves me hanging on her thigh. (77)

A different example of *ilinx* to be found in *East* is the mimed motorbike ride by Mike and Les. Mike says:

At a 150 a ton and a half of sublime speed tearing gut winded flailing flesh pulled – your glasses stabbing your eyes – ice ripping off your

face – the vibrations pulsating through each square inch of skin
between your thighs power lies – at 2000 cc my throttle-twist grip
lightly, oh so delicately held – not too much rev! We skate! We fly! (30)

In these instances the underlying desire of the participants is to liberate
themselves from the constriction of their social situation through vertiginous 'play'. The very temporariness of the thrills, however, emphasises
the socio-economic entrapment of the characters. They may 'dance' or
'skate' away from their dystopian surroundings for a short while but their
return is inevitable. And so the downward spiral continues.

The single mode of play from Callois's typology that is conspicuously
absent in these two dramas is *alea*, or games of chance. As we have seen,
Berkoff has been single-mindedly concerned with self-empowerment
and gaining, as the writer, director and producer of his plays, full control
over his 'product' and thereby his career. It follows, therefore, that *alea*,
which, as Callois (1961: 73) argues, "presupposes full and total abandon
to the whims of chance ... [and] the resignation of the will" has little or no
place in the schema of Berkoff's will-to-power. The two protagonists in
East and *West* express Berkoff's own oft-stated desire to achieve control
over his life and his art. As a consequence, the ludism of the two main
characters in these plays and of Berkoff in public life both on and off-
stage takes place on the most power and performance-related plane
delineated by Callois, namely the nexus where competition, simulation
and mimicry intersect. In other words, Berkoff and his proxies Mike and
Les have been engaged in 'power play'.

Far from setting out to create a factually reliable representation of
Cockney life and culture in *East* and *West*, Berkoff constructed a dystopian,
ludic working-class world – one which he then used to dismantle the
romanticised myth of the East End in order to cut his own tie to it.
According to the stage directions at the beginning of *East*, the first image
to greet the audience, before any action takes place, is an upstage screen
upon which is projected "a series of real East End images, commenting
and reminding us of the actual world just outside the stage" (7). This
authenticating convention is quickly subverted, however, at the very
opening of the play when the five cast members sing the well-known
Cockney music hall song 'My Old Man says Follow the Van' (7) "out of
order and in canons and descants" (7) to the discordant and broken
accompaniment of the off-stage pianist. Similarly, *West* opens with the
cast singing a medley of Cockney music hall songs "out of order" (49).
Both plays begin, therefore, with their possible worlds out of kilter.
Berkoff's parodic treatment of songs that have traditionally celebrated the

collective values of the working class can be seen as a swipe at the sentimental Cockney musical dramas staged at the Theatre Royal, Stratford East at the end of the 1950s.[7]

Dad is the leading voice of 'nostalgia' in the two plays. In Scene 8 of *East*, he eulogises the past: "Years ago things were good, you got value out of your money, a dollar was five bob, a summer's day was hot and sunny like a summer's day, you weren't short changed, you got your full twelve hours' worth" (21). Yet his repetition of the same mantra at the beginning of Scene 13 reduces this statement to meaningless prattle. Berkoff further demolishes this 'glorious' past by having Dad recall his participation in the anti-Semitic rallies and marches of Oswald Mosley and his followers (14–15). A 'typical' working-class tea-time with "steaming tea, a tureen of beans, [and] a packet of margarine" (12) becomes the locus of a frenzied re-enactment by Dad of the Battle of Cable Street that leaves the table in ruins. This scene, which destroys the myth of sunny days and good neighbourliness, can be read as an attempt on the part of Berkoff to avenge his own victimisation as a Jew by suggesting that the 'good old days' favoured only the Gentiles in the East End. Moreover, the wrecked tea table implies how, in Berkoff's view, the working class as a collective (as opposed to ambitious individuals like himself who 'escape'), has conspired to keep itself down.

The popular East End culture that is presented in these plays is not the oppositional culture of a politically conscious and active working class but the broken-down, self-destructive and self-confining culture of a racist and sexist *lumpenproletariat*, from which Berkoff has evidently wished to distance himself. In his autobiography he recalls:

> When I wrote *West* in 1978 I thought our working-class environment was fairly wretched but simple, with a couple of cafés and a few clubs and swimming pools, a few broken-down flea-pit cinemas, a sweaty old gym, a few parks in which to trot with your lady for a wintry squeeze. (*FA*: 66)

In this cultural wasteland, television, the "popular successor" of music hall (Drakakis 1997: 164), serves, alongside such diversions as bingo and shopping, to sedate the masses. Mum, in a moment of disturbing lucidity, describes herself as

> the other half of nothing fed with electric media swill – consumer me – *Hawaii Five-O – Z Cars – Coronation Street – University Challenge – Sunday Night at the London Palladium – On the Buses – Play of the Month – Watch With Mother* – tea, fags – light and bitter – ha! ha! and ho! ho! (26)

Similarly, Les articulates the sense of self-imposed waste in *East*:

> Why don't we chat up classy snatch? Why is it that we pull slags? We pull what we think we are Mike – it tumbled then – it dropped – the dirty penny dropped – that we get what we ARE. What we think we are, so when we have a right and merry laugh with some unsavoury bunk-up or gang bang behind the Essoldo we are doing it to ourselves. (29)

It occurs to none of the characters in these two plays, however, to initiate social change through political activity. Berkoff thus lit a fuse under the myth of a vibrant and progressive East End working-class culture. One critic of a 1991 revival of *East* writes that:

> Berkoff serves up the entrails of [the characters'] cockney sparrer culture over the trays of tea and it is not a pretty sight. To knees up piano accompaniment and performed within a claustrophobic fly-blown, fly-posted set you are taken on a crazy rip past the survivors of a burnt-out, white working-class way of life rooted in consumerism and fed on machismo thuggery, stunted sexuality, paranoid fantasy and reassuring myth. (Foss 1991)

I have argued that the characters in these dramas perform their play-related activities on the stage of a ludic 'East End' that is analogous to Bakhtin's carnivalesque marketplace. In this two-play self-destructive 'festival', they dance, sing, fight, fornicate, adopt alternative identities, use profane language and burlesque 'official' culture. Crucially, however, Berkoff's strategy was not counterhegemonic, since the ultimate target of these two plays was not the enslaving and exploitative ruling classes but the self-destructive working-culture of the East End itself. For Callois, the festival is "the paroxysm of society, purifying and renewing it simultaneously" (Callois 1961: 125–6). Berkoff and his alter egos, however, express no altruistic or self-sacrificial interest in purifying and renewing the working-class society of the East End and Stamford Hill. On the contrary, Mike fights and wins the battle for *himself*, just as his creator used *East* to exorcise his past and thereby purify and renew *himself* in the quest for mainstream recognition. Thus these two plays, far from being strategies to subvert the hegemony of the *status quo*, are discourses that seem to demonstrate Berkoff's belief in a working-class neo-Conservative philosophy of self-help individualism (see chapter 6).

Conclusion

With *East*, as he wrote in his preface to the play, Berkoff set out to "exorcize" the self-destructive aspects of Cockney culture from his life, to redirect, as it were, the 'teleological' trajectory of his career. The play was written at a time when he was still concerned with breaking away from his past and creating success for himself as a 'new' Berkoff, the 'de-proletarianised' theatre artist at home with the works of Kafka, Poe, Aeschylus and, most particularly, Shakespeare. Ironically, though, his performance in the original production and his projection of himself through the character of the juvenile delinquent Mike as a Cockney 'hard man' was so unexpectedly successful that, far from shaking off his past, he re-embraced his background with enthusiasm – so much so, indeed, that he repeated the strategy with *West*. And as we saw in chapter 1, he has been actively projecting himself as an East Ender ever since.

East and *West* are theatrical 'carnivals' in so far as they invert or at least assert equivalences between what are conventionally seen to be anti-podean registers of language and culture, namely Cockney billingsgate and Shakespearean dramatic verse. Yet Berkoff was not motivated by any counterhegemonic or macro-political intent but rather with empowering and promoting himself. Such a conclusion is supported by the following statement in his autobiography:

> In writing much of *East* in verse I was trying to arrest the ear. To reclaim the battlefield lost to movies and TV and to create a language or form that would prick up your ears. To attack the audience with an avalanche of language. To seize, attack, reclaim, hunt down, and generally say to them *listen to this ... watch this*, this is my territory (original emphasis). (*FA*: 236)

Significantly, he writes here not of "our territory," the territory of the LTG or the Cockney working class, but individualistically of "*my* territory". Just as *Metamorphosis* was a metatheatrical staging of Berkoff's physical constriction and escape, so *East* and *West* were similarly metatheatrical enactments of his own socio-economic constriction in the 'east' of his dark past and his individual escape to the 'west' of his bright future.

Berkoff's career might well indeed be described, to continue the geographic metaphor, as a continuous and nomadic travelling back and forth between the East End (the home of 'street theatricality', working-class vitality, and so on) and the West End (the home of the 'Shakespeare industry', mainstream success, and so on). In his autobiography he recalls that as a youth going 'up west' was a euphemism for doing something special and more elegant, of having a wonderful time and going on the town. You'd dress up to go 'up west'. It meant escape from the dreary slums or suburbs. Its very name gave a charge, as when Mum might say she was going shopping 'up west'. When you were in Stamford Hill going 'up west' still carried that aura of magic with it. (*FA*: 66)

We have seen that in 1959 Berkoff forsook his East End/Stamford Hill working-class Jewish culture in order to study drama 'up west', and that, for him, the West End represented (as it still does) the acme of success in the theatrical profession in Britain. As a postscript it is interesting to note that in September 1999 Berkoff celebrated the twenty-fifth anniversary of *East* by reviving it on the stage of the Vaudeville Theatre, thereby bringing his 'East End' to the West End. Thus his strategy of using his background as a stepping stone to individual mainstream success may be said, at least on his own terms, to have been successful. Yet a large question mark remains hanging over Berkoff's relationship with a working-class background that he once tried to "exorcise".

Notes

1 Quoted from Berkoff's notes to the programme of the 1976 Greenwich Theatre production of *East*.
2 The *Oxford English Dictionary* defines *Billingsgate* as follows: "The proper name (presumably from a name *Billing*) of one of the gates of London, and hence of the fish-market there established. The seventeenth-century references to the 'rhetoric' or abusive language of this market are frequent, and hence foul language is itself called 'billingsgate'".
3 In *West*, Berkoff notes, "there is not one swear word ... [not] one single four-letter word, since it was written for the Beeb" (*FA*: 70). This is true as far as the original script that Berkoff presented to the BBC in 1978 is concerned. In the subsequently published text, however, one finds the colourful phrase "Shit, cunt-face, scabby bollocks" (54). In this drama, the shock-effect of the linguistic wordplay is created by more extensive textual raids on Shakespeare.
4 All line references to Shakespeare's dramas follow *The Complete Works* (Oxford: Clarendon Press, 1988), edited by Stanley Wells and Gary Taylor.
5 Berkoff has staged the following revivals of Shakespeare's plays: *Macbeth* (The Place, 1970), *Hamlet* (Edinburgh Festival, 1979, and tour), *Coriolanus* (Public Theatre, New York, 1988), and *Richard II* (Joseph Papp Public Theatre, New York, 1994). He has also staged his one-man "masterclass in evil", *Shakespeare's Villains* (Theatre Royal Haymarket, 1998), and written and directed *The Secret Love Life of Ophelia* (King's Head, 2001).
6 *Locutionary, illocutionary* and *perlocutionary* are terms used by J. L. Austin in his speech-act theory (*How To Do Things with Words*, Cambridge, Mass.: Harvard University Press, 1962) to delineate three performative levels of

speech-as-action. Perlocutionary refers to the effect of an utterance upon the addressee or listener. Austin's theory has been applied by theatre semioticians in their discussions of dramatic dialogue. Keir Elam, for example, argues that "[t]heater has always been, or has always been thought to be, an essentially perlocutionary enterprise, its end and motivation lying in persuasion or delight or purgation or instruction" (Elam 1991: 51).

7 Two examples are Norman and Bart's *Fings Ain't Wot They Used T'be* (1959) and Lewis's *Sparrers Can't Sing* (1960). The latter was first adapted as the film *Sparrows Can't Sing* (1962), starring the Cockney actress Barbara Windsor, and then transformed by Bart into the musical *The Londoners* (1972).

6

BERKOFF AND THATCHERISM

It wasn't at all difficult this morning to vote Tory. In fact, it felt good, wanting change, and we have to change ... (Sir Peter Hall, *Peter Hall's Diaries*)

Britain in the late 1970s acquired the reputation of being the "sick man of Europe". Throughout the decade British society had been beset by a host of intractable problems, including high unemployment (more than 1 million in 1975); IRA bombing campaigns in English cities; bitter industrial disputes; and racist violence. The nadir was reached in 1978/ 79 with the so-called 'Winter of Discontent' during which widespread industrial action by various groups of public service workers led to the breakdown of Labour Prime Minister Jim Callaghan's pay policy. In the following May the General Election victory of the Conservatives saw Margaret Thatcher installed as Britain's first woman Premier (albeit with only 43.9% of the total vote). Her mandate, as she saw it, was to halt Britain's economic decline, rein in what she saw as recalcitrant trade unions, and establish a new consensus around the ideas of *laissez-faire* economic individualism and free enterprise. Thatcherism, the neo-Conservative ideology named after her, subsequently produced the greatest shake-up (or shake-down) of British society since the creation of the welfare state by the Labour Government of Clement Attlee in the second half of the 1940s. It marked the end of the post-war consensus, which Thatcher characteristically saw as an obstacle to progress, and its replacement with the dictatorial rule of an 'Iron Lady' who brooked no dissent, least of all from her own Cabinet colleagues. The far-reaching effects of Thatcher's autocratism and monetarist economic policies upon every aspect of the social, cultural, political and economic life of Britain in the 1980s (and after) have been extensively documented and analysed.

During the 1970s, politically committed playwrights on the Left such as John McGrath, David Hare, Howard Brenton, Howard Barker, David Edgar, Barrie Keefe, Caryl Churchill and Trevor Griffiths had attempted to diagnose the nature of the so-called 'British disease' in a variety of 'England-in-decline' plays. After the 1979 election, these same playwrights continued their socialist or Marxist critique of capitalism by turning their attention to the new threat of Thatcherism (Peacock 1999: 65–102). Berkoff's response (in public, at least) to the wrenching changes that came about in British society during the second half of the 1970s and during Thatcher's first term as Prime Minister was markedly different. In a 1977 interview published in *Time Out* magazine he outlined the 'apolitical' and 'selfish' nature of his work with the LTG:

> People say we're not political but the theatre of political observation is so limited to what's going on at present. It may inform a few people, it may illuminate a few facts but basically it becomes drab, locked in the scheme of the writer. Art belongs to itself; it's a selfish, grasping thing. (Grant 1977)

Such a view distanced him from the work of the left-wing playwrights mentioned above, and anticipated the virulently individualistic nature of neo-Conservative thinking, as encapsulated in Mrs Thatcher's famous dog-eat-dog dictum: "We don't belong to society, we are all just individuals doing the best we can for ourselves" (Gilmour 1992: 272).

Berkoff shifted to a more 'political' stance in the first half of the 1980s, however, as he used the social, political and economic changes that took place during the first Thatcher term as material for his dramas. Looking back in his autobiography at those years, he expresses bitterness at being criticised for his apparent lack of political engagement at a time of crisis for the Left in Britain: "I took great exception to the torpid lie that there were hardly any plays dealing with the Thatcher years, when what all my plays dealt with was those very years. *Greek, Decadence, Sink the Belgrano*"[1,2] (*FA*: 374). At the root of such criticism appears to be the assumption that political theatre can only be socialistic in orientation. A typical expression of this is Sandy Craig's narrow assertion that "[p]olitical theatre is, by necessity, a theatre of socialist political change" (Craig 1980b: 30). Here I proceed from the view that all theatre (indeed, all cultural practice) is political, but in different ways and with different orientations. Berkoff's treatment of Thatcherism in *Greek* (Half Moon Theatre, 1980), *Decadence* (Arts Theatre, 1983) and *Sink the Belgrano!* (Half Moon Theatre, 1986) and in his non-dramatic writings calls, however 'apolitically' framed, for socio-political change of a *certain* kind. That his analysis of British society is not socialist or Marxist but cryptically pro-Thatcherite (nowhere does he explicitly state his support of her policies) or, paradoxically, virulently anti-Thatcher, depending on the play, the issue and the timing, does not make his work any less political in nature.

In this chapter I examine how Berkoff did indeed 'deal' with the Thatcher years (or at least her first term of government) in the three plays just mentioned, and how this enabled him to construct and project his 'self' and his work in new ways. A key text that informs the following discussion is Paul Heelas's chapter 'Reforming the Self: Enterprise and the characters of Thatcherism' (1991), in which he presents a useful though perhaps rather reductive taxonomy of four distinct "characters" or models of the self: first, the 'enterprising self', "displaying initiative and responsibility in economic production"; second, the 'sovereign consumer', "exercising freedom to satisfy its wishes"; third, the 'active citizen', "concerned to contribute to the well-being of the community"; and last, the 'conservative self', "bearer of traditional or Victorian values" (Heelas 1991: 72–3). My concern below is to deconstruct Berkoff's ambiguous attitude towards Thatcherism according to these four "characters", particularly the first two, which are located at the more "selfish, grasping" end of the spectrum of neo-Conservative political philosophy.

Late capitalist society has become increasingly performance and commodity-oriented. In the catering, travel and retail industries, our leisure activities, and even politics, "human transactions are complexly structured through the growing use of performative modes and frames" (Kershaw 1994: 167), and commodities are purveyed and services offered with "a flick of performative spice" (166). At the same time that Thatcher was systematically dismantling Britain's traditional manufacturing industries, she was actively engaged in fostering the growth of service industries. During her tenure as Prime Minister the Arts Council of Great Britain became the instrument for coercing the theatre (indeed all the arts) into 'performing' (in the sense of working efficiently) according to the exigencies of the marketplace. In 1988 the then ACGB Chairman William Rees-Mogg could be seen clearly toeing the Thatcherite line: "We are coming to value the consumer's judgement as highly as that of the official or expert", he opined. "The voice of the public must ... be given due weight ... [and] the way in which the public discriminates is through its willingness to pay for its pleasures."[3] It may be said, therefore, that it was all part of Thatcherite orthodoxy to commodify the theatre, and to transform it, along with education and health care, into a service that had, first and foremost, to 'balance its books'.

This chapter is structured in the following manner. In the first section, I examine the ways in which Berkoff has embodied Thatcher's enterprise culture in his projections of himself as an 'enterprising self' and a 'sovereign consumer'. Whilst I discuss this primarily in the context of *Greek*, I also consider his non-dramatic writings, particularly his autobiography and his interviews. In the second section, I look at Berkoff's apparently *anti*-Thatcher response to the pernicious effects upon British society of her policies during her first term of government, namely the economic gulf that widened between the classes, the increase in civic disorder that resulted from it, and the resurrected myth of an Imperial Britain during the Falklands War, a military adventure that was initiated precisely in order to deflect attention from the failure of her domestic economic policies. The key texts that I examine in this context are *Decadence* and *Sink the Belgrano!* My purpose will be to show how Berkoff's pro-Thatcher support of the enterprise culture is a subject position that allowed him to celebrate his own entrepreneurial success. Conversely, his later anti-Thatcher stance enabled him to disassociate himself from the subsequent failure of her policies, and from the image of an Anglocentric Imperial Britain that she constructed at the time of the Falklands conflict.

Berkoff and the enterprise culture

At the core of Thatcher's programme for the 'renewal' of British society was the championing of the individual citizen both as entrepreneur and consumer. As Michael Heseltine, a former prominent member of Thatcher's Cabinet, put it in the *Daily Telegraph* (7 July 1987), "[w]herever possible we want individuals to control, influence and determine their own destiny". This is a sentiment that was and still is wholly consonant with Berkoff's self-oriented political philosophy. It was apparent, as we have seen, in his working methods with the LTG, and is expressed later in his autobiography, where he states that the most important thing in one's work is to achieve "control over your product" (*FA*: 95). *Product* is a significant lexical choice in this context. Berkoff's preoccupation, as playwright, director, producer, designer and lead actor, with commodifying his work and his 'self' in the marketplace is, I suggest, one of the chief defining characteristics of his whole career.

Greek was written during the Winter of Discontent (*FA*: 4), and performed in February 1980, a little less than a year after Thatcher's first election victory. In this play he reworks the Oedipus legend and tells the story of the protagonist Eddy's single-handed struggle *à la* Thatcher to defeat the plague infesting present-day (1978–79) Britain:

> Oedipus found a city in the grip of a plague and sought to rid the city of its evil centre represented by the Sphinx. Eddy seeks to reaffirm his

beliefs and inculcate a new order of things with his vision and life-affirming energy. (*CP*, I: 97)

Despite referring disparagingly to Margaret Thatcher in this play (and in *Decadence* and *Belgrano!*) as "Maggot Scratcher", there is a paradox, as we shall see, in the fact that *Greek* is a discourse of self-empowerment very much in tune with Thatcherite orthodoxy. His apparently anti-Thatcher stance is perhaps explicable in terms of a residual sense of himself as still belonging to the working class and thus reacting in an instinctively hostile manner to the party of the 'guv'nors'. Yet his pro-Thatcher position derives from his clear perception of himself as a 'self-made' man attempting to elevate himself socially and economically out of that very class. In what follows I examine Berkoff's neo-Conservative positioning of himself as an 'enterprising self' and as a 'sovereign consumer'.

Like Mike in *East* and *West*, Eddy in *Greek* is a Berkoff-alter ego. In his autobiography Berkoff repeatedly draws attention to the closeness of his identification with his creation. He writes, for example: "My love became Eddy's love, my hate Eddy's hate, my bile and pity Eddy's and so on" (*FA*: 4). Furthermore, Berkoff had originally cast himself in the role of Eddy, but opted instead to direct. He recalls that "I particularly liked that part since it was modelled around me and expressed what I felt around that time" (*FA*: 339). It is reasonable to assume, therefore, that the views expressed by Eddy in the play closely match those of Berkoff himself, both in the period 1978–80, when he wrote and staged the play, and around 1996, when he published his autobiography.

As is well known, Thatcher's election victory heralded the dismantling of the welfare state and the advent of a so-called 'enterprise culture' driven by "self-proclaimed achievers" (Marquand 1991: 187). These 'leaders' would now spread the gospel of "social Thatcherism" whereby "personal effort by the individual citizen benefitted the community" (Heelas 1991: 78–9) in what was supposed to be a trickle-down of energy and initiative. In 1982, shortly after the British victory in the Falklands, Thatcher declared in an interview in the *Daily Express* (26 July 1982): "We are looking for self-starters. We are looking for princes of industry, people who have fantastic ability to build things and create jobs." Eddy/Berkoff is the very embodiment of this successful Thatcherite self-starter, and *Greek*, for all his anti-Maggie posturing, is the dramatisation of Berkoff's own 'Thatcherite revolution', his own neo-Conservative manifesto, so to speak.

His metaphor in the play for Britain during the late-1970s and early-1980s is a poorly managed 'greasy spoon' café.[4] Indeed, as I show below, the café as a metaphor for society is a frequently recurring motif in

Berkoff's writings. In a key scene, customer Eddy, thwarted by bad service in his simple desire for coffee and cake, fights and kills the manager of the café and takes it over as his own business. He proceeds to run the operation along lean and 'efficient' Thatcherite lines, and, after a decade of hard work, he is able to boast of his achievements:

> I improved the lot of our fair café by my intense efforts ... got rid of sloth and stale achievement / which once was thought normal / I made the city golden era time / the dopes just died away when faced with real octane high-power juice / the con men that have tricked you all the while with substitute and fishy watery soup / went out of business and people starved for nourishment brain-food and guts just flocked to us. (*CP*, I: 121)

Here Berkoff can be seen moving very much with the late 1970s current of Thatcherite neo-Conservatism. Indeed, he was surging ahead of that particular stream, since the tone of Eddy's boast anticipated the Conservative Party manifesto in 1983, which trumpeted the Thatcher administration's 'achievements' in similar style: "When we came to office in May 1979, our country was suffering both from an economic crisis and a crisis of morale. British industry was uncompetitive, over-taxed, over-regulated, and over-manned ... This country was drifting further behind its neighbours. Defeatism was in the air."[5]

Eddy's café is an establishment that, in the best Thatcherite manner, claims to give its patrons value for money. In a word, it *performs* well. As such it may be seen as a symbol not only of Berkoff's answer to a plague-ridden and demoralised society but also to what he saw and still sees as the mediocre service and products offered by the institutional theatre, in both the subsidised and commercial sectors, in Britain. Already in 1978, one can hear the voice of Berkoff the neo-Conservative entrepreneur berating mediocrity:

> The theatre scene here has been so appalling that people are now inured [*sic*] to anything new and accept the general appalling standards ... Theatre in London has lost over a million people because the critics have helped sustain this turgid crap ... I've got a duty to London in a sense to give people somewhere to go where they can have a good time. (Elder 1978: 38)

He has been particularly scathing of subsidised theatre. Nearly twenty years later in his autobiography, and still in 'Maggie-mode', Berkoff continued to attack what he saw as the inefficient working practices of both management and unionised labour in the subsidised sector of the theatre:

In business a management would be sacked if the work methods produced such disasters on a regular basis and a new system would have to be installed to respond to the public taste and demands. However, the same boorish attitudes ensure that defunct and antique machinery is used. Like the ostrich attitudes of British industry after the war, where traditionalism impeded the need for change and lost Britain its markets, the theatre pursues the same hopeless and stale methodology. Why? Because it is largely a closed shop. It does not have to compete with foreign companies since the language barrier protects it in its insularity. (*FA*: 321)

By contrast, Eddy/Berkoff the crusading 'active citizen' boasts:

We cured the plague by giving inspiration to our plates / came rich by giving more and taking less / the old-style portion control practised by fat thieves went out with us / we put the meat back into the sausage mate ... now in our great chain we energize the people, give soul food and blistering blast of protein smack ... rid the world of half-assed bastards clinging to their dark domain and keeping talent out by filling the entrances with their swollen carcasses and sagging mediocrity. (*CP*, I: 122)

Berkoff comes close here to providing what Brecht (1964: 89), with a very different meaning, used to refer to disparagingly as "culinary theatre."

Berkoff's projection of himself, through Eddy, as an entrepreneur was both an established and a new subject position in his construction of 'self'. It enabled him to link up entrepreneurial aspects of his ethno-cultural heritage (what might be termed his 'Jewish immigrant' subject position[6]); his working-class East End background; his identification with such driven actor-managers as Edmund Kean, Henry Irving, Jean-Louis Barrault and Laurence Olivier; and his establishment and managing of the LTG as rungs on a 'teleological' ladder leading to his success as a playwright, writer, director, actor-manager, film actor and public figure. The culmination of his entrepreneurial activities perhaps came in 1996 when, "applying a warrior's zeal" (McAfee 1996), he became the self-financing impresario of the long-dark Mermaid Theatre.

A characteristic shared by Berkoff, Eddy and the "Pen King" (see chapter 1) is that they are all 'self-made' entrepreneurs, working-class Thatcherite meritocrats. Success for such individuals, as Berkoff himself argues, is always hard won. In his autobiography he has written of his own education in this "school of hard knocks":

By any definition it was a rough school, but a school which gave you the idea that it was down to you and not your dad, the state or any other charity that would bail you out. It was you. You had to give your all to whatever endeavour, since there was no one and nothing to fall back on except your wits and ability to improvise. (*FA*: 15)

Thus Berkoff has projected himself as financially self-sufficient and self-reliant. This, however, glosses over the fact that Berkoff and the LTG received Arts Council of Great Britain funding for a period of ten years from 1972 until 1982 (Coveney 1996; *FA*: 311).

With *Greek*, Berkoff appeals to an emotional connection with the working class. The play is written, he states, "in the language of the people, a demotic tongue" (*FA*: 4), and Eddy is a "working-class poet" (*FA*: 4). This, however, is the extent of Eddy/Berkoff's allegiance to the proletariat, since both of them embody the social Darwinist philosophy of the working-class Tory voter, the C2, the so-called 'Essex Man', who ensured Thatcher's electoral victory, particularly the second time around in June 1983 (Halsey 1989: 87–8). Eddy/Berkoff does not see the amelioration of society, as a socialist would, in the expansion of public services and a more equitable redistribution of wealth. Rather, his view – a *Thatcherite* view – is that society only moves forward on the backs of entreprenerial individuals such as himself who fight for personal survival and success. Characteristically, Berkoff couches his accounts of his own struggle to succeed in the martial language of combat and victory, and he describes his alter ego in *Greek* as "a warrior who holds up the smoking sword as he goes in, attacking all that he finds polluted" (*CP*, I: 97).

Thatcherite orthodoxy decreed that the individual be empowered and liberated by the freedom of the market "not only from the dependency culture of collectivism, but the old hierarchies of deference, status and taste" (Hewison 1995: 212). It follows from this that the neo-Conservative notion of the consumer's 'sovereignty' was predicated upon the "open-ended satisfaction of autonomous desires" (Heelas 1991: 78). Berkoff, it appears, has 'bought' this philosophy of "acquisitive individualism" (85) both in his very public 'private' life and in his approach to theatre as, first and foremost, an economic transaction conducted on the cultural marketplace. In *Greek* these private and public aspects coalesce in the figure of Eddy/Berkoff. In his private life, Berkoff, the self-made man, is the epitome of the empowered Thatcherite consumer. He has satisfied his consumer sovereignty, for example, in choosing to live in a luxury converted penthouse in Docklands, the symbol above all else of Thatcherite enterprise culture, and in driving a Jaguar (Appleyard 1989). In one interview he talks about the emporia in Los Angeles and New York where he shops for clothes (D'Silva 1990). Leaving such conspicuous consumption aside, however, it appears that for Berkoff, as for his *doppel-gänger* Eddy, consumer sovereignty operates on the more fundamental level of being able to get hold of a decent and well-served cup of coffee when he needs it. Eddy's inability to do this in *Greek* provokes the crisis that triggers his take-over of the café – his own Thatcherite revolution, so to speak. The scene is worth considering at length:

> EDDY: One coffee please and croissant and butter.
> WAITRESS: Right. Cream?
> EDDY: Please. Where is the butter so I might spread it lavishly and feel its oily smoothness cover the edges of the croissant?
> WAITRESS: Ain't got none. There's a plague on.
> EDDY: Then why serve me the croissant knowing you had no butter?
> WAITRESS: I'll get you something else.
> EDDY: I'll have a cheesecake, what's it like?
> WAITRESS: Our cheesecakes are all made from the nectar of the gods mixed with the dextrous fingers of a hundred virgins who have been whipped with bush rushes grown by the banks of the Ganges.
> EDDY: OK. I'll have one.
> [*she brings it*]
> ... I've finished the coffee now and won't have any liquid to wash the cake down with.
> WAITRESS: Do you want another coffee?
> EDDY: Not want but must not want but have to / you took so long to bring the cake that I finished the coffee so bring another ...
> WAITRESS: OK.
> [...]
> EDDY: Where's my fucking coffee? I've nearly finished the cheesecake and then my whole purpose in life at this particular moment in time will be lost / I'll be drinking hot coffee with nothing to wash it down with.
> WAITRESS: Here you are, sorry I forgot you!
> EDDY: About fucking time!
> WAITRESS: Oh shut your mouth, you complaining heap of rat's shit.
> (*CP*, I: 114–15)

In contrast to the shoddy service and inferior products offered by British eateries, Berkoff's 'perfect day', as he describes it in one newspaper article, can only be realised in distant lands. It revolves around early coffee at Venice Beach, breakfast on the Cote d'Azur, elevenses in Florida, lunch at Glen Coe, humous and falafel in the Souk at Jaffa, teatime in Madeira, dinner in Sydney topped-off with a late-night cocktails in Rio (Berkoff 1996b). Conspicuous consumption as lifestyle.

His reflections on the quality of service and range of products (or lack of them) offered by cafés and similar establishments in Britain and other countries appear frequently in his non-dramatic writings, and function as rather crude socio-economic barometers that register the pressure systems of a given society. In the (West) Germany he encountered as a young salesman in the late 1950s, for example, the troika of coffee, culture and consumerism united to satisfy his every desire. In his autobiography, he recalls:

> There was a great park in the middle of Wiesbaden and the long street of Friedrichstrasse where I could walk and be amazed at the things in the German shops already ten years after the war. I'd compare prices like any tourist and sit at a table in the great café and be served elegantly and watch the world and watch people and all in all find it most civilized. It's terrible how civilized countries are turned into mortuaries by people with ideologies. I am sure Germany was once one of the most civilized places in the world to live. There was an opera house and theatre in the town next to the *Spielhaus* [casino], which was my favourite café, so you could say that all senses were taken care of. (*FA*: 169)

In other words, Berkoff, a *Jew*, could look beyond Germany's recent past to become a participating consumer in a society whose return to health was proven beyond all doubt by the existence of an excellent café, shops bursting with goods, and an arch-bourgeois edifice of *Kultur*, the opera house. Thus satisfied, and unconstrained by ideology, Berkoff apparently had no questions to ask of a recently Fascist society that had gassed millions of his co-religionists.

Brazil, too, with its street children and economic apartheid, is rescued for Berkoff by its eateries. In his diary/travelogue *A Prisoner in Rio* (1989c), he relates the travail of working on the eponymous film and the solace he found in restaurants and bars:

> Paradoxically I am getting to like the night shooting, the bar around each corner and the iced *caiperena* and a juicy steak sandwich. The bars, as usual, are real sanctuaries, and around the U-shaped bar we sit, unable to resist comparing the deadened British pub and its dead people playing their ubiquitous slot machines with the welcoming Brazilian bar, with its smells of food and fruit juices, smoking meat, or just plain beer. But England has a health service which they don't have here; so Britain is a better place to be sick or to die in, but not too good for healthy people to *live* in. (*PIR*: 90–1)

Abundant consumerism can thus mask a multitude of ills. The culinary delights of Brazil can compensate Berkoff – but not, one imagines, the inhabitants of the *favellas* – for the lack of welfare provision. Britain, by contrast, is (or was before Thatcher) 'burdened' by universal health care.

Compared with Germany and Brazil, Britain (both in 1978–80 and more recently) is a wasteland awash with inferior food products and mediocre service which Berkoff lambasted in a newspaper article entitled, appropriately, 'The Coffee we deserve' (Berkoff 1990b). The nadir, for him, is reached in the dismal service offered by a certain chain of American fast food restaurants. In another article about revisiting Liverpool, Berkoff recalls that "I walked and saw a MacDonalds where a few dulled and depressed people sat at the plastic yellow tables and ate from their plastic boxes. They looked like animals in a zoo that would have been condemned by animal rights activists" (Berkoff 1991). Ironically, seven years after writing that, Berkoff would be responsible for seducing more human animals into culinary captivity with the voice-over work he undertook for TV commercials advertising Big Macs. The paradox (if not hypocrisy) here is that Berkoff actively participated in cultural practices that perpetuated the very dulling and depressing of the British population that he had previously deplored. It should also be pointed out that in so doing he broke an Equity boycott when he pocketed the "burger shilling" (Glaister 1998) for this work. Thus he may be said to have laid his pro-Thatcher cards on the restaurant table by simultaneously working against the collective union action of his fellow-actors and promoting the free enterprise of an American multinational corporation. Berkoff's 'active citizen' is thus totally eclipsed by his 'enterprising self'. In defence of his strike-breaking action, Berkoff informed one interviewer, "I never really cared much about the strike. Ninety per cent of actors don't get the chance to do voice-over, and this was a group of people with mobile phones racing from place to place earning up to half a million a year so I didn't feel morally defiled by breaking the strike but I was made a scapegoat"(Gibb 1999).

The success of Eddy in *Greek*, like Berkoff's in real life, has elevated him above the working-class lifestyle that he knew as a child. Eddy's relatives are now "boring turds" who "vomit up Guinness and mum's unspeakable excuse for cuisine all over the bathroom" (*CP*, I: 101). Mum goes to bingo, and Dad, with his "work-raped face", wears "tasteless shit-heap Burton ready-made trousers" and a "deadly drip-dry shirt" (*CP*, I: 103). By contrast, 'sovereign consumer' Eddy, like the Berkoff who describes his perfect day, has graduated to wine bars where he indulges in "a half bottle of château or Bollinger, some paté and salad served by a chick who looks as if she's been fresh frozen" (*CP*, I: 102). Proud of the degree to which he has transcended the limited lifestyle and expectations of his parents, he urges them to "[m]ove out that council flat where urchins' piss does spray the lift" (*CP*, I: 131–2) and live with him and his wife in suburbia where

> only the poodles drop their well-turned turds in little piles so neat. And au pair girls go pushing little Jeremys into the green and flowery parks / no ice-cream vans come screaming round this manor / all's quiet / just the swish on the emerald lawns close cropped like the shaven heads of astronauts. (*CP*, I: 132)

Yet Eddy/Berkoff's 'success', measured on his own terms as the increased sovereignty he enjoys as a consumer, demonstrates how far he has succumbed to what Marx termed 'commodity fetishism'. Kershaw (1994: 167), explicating this concept, argues that:

> The circulation of commodities is a phantasmagoria in which exchange-value banishes use-value and so occludes perception of the exploitative operations of capital in controlling labour for the extraction of surplus value. Thus consumption disempowers, the consumer has only a fantasy authority.

The seeming self-liberation through consumerism so valued by Thatcher, and indulged in by Eddy/Berkoff, therefore, is an illusion. It is, moreover, a 'freedom' that is bought, literally, at the expense of the less privileged in society:

> Freedom and independence derive not from civil rights but from choices exercised in the market. The sovereignty that matters is not that of the king or queen, the lord or the white man, but the sovereignty of the consumer within the market-place. It may be some time before there is a full popular understanding of the converse of this proposition, namely, the 'slavery' and indignity of poverty, the imposed loss of identity, the almost 'no person' status of those not able to make meaningful market choices or even present themselves as potential buyers. (Corner and Harvey 1991: 11)

In this sense, Berkoff may be seen to be a very political playwright indeed. His call for change is implicitly a call for greater economic enslavement so that society's self-proclaimed achievers might further increase their sovereignty as consumers. *Greek*, seen in this light, is almost a manifesto of Thatcherism; and Berkoff's career, an ideal of the neo-Conservative self-made man.

Berkoff and the darker side of Thatcherism

In contrast to *Greek*, in which Berkoff betrays pro-Thatcher leanings, he appears to adopt a more critical tone in *Decadence* and *Sink the Belgrano!*, although I wish to stress that his apparently 'on–off' attitude towards the Iron Lady and her policies cannot be so neatly compartmentalised according to the plays. In this section I argue rather that Berkoff's paradoxical stance towards Thatcher is built upon a contradiction that he has apparently been unable or unwilling to recognise, namely that the neo-Conservative enterprise culture that he supported in *Greek* must inevitably lead, through the privileging of a minority elite of meritocrats at the expense of welfare provision, public services and a functioning industrial base, to the kind of economically divided society that he depicts and attacks in *Decadence*, and to the jingoistic patriotism of the Falklands War that he satirises in *Sink the Belgrano!* In other words, yuppyism must lead to yobbism. In what follows I examine two key manifestations of the failure of Thatcher's brand of capitalism, namely an increasingly riven society and the aggressive nationalism that she manufactured to distract attention from it, and Berkoff's response to them in his plays *Decadence* and *Sink the Belgrano!*, and other works.

With the benefit of hindsight, it is possible to see that the catastrophic effects of Thatcher's policies upon the socio-economic fabric of British society were already beginning to emerge less than a year into her first term as the Prime Minister. Andrew Gamble (1994: 187) observes that in 1980 and 1981:

> the economy plunged into a severe recession. Output and investment slumped and unemployment soared. Sterling moved up sharply as did interest rates, and inflation accelerated. When riots erupted in several cities during 1981 some feared that Britain was locked into a spiral of decline which was leading to a breakdown of public order.

As a result particularly of the systematic dismantling of the welfare state, the population became more divided economically, and the communal values of civility and fraternity suffered commensurately. Halsey (1989: 176) makes the telling point that:

> If care and compassion for the weak is the mark of a good society, it is the least likely feature of an order of economic liberalism. Such an order forms classes, and liberty goes to those with power and advantage with respect to the market and the state apparatus. Such an order has the further insidiously self-fulfilling property of justifying inequality by blaming the poor for their poverty and

encouraging the strong to save themselves individually at the expense of the weak.

With British society thus apparently set to implode, Thatcher and her government became deeply unpopular, and opinion polls suggested she had little chance of gaining a second general election victory. The Conservative Party was internally split, and both Labour and the Social Democrats appeared to be regaining the support they had lost in the previous election. It is against this backdrop of social and political turbulence that Berkoff wrote his satirical play *Decadence*.

We have seen that in *Greek* Berkoff championed the aspirations and individual-centred lifestyle of the emerging Thatcherite meritocracy: Eddy, in short, is a classic yuppie. In *Decadence*, Berkoff completes his panoramic sweep of British society by dealing with the social classes above and below this expanding middle class. The two couples in the play, Steve and Helen, and Les and Sybil, are caricatures of the upper class and working class respectively. The antagonism between these two couples, and the classes they represent, is, according to Berkoff, a metaphor for Britain in the 1980s: "The two couples are a strange split personality in that the four characters are played by just two people, as if the very nation was one being split into two opposing halves and at war with itself like a schizoid personality" (*FA*: 348–9).[7] Yet the primary focus throughout remains on the upper-class pair. In his preface to the playtext Berkoff writes: "*Decadence* is a study of the ruling or upper classes, so called by virtue of strangulated vowel tones rather than any real achievement"(*CP*, II: 3).

The play consists of fourteen scenes that satirise the excessive and decadent (hence the title) lifestyle of these toffs. In Scene 3, for example, Steve recounts his experience of being abandoned by his parents at a public school, from which he is eventually expelled for indulging in buggery. Scene 7 is a celebration of foxhunting in which Helen 'rides' and whips Steve. Anti-blood sports protesters are described as "those left-wing bastards jealous as hell / to see their betters enjoying themselves" (*CP*, II: 23). The high-point of excess is reached in Scene 11, when Steve, in a long monologue, acts out a night of gourmandising in Giovanni's restaurant, at the end of which, having gorged himself on luxurious food and drink, he vomits, urinates and defecates simultaneously. In typical Berkovian style, the vignettes are painted verbally in extended monologues of obscene doggerel and physically in extravagant mime. Berkoff's method of satirising the upper classes here is to 'out-excess' their stereotyped excesses in order to show up their unproductive (unmeritocratic) and parasitic nature.

The working-class couple, Les and Sybil, function as the voice of vengeance and outrage, and demonstrate no redeeming or positive qualities in themselves at all. There is, to begin with, their manifest hypocrisy. Sybil plots to have Les, her husband, murdered because of his extramarital relationship with Helen, while she herself is committing adultery with Steve. Secondly, their negative attitude towards the upper-class couple is driven by very ugly emotions. In his autobiography, Berkoff writes:

> Hate, jealousy and vengeance became the rallying cry from the working-class couple as they planned and plotted macabre deaths for their elusive and luxuriating enemy who were seldom aware of them throughout the entire play whereas Les and Sybil, the proles, couldn't be more aware of them. Those of us who are forced to do without, who beg, plead, and whistle to be allowed to dip our spoon into the public soup bowl, can think of nothing less but vengeance. (FA: 348)

The phrase "those of us" aligns Berkoff with his spiteful creations. Berkoff's desire for 'social change' is founded upon an assumption that it is natural for the have-nots to seek vengeance, a selfish and divisive response, rather than to advance alternative policies, a responsibly social and inclusive approach. A significant point about this play, given that it was premiered on 14 July 1981, a little more than a week after there had been major riots in London, Liverpool and Manchester, is that the butt of the play's satire was not Thatcher or Thatcherism but an increasingly irrelevant aristocracy and an undeserving and recalcitrant working class. Indeed, in attacking these two targets, Berkoff was once again showing his neo-Conservative colours, since for Thatcher the upper classes (the Great and the Good) evoked images of "favouritism, injustice and propping up the status quo" (Thatcher 1993: 638), whilst the increasingly impoverished working classes got what they deserved through their refusal to pull themselves up by their own bootstraps, get on their bikes and shift for themselves.

Berkoff's reading of British society in the early-1980s, as it is expressed in *Decadence*, insists upon the traditional hierarchical social structure that had obtained until around 1945. As Tony Dunn (1996: 28) suggests, "the theme [of the play], the interdependence of sex and violence between aristocrats and workers, goes back at least to *fin-de-siècle* narratives by Stevenson and Wilde." Berkoff's treatment of British society in this play is based upon satirical stereotypes of social class similar to those that were used in the agit prop of the 1920s and 1930s. Modern

Britain, however, is a pluralistic society in which this traditional social hierarchy has been shaken up by affluence, access to higher education, consensus and the increase in social mobility, particularly since the advent of 'classless' Thatcherism. Hewison (1995: 293) observes that "[u]nder Thatcher the old social divisions of class had been replaced by an emergent meritocracy – even if that meant one form of stratification was replaced by another, and economic divisions between top and bottom became even wider." These economic divisions can no longer be mapped, as Berkoff attempted to do in *Decadence*, onto a simple and antagonistic dichotomy between the ruling classes and the proletariat. As Halsey (1989: 176) notes:

> The rich have become richer and the poor poorer in Britain since 1979. [Consequently] the odds of success or failure are lengthening along lines of social division – between the inner city and the prosperous suburb, between the North and the South, the white majority and the ethnic minorities, the privately and the publicly schooled. In short, not a simple division into two nations but a complex polarization of increasingly embittered inequalities.

In such a pluralistic society, therefore, in which ambitious individuals (like Berkoff) are crossing the borders of class, the 'enemy' to be attacked is not so easy to identify. Berkoff's caricatures of the upper class, reminiscent of the swine-faced capitalists in the drawings of Georg Grosz in the 1930s, are thus crude and obsolete instruments with which to attempt a meaningful examination of the New Britain under Thatcher.

By the early 1990s, as the full implications of a decade of Thatcherism were clear for all who were willing to see, even Berkoff, paradoxically, appeared to be joining the growing anti-Maggie chorus. In various nondramatic writings, he laid the blame for the deeper socio-economic divisions within British society at her feet. He deplored, for example, the modern wasteland of British cities in which, characteristically for him, the lack of coffee shops signalled a broken and benighted culture:

> Through increasing wealth and Thatcherite philosophy inner cities are now giant shopping centres, unenlivened by any relief from the relentless obsession to shop. No cafés filter through the ghastly endless arcades and giant windows, no cinemas break up the gloom. No alternative that might humanise the concrete wilderness. In other words there is nothing that might bespeak a creative act, like a bar or a café for conversation and to while away the time. Here in Orwellia you shop, and get back to the TV. (Berkoff 1991)

As a response to this consumerist dystopia, he expressed the hope elsewhere that in Britain "one day the herd will lift their heads from *EastEnders* and *Sunday Night at the London Palladium* and see what a slum the country has become and hopefully they'll wake up and kick the bitch [Thatcher] into kingdom come, and all the rot that goes with her" (*PIR*; 37). The irony inherent in a statement such as this is that it wholly contradicted his earlier embrace of Thatcher's enterprise culture. In other words, Berkoff wanted it both ways: on the one hand, he subscribed to the notion of empowered individuals contenting themselves with the accumulation of personal wealth in a society stripped of welfare provision and public services; on the other hand, he apparently refused to see that such a society, based as it is upon the jungle-reality of neo-Conservatism, must inevitably produce losers as well as winners.

One possible reason why Berkoff, in my opinion, missed the target with this play was that, for all its apparently outward social commentary, his gaze was still directed inward upon his 'self'. The "schizoid personality" of British society that Berkoff describes may perhaps be found closer to home, since in his autobiography he draws attention to what the play suggests about his own social, economic and cultural liminality: "There are flecks of me in Steve as well as touches of me in the disgruntled Les" (*FA*: 349). Steve and Les are, after all, shortened forms of Berkoff's two given names. As 'Steve', Berkoff clearly enjoys his sovereignty as a consumer. In a 1991 interview, he remarks that "Decadence was the delight and cornucopia of society" (McAfee 1991). His link to "disgruntled Les", however, suggests his ambivalent feelings, noted in the previous chapter, about the working class he has left, yet to which he still remained in some ways nostalgically tied. All that was left to Berkoff was to embrace the middle ground, the Thatcherite meritocracy.

Argentina's invasion of the Falkland Islands (las Islas Malvinas) on 2 April 1982 provided Thatcher with an opportunity to stem the mounting opposition to her failing domestic economic policies. Moreover, the victory in the short war that followed enabled her to regain a commanding lead in the opinion polls and secure a second term as Prime Minister with a greatly increased parliamentary majority in the July 1982 general election. Beyond all of this, however, the conflict enabled Thatcher to reinvent herself as the saviour and unifier of a Britain that was supposedly once again 'Great'. As Peter Clarke (1996: 375) observes, "Thatcherite triumphalism was born in the Falklands war." The historical details of this "last sad gesture of British Imperialist endeavour" (Bull 1994: 12) are well documented; my concern here is with what Paget

(1992: 156) calls "the sheer dramatic power of the Falklands as Event". In particular, my interest lies in the self-aggrandising performance strategies deployed by Thatcher herself as a war leader, and at Berkoff's own response to them in his satirical play *Sink the Belgrano!* and in other texts.

Both during and after the conflict Thatcher cast herself in the role of Commander-in-Chief not only of the British armed forces but also of a transhistorical and even legendary British military might. Her wide-ranging discursive strategy was to construct (and encourage others to construct) images of herself and contemporary Britain in terms of a mythologised past, to rework, in other words, old themes in the context of new realities and imperatives. As a result, both she and the conflict were projected in an intertextual relationship to other British war leaders and victories. Most notably, she exploited the collective British folk-memory of the 1939–45 conflict in order to resignify the Falklands War as a moral crusade against evil: "The Argentinian invasion of the islands allowed Thatcher to assume the anti-fascist mantle of Winston Churchill, mobilizing in the process much of the 'fighting for freedom' rhetoric of the Second World War" (Paget 1992: 10).[8] Indeed, she even attempted to 'out-Churchill' Sir Winston by projecting herself as the Warrior Queen of the British. Peacock (1999: 19) notes that Thatcher's

> self-aggrandizement exhibited monarchical tendencies. These were most clearly exemplified when, instead of the Queen, she took the salute alongside the lord mayor of London at the victory-parade of the Falklands Task Force. "What a wonderful parade it has been," she told those attending the lunch following the parade, employing what appeared to be the royal plural, "surpassing all *our* expectations." [Original emphasis.]

She was also identified with "Boadicea, an international figure in her martial chariot virtually invulnerable" (Hewison 1995: 217) and as a second Queen Elizabeth I, facing down a Spanish-speaking nation with a handful of ships. More mythically, she was widely seen as the "Iron Britannia" (Barnett 1982).

In the theatre, dramas dealing with the Falklands campaign in the immediate aftermath of the war threatened to be 'upstaged' by Thatcher's popular and populist performance in the drama of the Event itself, "making it particularly difficult to create any space from which to oppose the *Myth of Victory*" (Paget 1992: 160). Dramatists thus tended to focus on single issues or approaches related to the war and avoid the bigger target of the Prime Minister and her possible war guilt in ordering the unprovoked attack on the Argentinian battleship *General Belgrano*. The documentary-style *Voices of the Malvinas/Voces de las Malvinas* (Royal Court Upstairs, 1983), which remains unpublished, was "a searing indictment of the British expedition and its devastating effects on both the British soldiers and their families, as well as on those of the Argentineans [*sic*]" (Collier 1992: 144). Tony Marchant's *Welcome Home* (toured by Paines Plough, 1983) approached warfare as a "function of masculinity" (Paget 1992: 178), and Nick Perry's *Arrivederci Millwall* (Albany Empire, 1985) made an explicit parallel between football hooliganism and the Falklands War.

By contrast, Berkoff's *Sink the Belgrano!*, the title of which is an ironic echo of the jingoistic 1960 film *Sink the Bismarck!* (even down to the strident exclamation mark), is a direct attack amidships on the Prime Minister herself, on Thatcher-as-individual. His approach was to employ two powerful strategies to confront Thatcher and the whole myth of a resurrected Imperial Britain with which she cloaked herself. Firstly, he concentrated his attack upon the incident which initiated open hostilities, namely the unprovoked sinking by a Royal Navy submarine on 2 May 1982 of the *General Belgrano*, an act of aggression that resulted in the killing of 368 conscripted Argentinian sailors, and the opening of hostilities between the two countries. Berkoff based his play on Gavshon and Rice's book about the incident, *The Sinking of the Belgrano* (1984). Like Tam Dalyell MP in Parliament, his apparent purpose in casting doubt on the ethics of the torpedoing of the ageing battleship was to question the legality of the whole Falklands campaign and thus accuse Thatcher, as Commander-in-Chief, of committing a blatant war crime. Yet the play, as Berkoff himself has acknowledged, added nothing to what was already publicly known about the incident. Indeed, the critic Martin Hoyle (1986) commented that "Steven Berkoff the writer thuds into monotony and predictability with a desperately unfunny plod through an over-tilled field to which he can add nothing new." In this sense, then, Berkoff was playing safe.

The second strategy employed by Berkoff was to attack Thatcher and the gung-ho nationalism she personified by making *Belgrano!* into a loose parody of *King Henry V*. Shakespeare's play has lent itself easily to aggressively nationalistic interpretations. As Gurr observes, "[u]ntil very recently, all stage readings presented the play as an emotional voyage into patriotism, with Henry as the heroic helmsman that the Chorus makes him."[9] A classic example is Laurence Olivier's 1944 film adaptation, which used the drama of Henry's military expedition to France as a morale-boosting metaphor for the Allied invasion of German-occupied France that was in the final stages of preparation at that time. Gurr points out: "Inevitably, given that it was filmed in the months up to the D-Day landings, it was one of the last versions to present an unambiguously heroic Henry."[10]

In 1982 a similar transhistorical connection could readily be made between King Harry leading his small band of brothers-in-arms across the English Channel and 'Queen Maggie' dispatching her equally outnumbered soldiers to the South Atlantic. Adrian Noble interrogated this intertextual jingoism in his "post-Falklands" production of the play with the RSC in 1984. It was an interpretation that, according to one commentator, "endorsed the British liberal backlash against war in general and colonial campaigns in particular" (Collier 1992: 144). The same writer went on to observe that:

> its eerily contemporary look revolved around the soggy weariness and ultimate futility of colonial war. At that time, 1984, its resonances with the human costs and the political opportunism of the Falklands conflict were intensified by the opinion, frequently voiced while this production was being conceived and cast late in 1983, that Margaret Thatcher's landslide victory in her re-election earlier in 1983 had been attributable to the "Falklands Factor". (144)

Thus just as Shakespeare's play may become a powerful discursive weapon in the hands of aggressive patriots and nationalists, so it may be used with subversive irony as a reverse discourse to question the ethics of imperialistic war-mongering. On one level, *Belgrano!* appears to be a subversive reinterpretation of *Henry V*. Berkoff's satire rests primarily upon selected raids upon Shakespeare's text. A clear example of this is when the Chorus in *Belgrano!* declaims: "Oh for a brace of Exocet missiles / That would ascend the brightest heaven of invention / The sky would be their stage / Super Etendard jets to fly" (*CP*, I: 166). This is a parody of the opening lines of *Henry V*: "O for a muse of fire, that would ascend / The brightest heaven of invention, / A kingdom for a stage, princes to act, / And monarchs to behold the swelling scene" (Prologue, 1–4). The satire also rests upon parallels in the plots of the two plays. The sophistry employed by Maggot Scratcher's ministers to justify Britain's historic claim to the Malvinas (*CP*, I: 158), for example, parodies Canterbury's dubious invocation of Salic law in i, 2 of *Henry V* to sanction Henry's expedition to France. Also, the voices of the submariners in *Belgrano!*, which are heard throughout the play either supporting or criticising the morality of the

Falklands campaign, recall the range of opinions expressed by Henry's soldiers in the English camp on the eve of Agincourt.

A parody of *Henry V* was certainly an efficient discursive weapon with which to attack Thatcher as military C-in-C since it struck at the head of the enemy, so to speak. As Tennenhouse (1985: 120) argues, Shakespeare's drama hinges on the very person of the king himself:

> In certain respects, *Henry V* can be called a piece of political hagiography. Henry discovers domestic conspirators as if by omniscience and punishes them, he secures his borders against Scottish invaders, unifies the dispirited and heterogenous body under his authority, and wins the battle of Agincourt, thus taking control of territory which had been claimed by French inheritance law and contested by English laws of succession.

Similarly, as Paget (1992: 165) notes, Thatcher's implied projection of herself as a second King Harry represented the "apotheosis of Thatcher-as-individual"; it was a strategy that "legitimate[d] her political handling of events." In his play Berkoff set out comprehensively to strip the Thatcher-hagiography of its myth by caricaturing her mercilessly as the ignorant, boorish and racist yob called Maggot Scratcher, "the master bitch" (*CP*, II: 177). She is shown to be ignorant of colonial geography: "By the way Pimp ... where is the Falklands?" (151);[11] fearful of domestic opposition: "the barometer of fate / Has placed us in the opinion polls / Behind the scummy Socialist crud" (161–2); obsessed by personal power: "I don't intend to move [from No. 10], / I just redecorated the place" (169); contemptuous of the British working class: "The Brits are such a lazy bunch of sods / No wonder there's three million unemployed" (161); militaristic: "Call out the Fleet, get planes / and tanks, I love to have a crisis on my hands" (150); racist: "those greasy Argy wogs" (150); autocratic: "Stop whining, you sickening spineless wimp" (175); duplicitous and Machiavellian: "If we let UNO back in, / Sit down for weeks with Garlic Chops / debate our terms with the gangster mob / We'll look like we've been shat upon" (168–9); and unrepentant: "I would do it again" (185).

In his autobiography, Berkoff describes *Belgrano!* as "an anti-war play, not merely a Thatcher-knocker" (*FA*: 373). Pacifist sentiment in the play is voiced on occasions by Sailor I, who at one point declares to his fellows:

> Here, hang about and just a mo'
> Before we get all bleedin' hot
> Now sod all this, don't swallow shit

Don't gulp down all you hear you fool
You ape, you asshole that is used
By others who make up the rules
'You're just a soldier now, go kill'
'Go Fido, fetch'. Don't think mate, no,
Don't use no skill ...
Just obey orders that's your job
Become a murderer's right hand ...
Don't dare to question what we do
For what we are protecting and for who!

(*CP*, I: 155)

Other characters, too, express a general humanity in their concern with the lives and deaths of their Argentinian counterparts (*CP*, I: 185). On the basis of this play alone, however, it is doubtful if one could describe Berkoff as a writer committed to pacifism, since, to put it bluntly, he has consistently lacked throughout his career what might be called dovish credentials. While acting at the Royal Court in the early-1960s, for example, he recalls the distance and sense of alienation he felt from the anti-nuclear activities of the other theatre workers there who were, according to him, "merely making the correct political gesture" (*FA*: 187). At the time of the Six-Day War he had been prepared to fight for Israel (Church 1994). Furthermore, as we have seen, the language used by Berkoff to describe his own journey along the 'difficult' path to success, and his remedies for curing a diseased British society, is saturated with martial imagery. Finally, his claim to be taking up an anti-war position with *Belgrano!* is weakened considerably by the apolitical stances he has previously adopted and by the fact that this play and his performed poem 'Requiem for Ground Zero' (2002) are the only works in which he deals overtly with contemporary political events.[12] His way of dealing with these issues, however, was superficial. His primary concern in creating *Belgrano!*, I suggest, was once again with projecting *himself* in a certain light. If this was so, what did he hope to say about himself with this apparently anti-Thatcher discourse?

There are, I believe, three plausible reasons for his seemingly aggressive 'anti-Scratcher' stance in this particular play. Firstly, her war-mongering in the South Atlantic, unlike her domestic economic policies, did not address the individual, as an economic entity, but rather a strong British state, which, by definition, places constraints on individual free-dom. In other words, Berkoff cryptically supported Thatcher's policies only to the extent that they served his own individual interests as entrepreneur and consumer. Where the Thatcherite state eroded the rights and freedom of the individual (by sending young and often working-class men to war in the Falklands, for example) he expresses dissent.

Secondly, it seems likely that Berkoff, who has consistently projected himself as an outsider in British society, was literally alienated by the image of an Imperial and Anglocentric Britain that Thatcher constructed before, during and after the conflict. The war, as Tana Wollen (1991: 179) observes, was used by Thatcher to (re)define 'Britishness':

> [The 1980s] has been a decade in which definitions of what it is to be British have been viciously contested. The Falklands/Malvinas war in 1982 and the miners' strike in 1984 were the most overtly political arenas where the whips of patriotism were cracked.

Indeed, Thatcher herself stated: "The lesson of the Falklands is that Britain has not changed and that this nation still has those sterling qualities which shine through our history" (Barnett 1982: 149). Britain, however, had changed, and there was a deep contradiction between the 'old' identity centred on national sovereignty and a strong state embracing white, Anglo-Saxon, imperial values and the 'new' identity that had emerged from a nominally classless, property-owning, multicultural society. Berkoff, a working-class, third-generation immigrant Jew, had flourished during the years of Thatcher's premiership because the government's economic liberalism served his goal of personal success. Indeed, he had lived out the neo-Conservative ideal of the self-made proletarian. The Falklands conflict, however, enabled Thatcher to resurrect some of the worst values of the Old Britain – racist, violent, Anglocentric values – all of which, from a Jewish perspective, had contributed to the anti-Semitism of the 1930s and before.

Thirdly, in writings that have appeared since *Belgrano!*, Berkoff has attacked Thatcher for the civil disorder and yobbism that increased during her years in 10 Downing Street. In the preface to *Brighton Beach Scumbags* (Sallis Benney Theatre, Brighton, 1991), Berkoff's play about anti-gay violence, for example, he describes his thuggish characters: "They are British archetypes representing a programmed beast that at heart is still innocent in its beliefs but has been corroded by the deadening effects of a rotten sub-culture, cheap tabloids, easy racism and slobbering consumerism" (*CP*, II: 148). In his one-man-and-a-pitbull play *Dog* (Warehouse Theatre, Croyden, 1993) (see Figure 14), he sinks his teeth into what he refers to as "the British low-class yob culture [that was] more prevalent in the Thatcher years as class-division widened and the social fabric decayed" (*CP*, II: 219). Finally, in an article entitled 'From balcony to bedlam', he declares that "There are millions of yobs in England, breeding like flies across the length and breadth of the country. They are in no way led to believe in anything. They have no example of anything but a merciless Thatcherism, supermarkets and yobbo television" (Berkoff 1992c). For Berkoff, Thatcher did not merely preside over this general increase in yobbish behaviour, she encouraged it with her own xenophobic and Anglocentric posturings, particularly during the Falklands crisis, and in her support for liberalised commerce and consumerism.

Berkoff is not alone in this view. The social historian Arthur Marwick, for example, discussing British society in the 1980s, argues:

> Football hooligans at home saw themselves as fighting for their own particular community; football hooligans abroad, ironically, saw them-selves as demonstrating British might. All this was, however distortedly, in keeping with the values of the aggressive market place and the Falklands War. (Marwick 1990: 351)

14 Berkoff as the pitbull-loving yob in *Dog*

Similarly, Paget, in his discussion of plays about the Falklands conflict, observes that "the equation of football hooliganism and the Falklands war proposes the solution that both are peculiarly English types of behaviour – but only one is politically sanctioned (and therefore respectable)" (Paget 1992: 177). As a 'pretender' to the throne, as the *de facto* Queen during and after the conflict, Thatcher was in a position to give her 'royal' seal of approval to what could be called the 'state-sanctioned yobbism' of the military action against the Argentinians. It is perhaps not an over-statement to suggest that Thatcher represented the culture of insular yobbishness that had threatened Jews in the past and from which Berkoff had tried to escape by abandoning the East End for the acting profession. These rather than the dubious ethics of waging war on Argentina were the reasons why in *Belgrano!* Berkoff attacked Thatcher so virulently.

Conclusion

There is a paradox at the heart of Berkoff's claim to despise Thatcher/ Scratcher and her policies, since in many ways he has been the very embodiment of Thatcherism, the self-made Essex Man of the theatre. In *Greek* and in various interviews, as we have seen, he echoed and epitomised those aspects of Thatcherism that were directly concerned with empowering the individual as entrepreneur and consumer. Yet it was precisely those policies, which stripped the less privileged in society of welfare provision whilst encouraging the yuppie class to enrich itself, that brought about the divided society that Berkoff depicted satirically in *Decadence*, although in that play he does not seem to make such a connection. Apparently, Berkoff has been unable or unwilling to recognise that yuppies and yobs represent, to use a monetary metaphor, the two sides of the same Thatcherite coin.

Ironically, Berkoff has been perceived by some commentators as a committed political (i.e. socialist) playwright. Monique Prunet, for example, bases her naïve reading of *Belgrano!* upon the assumption that Berkoff was convinced of the "wickedness of Thatcherism" (Prunet 1996: 91), and that he was, along with David Hare, one of the "politically committed playwrights who had emerged from [quoting John Bull] 'the bruised dreams of the sixties counter-culture'" (91). Yet Prunet has evidently considered *Belgrano!* in isolation and without reference to his other works and public statements. In one of these statements in 1990 Berkoff attacked overtly anti-Thatcher playwrights, notably Howard Brenton, for rejoicing in the demise of Thatcher when, as he argued, they needed her as an ideological adversary. Berkoff asks with characteristic acerbity: "What targets will you have to pit your angst against now since it was Thatcher who gave you spice and drama, gave you a dragon for every little St George to dip his little pen into and polish his little anti-Thatcher medal worn alongside the 'I am a good liberal medal'?" (Berkoff 1990c). As for Berkoff, he, like Thatcher, needed the 'British disease' against which to offset his striving individualism. Unlike Brenton, he did not need Thatcher to "pit his angst against" because, as we saw, particularly in the case of *Greek*, he implicitly agreed with her economic policies. His claim above that "those who most condemn Thatcherism are those who most reflect her aims" could with a good deal of justification be applied to himself. Far from being a critic of Thatcher or her policies, Berkoff, I suggest, has actually embodied the spirit of Thatcherism in his working methods as director, the individualistic ideology in his plays, his overt consumerism, and his stated impatience with unionism, collective welfare and subsidy.

Notes

1 In a letter (12 November 1999) to this writer, Berkoff stated that the author of this "torpid lie" was Michael Billington in the *Guardian*. He was unable or unwilling to supply precise details of publication, however.
2 In passing it is worth noting that D. Keith Peacock, in his book *Thatcher's Theatre: British Theatre and Drama in the Eighties* (Westport, Connecticut, London: Greenwood Press, 1999), makes only a very brief mention (eight lines) of Berkoff and his work. He writes: "In 1986 Steven Berkoff, whose distinctive physical productions began in the 1970s, also adopted the current fashion for literary adaptations with his theatrical version of Kafka's *Metamorphosis*" (Peacock 1999: 209). This is incorrect, since Berkoff had already staged literary adaptations in 1968 and 1969 (*In the Penal Colony* and *Metamorphosis* respectively). Peacock appears to have confused the 1986 revival of *Metamorphosis* at the Mermaid Theatre with the original Round House production in 1969. Furthermore, his opting to write about this particular play, which has no relevance to the Thatcher years, is certainly baffling.
3 From the *43rd Annual Report and Accounts* (London: Arts Council of Great Britain), 2–3.
4 In this, Berkoff may initially have been influenced by CAST's *Harold Muggins Is a Martyr* (1968), which deals with the proprietor of a café that is used as a symbol for Britain.
5 Quoted in Gamble (1994: 187).
6 At the beginning of the twentieth century, the social investigator Beatrice Potter (1904: 191–2) was moved by her discovery that "the immigrant Jew ... seems to justify by his existence those strange assumptions which figured for

man in the political economy of Ricardo – an Always Enlightened Selfishness, seeking employment or profit with an absolute mobility of body and mind, without pride, ... without interests outside the struggle for the existence and welfare of the individual and the family." Berkoff draws upon this tradition of the Jewish immigrant's proud work ethic and self-sufficiency: "I've worked since I was 14. My ethos is to graft. My father taught me the value of work" (McAfee 1996).

7 In the original production Berkoff and the actress Linda Marlowe doubled up to play all four characters.

8 The mantle was besmirched in 1998 by Baroness Thatcher's vociferous support of the fascist former dictator General Pinochet in his legal battle to avoid extradition to Spain to face charges of human rights abuses in Chile. As grounds for her support, she has cited the intelligence assistance that Chile provided Britain with during its conflict with Argentina.

9 From Andrew Gurr's introduction to The New Cambridge Shakespeare edition of *King Henry V* (Cambridge: Cambridge University Press, 1992), 38.

10 *Ibid.*: 52.

11 Francis Pym and John Nott, the Foreign Secretary and the Defence Minister respectively at the time of the crisis, are caricatured as the obsequious Pimp and Nit.

12 As with *Sink the Belgrano!*, 'Requiem for Ground Zero' (Edinburgh Festival, 2002), Berkoff's poetic response to the deadly terrorist attack on the World Trade Center in New York on 11 September 2001, lacks any new or enlightening interpretation of the tragedy. As critic Brian Logan noted, the poem would be "gripping viewing if you'd been holidaying on the moon since September 10 2001", for it "rarely tells us anything we haven't heard many times before." The epic narrative, Logan adds, leads Berkoff "to simplify the incident, to present it as an emotional, not a political, drama" (Logan 2002).

7

BERKOFF'S 'INNER SELF'

If in one way he seemed much more human, more normally fallible, than before, that was tainted by what seemed like a lack of virginity in the telling. Calculating frankness is very different from the spontaneous variety; there was some fatal extra dimension in his objectivity, which was much more that of a novelist before a character than even the oldest, most changed man before his own real past self. (John Fowles, *The Magus*)

The overarching theme of Berkoff's *œuvre* – its driving force, I suggest – has been his need to reveal and explain himself. Berkoff has repeatedly drawn attention to what he characterises as the autobiographical nature of his work in general: "The evolution of my life goes through my plays", he declared in one interview (McAfee 1991). Yet he has highlighted this quality not only in the writing of those plays but also in his performances in them: "All acting is a quest for self", he states in *I Am Hamlet* (44). "What is vital to the spectator", he writes in his 'Three Theatre Manifestos', "is your core, the inner part of you" (8). In the special case of an artist such as Berkoff, who has combined the activities of writer and actor, the writing and enacting of the 'self' are indivisible. In the story entitled 'Big Fish', Berkoff, pondering this inseparability of the written and performed acts, asks through his alter ego protagonist, the young, Cockney actor Harry, whether it is "the actor interpreting the writer, or the writer interpreting the actor, allowing the actor to understand himself?" (*G*: 47).

In his apparently uncompromising desire or need to reveal and explain himself through his *œuvre*, Berkoff has explicitly set out to stake a special claim to truth, objectivity and authenticity. On the South Bank Show in 1989, he declared:

Basically, I operate in the same mandate that you must say what is inexpressible, you must confess your deepest secrets, you must express your deepest and most fundamental passions, you must express things that nobody else will even hear about, that you wouldn't tell your closest friend, the most abominable kind of imagination.

Imaginings you have, the worst things you can imagine, the best things you can imagine. That is the domain of theatre, to open the skull and put out on the stage those writhing cans of worms.

Berkoff has not always taken such a direct approach in his drive to explain himself, however. In his early theatrical works, he tended to relate aspects of his 'self' to external factors. We have seen how he identified himself with a diverse range of individuals that included Franz Kafka, Kafka's victimised protagonists and Jean-Louis Barrault (*Metamorphosis* and *The Trial*); with events such as the persecution of Jews in medieval Lincoln (*Hep, Hep, Hep*) and the Six-Day War (*In the Penal Colony*); and with his working-class background (*East, West* and *Greek*). By contrast, in his later works, Berkoff increasingly directed his apparently self-revelatory project inward. In this shift of focus from the external to the internal, he has drawn near to creating what John Sturrock (1993: 257–61), in *The Language of Autobiography*, terms *autopsychography*, which is to say the chronicling, explicating and, particularly in Berkoff's case, performing of one's own psyche, one's own *inner* self.

An early indication of this tendency in Berkoff's career was his production of Shakespeare's *Hamlet* (1979) in which he claimed to use his own performance in the lead role as a means of metaphorically stripping himself naked on the stage. In *I Am Hamlet*, his commentary on that production, Berkoff writes:

YOU ARE THE SACRIFICE AND YOU DISSECT YOURSELF WITH THE SCALPEL CALLED HAMLET AND PEEL OFF THE FLESH AND NERVES RIGHT IN FRONT OF THE AUDIENCE. (*IAH*: 24)

The metaphor of the scalpel, though not original,[1] is very appropriate in the present context. During the early part of his career, as I have just mentioned, Berkoff attempted to construct, project and explain his 'self' by adopting subject positions *accretively*, namely by covering himself with layer upon layer of identities. With his performance as the Danish prince, by contrast, Berkoff apparently set out to reverse this approach by removing these external 'skins' in order to reveal what he evidently believed to be the essential 'core Berkoff' within.

The total revelation of the 'self' may be a dangerous undertaking. Berkoff's awareness of this is clear in one interview in which he declared:

The more naked I make myself the more audiences identify with me. Of course there's an element of risk and humiliation: many writers would rather be witty or charming. I go for the most embarrassing things that ever happened to me, things so humiliating that you would never tell a single living soul. That's how I write, or have written. (Christopher 1993)

The potential for "risk and humiliation", I suggest, has persuaded Berkoff of the need to conceal in various ways the very 'self' that he has declared it his business to reveal. Indeed, as Berkoff appears to see it, the most effective self-baring takes place, as in Christian confession, when the penitent's face or identity is hidden from view. In his travel diary *Shopping in the Santa Monica Mall* (2000e), there is a passage that is indicative of Berkoff's thoughts regarding this process. He recounts watching the movie called *The Mask* while on a flight to America:

> It's a tale that's brilliantly told about a man who finds his inner being when he is able to hide his face behind a mask and I immediately identify with this man who becomes wild, mischievous, demonic, surreal and a brilliant dancer to boot. The mask is the very thing we used to play with in our early drama classes since it would free us from the constraints that help us to 'adjust' to the norms of society. (*SSMM*: 2)

In this chapter I look at three key works in which Berkoff has explicitly set himself the task of revealing what he considers to be his inner self: the two plays *Harry's Christmas* (Donmar Warehouse, 1985) and *Kvetch* (Odyssey Theatre, Los Angeles, 1986) and his autobiography, *Free Association* (1996). My purpose will be to examine the extent to which Berkoff really strips his 'self' bare and the extent to which he adopts masks to elude that metaphorical nakedness.

The 'self-revelatory' project in these works, I shall argue, is problematised by the shifting qualities of Berkoff's reflexivity and the equally ambiguous qualities of the discourses and texts. With regard to his reflexivity, my concern will be to demonstrate the ways in which Berkoff appears to position himself both 'in' the texts (either as 'himself' in *Free Association* or through his alter egos in the plays) and 'above' them as an omniscient author. The ambiguity of his presence/absence in these texts is multiplied by the freedom that Berkoff permits himself in his shifts between 'fact' and 'fiction'. Whilst I separate my discussion here into two main sections that deal with Berkoff's nominally fictional and non-fictional accounts of his 'self', I do not accept that these two modes of representation exist in any absolute or mutually exclusive sense; rather, I will show how, particularly in Berkoff's case, they blur and merge into one another. Thus I do not approach the 'confessions' in his stories and plays solely as fiction nor do I accept the 'revelations' in his autobiography as absolute fact: both modes of discourse will be accorded equal status as strategies deployed in a very slippery undertaking that becomes ultimately, I suggest, a vain attempt to achieve closure in the revelation and explication of his 'inner self'. In what follows, I will necessarily refute Paul Currant's (1991: 186) assertion that "[w]hatever genre Berkoff chooses to work in, he uses it to bring out the psychological truth of the events. No other truth is more important to him than this."

This chapter is in two main parts. In the first section I focus upon *Harry's Christmas* and *Kvetch* in order to examine how and why Berkoff sets out to construct but ultimately escapes from representations of his 'inner self' through the fictional mode of the discourses. In the second section I turn to Berkoff's supposedly factual account of his inner self in his autobiography. I have used *Free Association* so far in this book as a point of reference in my discussions of Berkoff's self-construction and career; here, I analyse it in its own right as an apparent discourse of self-revelation. Finally, I should emphasise once again that I do not propose to embark here upon a psychoanalytical investigation of Berkoff's 'inner self' but rather to pursue a discursive analysis of the various subject positions adopted by him in the process of his 'autobiographical' project.

Berkoff the fictional 'confessant'

In his plays *Harry's Christmas* and *Kvetch*, as well as in the *Gross Intrusion* stories and his autobiography, *Free Association*, Berkoff has drawn on and exploited the performative quality of confession. John Sturrock (1993: 158) notes that:

> Confession in our [sic] Christian culture is a very strongly performative, a solemn performance rooted in church ritual and made dramatic by the avowal within it of shameful actions, thoughts and feelings which the person confessing would in all other circumstances have kept to himself.

With his (albeit secularised) Jewish background, of course, Berkoff stands outside the Christian tradition of confession. In its place, he has attempted to link himself to the no less performative tradition of confession that is identified with Freudian psychoanalysis. This strategy is particularly in evidence, as we shall see, in the works under consideration in this chapter.

The short one-man play *Harry's Christmas* consists of a seventeen-page soliloquy spoken by the eponymous protagonist. On a bare stage, Harry (played by Berkoff in the premiere) sits on a chair and discloses his failings and weaknesses to an implied confessor, the audience. The drama is set in Harry's bed-sit during the final week leading up to Christmas, and opens with him counting the paltry number of greetings cards that he has received. This self-destructive act sets in motion a systematic and pathological analysis of the total lack of love and intimacy in his life and of what he perceives to be his own unpopularity:

> Four, five, six. That's all. That's the lot ... but there's some from last year ... let's see. (*Looks through last year's.*) I could maybe add a couple ... No you shouldn't do that ... that's silly ... to make it look better ... who cares? But it looks a bit thin. YOU WORRIED WHAT PEOPLE MIGHT THINK? Yeaah! PEOPLE WHO MIGHT DROP IN, MIGHT THINK, POOR HARRY, NOT VERY POPULAR? Something like that yeah. LOOK AT THE CARDS AND PITY YOU? Maybe, yeah maybe. THINK, WHAT HAS HIS LIFE BEEN – TO HAVE SO FEW CARDS? Maybe yeah. WHO AND WHAT DOES HE MEAN TO THE WORLD? Christmas tells you ... that you have sweet FA. (*CP*, II: 129)

The 'festive' season thus becomes a personal hell for this lonely and tormented figure, as the guilt he feels at his social rejection takes him on a downward spiral of depression and despair that leads ultimately to suicide.

Berkoff has explicitly related the character of Harry to himself and the play to his own experiences. In a 1985 interview with Berkoff, Steve Grant writes: "[Berkoff] says he wrote [the play] in three days after a particularly miserable Christmas in 1982. 'I always write about my own experience and I'd split up from my wife. I didn't suffer like Harry, obviously as I'm still here, but it did make me think about things a lot'" (Grant 1985). In the same interview, Berkoff describes his tormented alter ego as he appears in the play:

> Harry is a normal guy in his forties who's run out of friends, through no fault of his own. Christmas comes along like a searchlight and everyone runs and hides and people like Harry are left with this feeling of guilt simply because they are lonely. Christmas is society's rejection of him – Christmas symbolises Christ's atonement of sin and two thousand years later that celebration can make people suffer for that very reason. Suddenly there's a level of intimacy which some people can't partake in because they aren't married with two kids, or because they have no family, feel inferior, shy.

Berkoff invites his audiences and readers to accept that he is parading the unvarnished reality of his own neuroses through the medium of 'Harry'. Such a view is encouraged by the rock musician Pete Townshend, who comments in his foreword to the published script that the play is "so revealing of Berkoff's own deeply felt lonely times, and the way they made him aware of his self-obsession and insecurities."[2] The textual construct 'Harry' is Berkoff's fictional alter ego not only in this play but also in his two collections of short stories: he is the protagonist in most of the *Gross Intrusion* stories (1979), and the central figure in the more explicitly 'autobiographical' *Graft* collection (1998), which deals with Berkoff's experiences as a beginning actor. The lack of love and friendship in Harry's life, the central factor in the play and the stories, parallels what Berkoff has acknowledged as the lack of satisfying intimate relationships in his own life. In his autobiography, as we shall see, he retrospectively elaborates this theme of emotional outsiderdom into one of the major patterns shaping his life and his art.

Berkoff's performance in the original production of *Harry's Christmas* was a strategy that enabled him to enact vicariously, through the 'Harry' construct, aspects of his life and subjectivity that he would normally have repressed: "I showed a solitary man in his room taking a crap, wiping his arse and performing the things one does in ones [*sic*] private world", he writes. "And the audience laughed, since I was miming it, and could then comment even on the way one performs these private moments" (*PIR*: 97). There is a link here to a key component of Jacques Lecoq's pedagogical method, namely the "personal clown", which Berkoff would have encountered during his summer sojourn at the mime school in Paris in 1965. The personal clown, as Thomas Leabhart (1989: 99) describes it, is 'inextricably related to one's essential weakness, which one must "recognize, bring out, hold up, publicly make fun of, and incidentally, make people laugh"'. Frost and Yarrow (1990: 118–19) observe that "[h]ere one confronts and confesses by sharing what one normally represses: brings out one's 'shadow', as it were, and lets it dance in the light." The personal clown, paralleling Grotowski's notion of the "total act" – "the act of laying oneself bare, of tearing off the mask of daily life, of exteriorizing oneself ... is a serious and solemn act of revelation" (Grotowski 1992: 178) – thus implies complete psychological nakedness before the audience. It involves the total presentation of the actor's 'self', assuming (which I do not) that such an entity exists. It is a means of rendering one's pain, for want of a better word, into a performance that may be seen as authentic from the *emotional* rather than from any supposedly factual perspective.

Whilst Harry/Berkoff appears to confess his feelings of worthless-ness, loneliness and despair, the 'self' that is revealed in front of the audience is ultimately and, for Berkoff, cathartically, dispersed into non-existence. The stripping away of every layer leads to Harry's textual death through suicide. In the middle of his confession Harry declares: "DEATH IS THE FINAL SOLUTION OF TAKING YOUR PAIN TO YOURSELF AND HUGGING IT TO DEATH ... DEATH IS YOUR PAIN TAKEN TO THE END" (*CP*, II: 141). Similarly, in the story entitled "Hell", a spin-off from the play that was published in the second and expanded edition of the *Gross Intrusion* tales, the unnamed first-person narrator, like Harry, dwells pathologically on his loneliness. The story, like the play, ends in his suicide, the ultimate negation of one's selfhood. In the story the protagonist despairs:

> You can't use any of yourself and when that happens you have an ache ... in your stomach, and you feel like a non-being. So since you can't speak. Hold. Make love. Dance. Play. You die. You drink. You smoke ... And I have to keep smoking. Keep drinking to fill the hole of emptiness. (*GI*: 1)

Both *Harry's Christmas* and the story "Hell", then, point away from a substantial existence to lack, "non-being", insubstantiality and death. Both apparent confessions are vain attempts at signifying an inner self that drains away in the "hole of emptiness".

Yet the original title of the play, *Death and Transfiguration* (*FA*: 353), hints at redemption and catharsis – not for Harry, who dies in self-destructive misery, but for Berkoff. 'Harry', I suggest, is the textual alter ego that Berkoff constructs and sacrifices in order to demonstrate, as the advertising blurb on the back cover of the *Gross Intrusion* stories proclaims, that "no act or thought is too private or taboo" for him to reveal. 'Harry' is a skin that Berkoff the scalpel-wielding 'confessant' strips away. As in the case of the original production of *Metamorphosis*, in which Berkoff used Gregor's disablement and death to project his own enablement and phoenix-like survival, so, too, I suggest, he exploits Harry's 'confession-to-death' to justify his own special claim to authenticity in his 'self-revelation'. In other words, Berkoff creates the impression that he is engaging in no-holds-barred self-revelation whilst metaphorically dancing free of the guilt, loneliness and worthlessness that dies with 'Harry'. It is a therefore a 'win-win' strategy for Berkoff, as he appears to benefit both from the kudos of 'authenticity' and from the catharsis implicit in the performance of his own redemption.

I turn now to *Kvetch*, a play that Berkoff describes as "a study of the effects of anxiety" (*CP*, II: 46). As in the case of *Harry's Christmas*, he has presented it self-referentially as a product of his own 'inner' turmoil, describing it as "a play hewed out of every pain I ever felt. Every angst that gnawed away inside I put outside" (*PIR*, 178). Set in the Jewish East End of London,[3] the first half of the play centres around a disastrous impromptu dinner party that becomes, in the words of the critic Jack Tinker (1991), "a nightmare of individual embarrassments, with each character locked into his or her private hell". The main character (played by Berkoff in the British premiere) is Frank, an anxiety-ridden Jewish fabric salesman, who brings his colleague Hal home one evening after work to a supper of stinking, burnt food. During the meal Frank agonises over when to tell the only joke he knows and whether or not he will be able to remember the punchline; his wife Donna worries endlessly about the food; and the recently divorced Hal about how to answer Donna's incessant probings about how he gets through the nights alone. The second half of the play becomes more fragmented, with the action moving out of the home to depict the characters' wider lives in a series of vignettes in which they appear to obey their 'real' but repressed instincts: Donna leaves Frank for George, one of her husband's clients, and Frank and Hal, more improbably, become partners in a gay relationship.

The premise of this play as with *Lunch* (King's Head, 1983),[4] one of Berkoff's earlier 'confessional' plays, is that there are different qualitative orders of truthfulness or authenticity in the way people communicate with each other and 'perform' in daily life, and that as socialised animals we tend to repress our 'real' feelings and impulses. Berkoff makes this point explicit in his preface to the published text of the play:

> How often when we speak we have some background dialogue going on, sometimes to guide us and sometimes to protect us. Sometimes, though, the dialogue in the back of the head is truer than the one in the front. If only we could always speak the thoughts in the back; how much truer our communication would be. We are like icebergs slowly moving through life and seldom, if ever, revealing what is underneath. (*CP*, II: 46)

In this drama Berkoff allows his five Jewish characters to express these hidden thoughts by employing the theatrical device of the unheard 'blind' aside that is directed at nobody in particular and heard only by the audience. As a character on stage 'confesses' unspoken or unspeakable thoughts or emotions (printed in italics in the published text), the actions of the others are, as Berkoff describes it, "frozen in the last position they were in and held for the duration, almost like a freezer-frame" (*CP*, II: 45). The American playwright Eugene O'Neill is considered to be the innovator of this technique in his drama *Strange Interlude* (1928). Following the impact that Freud's writings made after the First World War, O'Neill sought to establish a new "Freudian dramaturgy of the Self and the Other" (Orr 1991: 12). The extent to which he succeeded in this aim falls outside the scope of this discussion. What is important here is that O'Neill, whom Berkoff has described significantly as "one of the most powerful and awesome describers of the human condition in its naked state" (*Guardian*, 28 August 1989), evidently provided the latter with a model or method for creating a 'psychoanalytical' or 'confessional' type of drama. Where O'Neill aimed for a tragic dimension, however, Berkoff opted for the deflecting shield of comedy. The following two extracts may serve to demonstrate this.

At the beginning of Scene 2, as Frank and Donna begin to make 'love', Donna's head is filled with fantasies of being ravaged by the refuse collectors:

FRANK: ... [FRANK kisses DONNA perfunctorily and climbs aboard.] There ... there ... ouch ... ow! what are you wearing? ... ouch! ...
DONNA: Ouch ... ow! ... here let me do it ... there ... *I want to be raped ... Sometimes I want the garbagemen to throw me on the bed in the morning after the lump has gone to work and just use me ... the three of them ... and I know they've been eyeing me ... They empty the garbage cans and I'm still in my nightdress ... I know they're horny for me ... They smile and talk after they've gone about the dirty things they'd like to do to me ... tear my nightie off ... put their hands all over ... grab me and tear me to pieces ... examine and explore me ... all hungry and sweaty and dirty ...* (CP, II: 69)

The dubious humour in this scene arises from Donna achieving her subsequent orgasm not through the 'attentions' of her indifferent husband but through giving herself up to a fantasy of being gang-raped. In passing, we can see once again how Berkoff compels his female characters to express their sexuality through a self-negating subservience to male sexual fantasy. Thus Donna's inner thoughts are no freer for having been expressed, since they are framed in what is evidently a *male* sexual fantasy served up as comedy.

Further on in the same scene, Frank also achieves his climax by yielding to previously repressed fantasies – first, in another echo of *Lunch*, of an unknown woman he once saw on a beach, and then of his male co-worker:

FRANK: ... *now my hands are climbing higher, higher and her legs feel stronger and the thighs powerful and suddenly I feel this enormous ...*

> *What's happening here? ... Why are you in my fantasy, Hal? ... Go*
> *away ... I want the soft squishy succulent ... not this hard thick big thing*
> *... go away ... get out of my fantasy.*
> HAL: *But I am your fantasy .. Relax, don't fight it ... No one knows ...*
> *only you ... Even I don't know ...*
> FRANK: *You sure?*
> HAL: *Of course. I'm only a fantasy ... They're supposed to be good for you ...*
> FRANK: *But only in fantasy, you understand ... This is to go no further ...*
> *I couldn't even think of it in reality ... Phahhh, it would make me sick ...*
> *yuk!* (CP, II: 70)

Protected by the implicitly homophobic 'humour' of this scene, Berkoff is
able to play with and perform different modes of sexuality – "but only in
fantasy". There are similar instances in which Berkoff, pleasuring
himself with sexual fantasies, appears to dance on the fringes of sexual
otherness in his *Gross Intrusion* short stories.

In chapter 2 I discussed the homosexual scene in 'Gross Intrusion'
in the context of Berkoff's interpersonal relationship with 'Olivier'. In
another story entitled 'Daddy', the unnamed and apparently heterosexual
protagonist relishes an anonymous gay encounter in a steam bath. As he
is being fondled, he reflects with pleasure on

> the strange warm satisfaction of a man's fist, heavy, large, seeking
> out one's shame ... that's what's so good about it ... so secretive ...
> not open, accepted naturally . . . meet the folks . . . but mysterious ...
> dirty ... unaccepted ... even by oneself in the cold light of day ... there,
> clothes describe the owner's taste, class, personality ... too much
> given away, too much to risk ... only in the steam room protected by
> the blankets of mist rising and the neutral anonymity of nakedness
> can you surrender to the full, the implications and impulses the
> clothed conscious daylight being would reject. (GI: 35)

Anonymity, the principle that underpins Roman Catholic confession,
makes the revelation of things that the conscious mind would normally
refuse to recognise easier and less threatening. It also allows one to deny
that the event or the act impinges upon one's socially accepted
subjectivity. Steam, anonymity, evasive humour and fictionality are all
masks from behind which Berkoff appears to own up to what he hints
teasingly may be repressed aspects of his own sexuality. Just what these
aspects may be need not detain us here. What is germane to the present
discussion is that one senses the artifice with which Berkoff *plays* with
aspects of an 'inner' self which he then *eludes* by relegating them to the
non-real status of a fantasy embedded in a fictional performance. One

sees again the ambiguity of Berkoff's reflexivity, namely that he is both inside and outside the 'self-revelatory' discourse that he constructs and then disperses.

The very title *Kvetch* signals that the possible world on stage is first and foremost a neurotic Jewish environment. The *OED* defines *kvetch* as a Yiddish loan word that means, as a noun, "a person who complains a great deal, a fault-finder", or, as a verb, "to complain, to whine". Berkoff set out to show unequivocably that the characters, particularly the chief kvetch Frank, are to be seen as stereotypically *Jewish*. To this end, once again, Berkoff erred on the side of caricature in his characterisation. A measure of this is the comment by John Gross in his review of *Kvetch* in the *Sunday Telegraph* (13 October 1991) that Berkoff "overdoes his sing-song Jewish accent".

Berkoff's stereotypical use of self-deprecating humour in *Kvetch* locates him in the tradition of Jewish stand-up comedy. In his auto-biography he writes that "Jews are born satirists anyway, or comedians. It's one of the most effective defences against pain that there is" (*FA*: 356). The following scene in which Frank attempts to tell his joke is a typical illustration of this self-belittling strategy:

> FRANK: So there was an English, and Irishman and Jew ... *Ah, they're smiling . . . like I hope we'll enjoy ourselves . . .* And they meet in a bar ...
> DONNA: You know Jews don't go to bars ...
> FRANK: I have never been to a bar!? Eh! You have never seen me in a bar?
> DONNA: Yeah, but you're not a real Jew ...
> FRANK: What?
> DONNA: No, no, I mean, not like those Jews ... er ... real ones like ... *Oh shit, why does he embarrass me? ... He knows what I mean ... he knows I mean Jews like his father who wear a hat in the house and dandruff over their coats and smell of onions, yellow flaccid ones with round backs and beards ...* You know, like Orthodox ... (*CP*, II: 63–4)

Kvetch, like Woody Allen's films *Annie Hall* (1977) and *Manhattan* (1979), unfolds in a Jewish *milieu* in which self-psychoanalysis has become obsessive. The overt Jewishness of this play has enabled Berkoff to draw upon two interconnected discourses in his apparent self-revelation, namely the introspective fiction of Kafka once again, and, more impor-tantly in the present context, the tradition of psychoanalysis that is linked inextricably with Freud.

Berkoff writes in his autobiography that he identified strongly with Kafka's "dream-like stories and his acute perception of detail, detail that is not ordinary and programmed, the detail of the life beneath the frustrations. The life within. Closer to dreams and closer to Freud" (*FA*: 103). Such ideas feed into his own conception of theatre in general:

> I have always imagined theatre to be the last resort of an over-burdened imagination, a hothouse of profanity, an opening of Pandora's box, but most of all an examination of us in all our warts, wounds and blemishes. Closer to Freud than to the political columns of the *Daily Rant*. (*FA*: 5)

In both of these quotations Berkoff can clearly be seen attempting to position himself and his dramas "closer to Freud". The irony here, though, is that nowhere does he publicly discuss or engage with the latter's works or ideas. Rather, he contents himself merely with invoking Freud's iconicity in order apparently to claim a common 'outsiderdom' through their shared cultural Jewishness (Hitler banned psychoanalysis in 1933 because of its Jewish associations) and, more importantly, a privileged and 'authorised' access to the "life within". Berkoff may be seen to deploy 'Freud' (by which I mean his monologic reading of the historic Sigmund Freud and his theories of psychoanalysis) to underwrite his own 'self-revelation'. As we shall see in the next section, Berkoff uses this strategy most explicitly in the context of his autobiography.

Berkoff the 'self-psychoanalyst'

Berkoff took the performance of his 'inner self' to what is perhaps the logical extreme by giving his autobiography the title *Free Association*, implying that he has placed himself metaphorically as an analysand on Freud's famous couch, the iconic site of unencumbered self-unburdening. The conceit, however, was not original: Ernest Jones, Freud's disciple and official biographer, called his autobiography *Free Associations* (1959). Berkoff's stated purpose with this account of his life was not only to lay bare his unconscious mind and present the unadorned truth about himself but also to give it coherent form and interpretation. In other words, he set out to become not only his own chronicler but also his own analyst. He made these ambitious objectives clear in his preface to the autobiography, which I quote here in its entirety:

> When I started to write these memoirs I had in mind all those I had waded through in the past and my impatience with their order of events. I was keen to get to the personality I knew, to bite into the mature fruit rather than be made to wait. It seems that everyone is

born, has parents, goes to school and it's not too much of a generalization to say that everyone resembles one another but for a few details here and there. It is when the struggle begins and one is released from a life that has been organized that the aspects of personality begin to emerge, and one makes certain choices as to how one deals with the chaos that is the stimulus of life and how to give it form and interpretation. I did not wish to leave out my early years, but rather to try to put them in an order that would show a causal effect within the later years. So I free-associated, as one does in conversation, letting one thought spark off another, so that my life unravelled in this way rather than in a sequential order. A chronological order may be clearer and certainly less of a headache to write but the more spontaneous method produced unexpected links and the development of certain themes. If this is sometimes frustrating I apologize in advance and hope the reader with a dash of patience will be rewarded for it. This is the first volume and this is my life as I remember it. (*FA*: ix)

In this section I propose to examine the status of the apparently factual discourse of *Free Association* and Berkoff's authorial relationship to it by addressing some key points that suggest themselves in this extract. First, I will interrogate the conceit that Berkoff is free-associating in the first place, and that the non-linear chronology of the narrative emerges spontaneously with the 'flow' of his memories. Second, I will examine Berkoff's omission from his account of certain very important aspects of his life and personality and explore the implications of this selectivity for his apparent self-revelation. Third, given that Berkoff's 'censored' autobiography doomed his supposedly self-revelatory project to failure from the outset, I will seek to show that he had another purpose in writing his autobiography, namely to justify himself through an artfully constructed 'teleological' account of his career – despite its apparently fractured and random quality.

Conventional autobiographies are structured around a linear chronology. As Sturrock (1993: 256) observes:

The rule is for autobiographers to serve as their own biographer and to write their lives as a narrative, starting as far back in time as they care to go and advancing chronologically towards the present. They have followed biographers without serious question in presuming that a life lived in time is best projected on to the page orthogonally, the order in which events are told repeating in the main that in which they occurred. The Memory that the autobiographer makes to Speak invariably does so with its eye on the calendar.

Berkoff's decision to 'free-associate' liberated him from what Sturrock refers to as the "the linearity of public time" (256). The leaps in the narrative from memory to apparently associated memory necessarily fracture the chronology of his autobiography. Thus Berkoff gave himself *carte blanche*, as it were, to move freely and flexibly through the textuality that he created of his 'life'.

Free-association is the name in English for the key psychoanalytical tool pioneered by Freud for reaching the repressed memories of his patients. In *A Critical Dictionary of Psychoanalysis* Charles Rycroft (1968: 54) describes it as

> [Abraham Arden] Brill's mistranslation of Freud's *'freier Einfall'*, which has, however, become the accepted term in English. *Einfall* means 'irruption', 'sudden idea', not 'association', and the concept refers to ideas which occur to one spontaneously, without straining. When used as a technical term, free association describes the mode of thinking encouraged in the patient by the analyst's injunction that he [*sic*] should obey the 'basic rule', i.e. that he should make no attempt to concentrate while doing so.

Thus free association, however imprecise or unfelicitous a term in English, has come to describe the act of spontaneously expressing whatever thought or memory comes to the analysand during a therapy session. As with confession, it is a process that requires two parties, the analysand and the analyst, in what may be seen as a *performance*. As Mark Fortier (1997: 61) observes:

> Classical [i. e. Freudian] psychoanalysis deals with verbal symptoms, but it is only actualized in the analytic situation, with the enactment of the analysand in the presence of the analyst, with the emotional investments in transference and countertransference, and the repetition of sessions at regular intervals. Analysis so described is obviously a performative practice as well and has much in common with theatre.

This process is made problematic (if not impossible) if, as in the case of Berkoff's 'autopsychography', the analysand and the analyst are one and the same person. Such 'self-psychoanalysis' may be judged to be a flawed project if one is concerned solely with what Paul de Man, in his article 'Autobiography as De-Facement' (1979), terms the "cognitive" order (the historical 'facts') of autobiographical discourse. A different conclusion may be reached, however, if one investigates what de Man calls the "performative" order (the autobiographical act of recounting the 'facts') of autobiographical discourse. My focus in what follows will be upon this latter order as I examine what Berkoff set out to *achieve* with the 'performance' of his 'self' through the discourse of his autobiography.

It is necessary, to begin with, to look at how Berkoff's supposed use of free association operates as a trope. Two typical examples from the text may suffice to demonstrate this. The section in his text entitled 'Zoot Suit – Childhood, 1950' begins with the statement that "[t]he first production of *Greek* at the little Half Moon Theatre in Alie Street in 1979 took me back to my youth there" (*FA*: 5). This recollection then sets up what appears to be an unproblematic flow of reminiscences about his father's tailor shop, his time spent at primary school, and the rehousing of his family in the council estate in Stamford Hill (*FA*: 5–8). Quite simply, his approach, as he states in his preface, is to let "one thought spark off another" in a 'conversational' style. In another instance, Berkoff uses a memory of his second wife, the dancer Shelley Lee, as the link between two sections dealing with *East* and *Agamemnon*. The memory of his unease at her witnessing a rehearsal of *East* in Edinburgh leads him to recall the occasion on which they first met, when he was "trying to put together a production of *Agamemnon*", which in turn serves to introduce a new section entitled "The Discovery of Agamemnon – RADA 1971" (*FA*: 50–1). Once again, Berkoff presents these events in the form of a natural and unimpeded flow of reminiscences. The crucial question, however, is this: Did Berkoff really free-associate as one would in psychoanalysis or did he employ Freud's therapeutic method simply as a narrative strategy?

It is certainly possible that Berkoff used an approach akin to free association as an initial tool for gathering together his assorted memories in these two instances and, indeed, elsewhere throughout the text. Furthermore, it may be that as Berkoff was sketching out the first draft of his narrative the memories of his early life in the East End and of his wife flowed spontaneously from the thoughts that first triggered them and provided him with a pattern of ideas that could be rendered into the narrative of his text. Such a conclusion would be encouraged by Berkoff's use of a fractured chronology. This, we may tend to agree, is the way the 'butterfly mind' operates in everyday life, flitting incessantly from thought to impression to memory. The language in which Berkoff couched the apparent spontaneous leaps back and forth in time, however, alerts one to the authorial control that he exerted over his material.

After one digression in the flow of his narrative, for example, Berkoff declares: "I return to the crossroads of Stamford Hill where the sensitive youth is struggling to assert his frail ego amidst the boisterous blades and tearaways; where he voyages from pillar to post, seeking at each station some clues to his identity" (*FA*: 29). The language in this extract, which demonstrates above all else the presence of a omniscient author (or, to use a theatrical metaphor, a master puppeteer, who objectifies and toys with his marionette-like hero) appears almost to parody the wordy preambles to chapters in the picaresque novels of the eighteenth century. Berkoff clearly takes up a privileged position *vis-à-vis* his younger 'self' not just in terms of the omniscience which hindsight confers but also, and more importantly, in terms of the way he positions the "sensitive youth" as an earlier incarnation of himself in an evolving 'teleology'. In other words, there is no randomness in this account because it is manipulated in such a way as to explain most effectively the 'Berkoff' he has become or rather wishes his readers to believe he has become. Once again, then, Berkoff may be observed to be both 'in' the text, living in the virtual present of his unfolding memories, and 'above' it, manipulating and interpreting its every twist and turn.

In other cases, Berkoff uses a style of chronology-hopping that is akin to cinematic editing with its fades and dissolves. Reminiscences of the idols of his teenage years, for example, prompt a memory of a particular hero, the crooner Johnnie Ray, whom Berkoff once "worshipped" (*FA*: 151) at the London Palladium. This segues into the next section of the text, 'Fast Forward to 1984', a description of the next occasion on which Berkoff witnessed Ray singing in a bar in Hollywood. Thus the 'Johnnie Ray' of the mid-1950s is match-cut with the 'Johnnie Ray' of the 1980s. Despite the smoke screen of apparent spontaneity, one senses again that the narrative, like the sequence of shots in a film, has been artfully manipulated with an authorial or directorial eye on the whole structure. Freed from a linear chronology, Berkoff may hop to whatever memories best serve and further the plotting of his story. Since Berkoff's 'free associations' and 'spontaneously' non-linear chronology are evidently narrative conceits, one is prompted to ask what has motivated him in his use of these textual strategies. Primarily, as I suggested in the case of *Harry's Christmas*, Berkoff has been concerned with creating a sense of *authenticity* in order to validate what appears to be his self-revelation. In other words, he has sought to create the impression that he is holding nothing back from his readers and audiences – that, with his right hand placed on the works of Freud, he is revealing the Berkoff, the whole Berkoff and nothing but the Berkoff.

A further strategy employed by Berkoff in the shaping of his 'autobiographical' narrative is his obvious omission of certain important aspects of his personal life. As Michael Billig cautions in his chapter entitled 'Rhetoric of Social Psychology' (1990), in deconstructing any accounts, not only autobiographies, we must look not only at what is being said, but also at what is being rejected. What one misses most in *Free Association* is any mention by Berkoff of intimacy, whether in the form of friendships, his two marriages, or his relationships with lovers or his daughter, that lasts much longer than a single sentence. With regard to friendships, he occasionally mentions the name of a friend in the context of a specific activity remembered from his childhood or youth – swimming with "my mate Cornelius from across the road"(*FA*: 9), for example, or playing truant with Maurice Hope (*FA*: 14) – but he never describes anything that could be considered as a deep friendship that endures beyond these isolated moments. Cornelius and Maurice make no further appearances in the narrative. This absence of friendships continues throughout the text. One straightforward explanation for this may be quite simply that he has had no deep friendships in his life. Recalling the heady days of Swinging London, when for many young people interpersonal relationships and social behaviour became much less inhibited, he describes himself as "a quiet soul given to few friends" (*FA*: 275). His lack of friendships comes through clearly in his recollection of the joys of working with the ensemble in the production of *Agamemnon*:

> It was perhaps feeling the warmth of camaraderie that I had missed for all those years in my youth and lonely school days. Now I had my eight male mates around me, plus of course Teresa D'Abreu as Clytemnestra and Judith Alderson as Cassandra. It was tremendously satisfying to sense that I had found friends. (*FA*: 323)

The memory ends here suddenly, however, with no further mention anywhere else in the text of these particular friends or of what part they might have played in the unfolding of his emotional or artistic life.

Memories of romantic relationships also fizzle out. Looking back to his youth in the mid-1950s, Berkoff writes with a coyness not usually associated with him that in "those far-off days I had what I might dare to interpret as a romantic streak" (*FA*: 169). The flow of free associations that one might expect to follow such a tantalising admission, however, is abruptly dammed, and the reader receives no further information. Similarly, Berkoff writes that *Greek* was "inspired by the pain of a bitter relationship I was going through" (*FA*: 4). Yet once again the flow ceases at the very point where he might have been expected to describe a key moment in his emotional and creative life. In another passage, in which he recalls the circumstances in which he wrote the *Gross Intrusion* stories in Brighton, Berkoff achieves what appears to be unintentional bathos when his exultant memory of one former lover leads him, in a reversal of Proust's *madeleine*-induced reverie, to a humble sandwich. The recollection of his "delightful pre-Raphaelite Annie, her long, silken, chestnut hair reflecting glints of sunlight" is outshone by the more dominant memory of the "cheese and salad sarnie in [his] mitt" (*FA*: 191–2), and so another intimate moment is abruptly smothered. More surprisingly, perhaps, Berkoff provides no details whatsoever concerning his two marriages, the two divorces that followed them, or his relationship with his present partner, the German pianist Clara Fischer. As for the relationship with his daughter, his autobiography provides no information whatsoever.[5]

Sex is the most conspicuous absence in *Free Association*. This is most ironic given that Berkoff has sought to position himself "closer to Freud," for whom memories of sexual activity and desire, particularly during infancy, played such a key part in his psychoanalytical theory and practice. It is ironic, too, given that, as Foucault (1990: 61) argues, "[f]rom the Christian penance to the present day sex was a privileged theme of confession". The journalist Nick Smurthwaite (1996) seized on this self-censorship in his interview with Berkoff:

> In his plays and writings, Berkoff isn't exactly sparing with sexual imagery and allusions, but in his own life story sex is the one glaring omission. I'm treated to Berkoff's best rottweiler face when I bring this up. "Where I dip my wick is my business," he barks. "Sex is such a delicate and profound experience, it's very private for me, not meant to be put in print. I'll leave the kiss and tell stuff to Rod Stewart."
> But [Smurthwaite persists] don't a lot of actors and dancers find sexual energy and the performing instinct indivisible?
> He warms to the theme. "If I wrote about my love life it would take a thousand pages at least. It's my source of being and energy, my salvation, my mental stability, my security, it's what drives me, it's my core."

Given the central position that sex, by his own admission, occupies in his creativity, and that it is his "core", it is indeed striking that Berkoff fails to include a single mention of a sexual encounter in an autobiography that purports to reveal his real and essential self. By contrast, one would have to note that his 'confessional' stories and plays are saturated with sex, particularly instances of onanistic and homosexual sex. This apparent lack of intimacy in his life may be seen as an intentional pattern in the way Berkoff has projected himself, namely as an 'outsider', a 'reject', a 'loner'. Love, intimacy and sex, he tells Smurthwaite, are present in his life – are, indeed, key elements in it. He evidently exercises his authorial veto, however, to pass over them in silence. Describing and dwelling upon the *lack* of love in his life has, I suggest, better served the narrative of his 'autopsychographical' project.

At the moment that the analysand forsakes spontaneity in the psychoanalytical process in order to reflect upon her or his own utterances, or escape the flow of memories and thoughts that they release, the associations are no longer free but mediated through consciousness. This is where Freud speaks of the patient placing a resistance in the path of the flow of associations, and observes that "[w]e are certainly right in thinking that the longer and more roundabout the chain of associations the stronger the resistance" (Freud 1973: 42). As Rycroft notes, "resistance is minimalized by relaxation and maximized by concentration" (Rycroft 1968: 54). The concentration that Berkoff brought to bear in shaping his supposedly free associations is evident in his acknowledgement in the preface quoted above, that the autobiography was a "headache to write" and that he had considered "how to give it form and interpretation". It is also evident in the authorial manipulating of his apparently spontaneous memories discussed above. In instances such as these Berkoff loses what Abbott (1988: 602) calls the "innocence" of the narrator/confessor and becomes an omniscient and controlling author. In situations like this we do well to heed Sturrock's (1993: 159) caveat that "[w]e read autobiography intelligently when we keep in mind that our one access to the 'cognitive' order of the writer's is by way of the performative, that whatever 'facts' the text contains are there by authorial fiat". Conversely, the absence or suppression of 'facts' is also a function of authorial control. In contrast to what he proclaims to be the unbounded baring of his inner self in his plays and stories, it is clear that Berkoff has found that some acts and thoughts were indeed too private or taboo to be included in the pages of his autobiography.

To step outside the specific context of his autobiography for a moment, Berkoff as an 'analysand' may be seen in other 'confessional' situations to offer resistance to unfettered self-revelation, particularly where sex is concerned. One example is the 'therapy session' he underwent with Professor Anthony Clare on the BBC Radio 4 programme 'In the Psychiatrist's Chair' broadcast on 11 October 1998. During their conversation Clare repeatedly drew attention to what he perceived to be Berkoff's evasions, even noting on a number of occasions for the benefit of his listeners how Berkoff appeared to be smiling with knowing irony as he gave certain responses. The operation of resistance is manifest in the following exchange concerning Berkoff's teenage years:

> BERKOFF: I love fashion, I love style, I love dressing up, and –
> CLAIR: – and [your father] would have seen this as very effeminate?
> BERKOFF: Oh, absolutely. Yes. Feared that ... yes, terrible.
> CLAIR: Did you worry about your sexuality? That sometimes happens when someone questions it –
> BERKOFF: – Not ... not ... not ... no, didn't have any problem with that ... not really. No, because I was attracted to girls at a very, very early age. Because we lived in Stamford Hill , and all the girls kind of ... they were ... they were rutting, you know, Jewish girls, and, er, we used to go to the cinema on Sunday afternoon and they ... everyone used to walk up and down the aisles and seats looking for someone, and you sat there and you put your arm around them and if they accepted it and the rest of the film you just spent plonking these gigantic suction French kisses on them. That's all you heard in the cinema. You might get a little squeeze of breast but that was very, very, very, very rare and very daring and of course a source of great pride afterwards when you leave the cinema and you go to the cafe or you stand outside with your mates and they say: "Did yer get any tit?"

Of course, one could object that this is not a real therapy session at all but a 'psychoanalytic chat show', and that Berkoff, perhaps justifiably, did not relish the thought of millions of Radio 4 listeners eavesdropping, as it were, on his private thoughts regarding his own sexuality. Nevertheless, Berkoff's *performance* of his elaborately long-winded and evasively 'humorous' response – he speaks rapidly in a variety of accents, gives histrionic emphasis to certain phrases, and imitates the sounds of slurpy French kisses – does conform rather closely to Freud's notion of resistance, or more exactly to his concept of "screen memory," whereby "one memory 'covers up' another, more significant one" (Marcus 1994: 82). This, Marcus adds, "has such radical implications for autobiographical memories" (82). My point in this digression has been to show how Berkoff, when in situations of extreme exposure, commonly employs strategies of resistance in the construction of his 'self'.

The genre of autobiography, although commonly held to be an objective account by an individual of her or his life, is more akin to that of the novel. In his *Anatomy of Criticism*, Northrop Frye (1957: 307), drawing attention to the fictional quality of autobiography, suggests that

[m]ost autobiographers are inspired by a creative, and therefore, fictional, impulse to select only those events and experiences in the writer's life that go to build up an integrated pattern. This pattern may be something larger than himself [sic] with which he has come to identify himself, or simply the coherence of his character and attitudes.

What, one may ask, is the "something larger than himself" with which Berkoff identified himself in his autobiographical project, and what might his motivation have been? One answer, I believe, is Berkoff's concern with constructing something analogous to what Joseph Campbell has called a "monomyth," a concept that Mary Gergen (1994: 23) explains in her chapter entitled 'The Social Construction of Personal Histories':

The ideal protagonist of the conventional autobiography is the hero. The plot is formed by his [sic] struggle to attain success in terms of a valuable social goal. This formulation adheres to the classical lines of the "monomyth", a form that classicist Joseph Campbell (1956) has designated as the single basic story of Western civilization. In its clearest form, this heroic myth centers on the theme of the triumph of spirit over flesh; of good over evil; of mind over matter. The central plot of the monomyth describes the hero's life, from being chosen as a heroic figure, embarking on a quest, struggling against various adversaries and temptations, to gaining a final victory and being recognized for his achievements.

It is in such a light, I suggest, that Berkoff's autobiography project may be best understood. His concern with his own 'heroic' quest in life – the triumph of the victimised, working-class Jew Steven Berkoff over the hegemonic, middle-class theatre Establishment – may partly explain why his narrative contains little or no detail about friendships, intimate relationships, the joys and satisfactions of fatherhood and sex, and why instead he has dwelt almost obsessively on patterns of hardship, exclusion, rejection, loneliness and his compensatory will-to-power. In other words, the project of revealing his 'inner self' through a process of spontaneous free association is totally eclipsed by what has evidently been his primary concern, namely justifying and validating himself by showing how he has hewn his way to success against all the odds. Sturrock's notion of self-justifying autobiography is useful here:

Autobiography is self-evidently not the way of the quietist, but an expedient by which the writer can reply to the injuries that have been done to him ... The autobiographer can stand up in court and vindicate himself against whoever may have harmed or defamed him in the course of his life, as well as against the impersonal hindrances that might have kept someone less pertinacious than himself from winning prominence. He is a narrator who has won through and has correspondingly much to gain from showing how hardly his reputation has been gained, in spite of a grudging fortune and of human contrariety. (Sturrock 1993: 49–50)

Berkoff's *Free Association* fits this description, and the account that he offers of his life is best categorised as a *via travagliata* or 'life of travail' in the manner of Benvenuto Cellini's *Life* (Sturrock).

Berkoff's self-vindicating 'Finale' to his autobiography supports such a conclusion. Apparently piqued by his exclusion from theatre critic Irving Wardle's round-up of the best playwrights of the 1980s, Berkoff writes bitterly:

Now let me look at this objectively, as if I were someone else. I ask why am I not included? Is it because I'm also an actor and director and we mustn't be seen to be too busy must we, eh? Who cares, I always say to myself, but some part of me weeps inside, even if the outside is scarred and weathered like old leather. I look at Mr Scribblemuch rounding up the decade's writers and not mentioning me once and I think, bollocks. I think even a little squib would do, but nothing! Not for *Decadence*, not for *Greek*, not for *West* and not for *Sink the Belgrano!* I feel like those artists in the Third Reich who were cut out of the history books.

But actors want to perform my plays over and over again. And they do. They perform my plays at the Edinburgh Festival. I am performed in every campus, university, college and prison in the country. Hey, that's quite an achievement. (*FA*: 388–9)

This rather desperate parting shot from a disgruntled Berkoff demonstrates that *Free Association*, far from being the spontaneous account of his 'inner life' that he stated it would be in his preface, is a defensive and self-justifying account of his career. Rather than an autopsychography, therefore, it is best seen as an example of what Michel Neyraut terms a "periautography", namely a narrative describing the origins and development of a professional or intellectual career (Marcus 1994: 82).

Conclusion

In this chapter I have discussed the paradoxical situation whereby the very works that Berkoff singles out explicitly as being the most revealing of his 'inner self' – the works in which he takes the metaphorical scalpel to himself – are texts that point instead to his own fugitive and slippery subjectivity. We have seen that in the two plays *Harry's Christmas* and *Kvetch*, as well as in the stories 'Hell' and 'Daddy', Berkoff gave his alter ego protagonists what appears to be almost total freedom to explore repressed areas of their subjectivities, particularly where sex is concerned. Harry and the protagonist of 'Hell' are permitted to open the Pandora's Box of their loneliness, and are then sacrificed. Frank in *Kvetch* is allowed to play with his latent homosexuality but only in so far as it is presented farcically as an aberrant and atypical fantasy. Lest readers and spectators be tempted to draw literal parallels between these fictional characters and their creator, we have seen how Berkoff, like a master illusionist, pulls off textual disappearing acts.

In contrast to these fictional discourses, Berkoff has presented *Free Association* as no mere conventional autobiography but as a text in which he set out to display his inner self with all its "warts, wounds and blemishes" in an unfettered way, as if unburdening himself to an analyst. His purpose, I suggest, was to create and project what Orr, in a different context, has called a "performance of authenticity" (Orr 1991: 13) as a means of validating his whole self-revelatory project, indeed his entire self-referential *œuvre*. As we have seen, though, the revelations of auto-psychography yield to the exigencies of periautography. In other words, far from stripping himself psychologically naked, Berkoff sets out to justify himself and his career by selecting, elaborating or excising certain themes and patterns in his life. In this text, Berkoff may be seen to adopt subject positions that reflect his ambiguous reflexivity: as a 'confessant' he represses and omits crucial information about his 'inner self' and as an 'analyst' he manipulates and interprets his accounts. The 'self' that emerges from this apparently factual discourse, therefore, proves to be just as fugitive as the alter ego 'selves' he presents in the fictional works.

Does Berkoff reveal or conceal himself in his autobiographical project? The cover photograph of *Free Association* offers a tantalising clue. It depicts Berkoff in the process of making himself up as the character Titorelli in *The Trial*. The image captures Berkoff in a cosmetic limbo between two identities, as it were, with half his face painted with a twirl-ing Daliesque moustache and the other half unpainted as himself. It is a moment that encapsulates the promise and the failure of his auto-biography, since we catch a glimpse of the Berkoff 'self' but a self that is half-masked in fictionality. The character of Titorelli is particularly interesting in this context since in the play he is first seen trapped by his own contrivance inside a picture frame. When he is extracted by K., he exclaims: "Thank you very much. I got stuck inside a self portrait. That's very dangerous. Once I got stuck two days before someone came" (*TT*: 58). With his autobiography, I suggest, Berkoff gets himself stuck inside a self-portrait, one that is constricted by the logocentric frame of his authorial control and his 'periautographical' motives. In this chapter I have attempted to pull him out of that 'frame'.

Notes

1 There is an echo here of Grotowski's assertion, made in his discussion of *Hamlet* in his groundbreaking book *Towards a Poor Theatre* (first published in 1968), that "[f]or both producer and actor, [Shakespeare's] text is a sort of scalpel enabling us to open ourselves, to transcend ourselves, to find what is hidden within us" (Grotowski 1992: 57).
2 Quoted from Pete Townsend's introduction to Steven Berkoff, *West and other Plays* (London: Faber & Faber, 1988), 8.
3 The original production of *Kvetch*, which Berkoff describes as his "first 'American' play" (*CP*, II: 46), is set in the Jewish community of Los Angeles. The later switch to the Jewish East End required him, as he put it, to make only "a few changes of idiom and brandnames" (*ibid.*).
4 Originally entitled *Mr Prufrock's Songs*, this play was Berkoff's second original script. He wrote it in 1966, but it remained unstaged until 1983 when it was premiered at the King's Head Theatre Club under the new title *Lunch*. The two characters in this play, a man and a woman, meet by chance on a beach and converse 'past' each other in monologues that express their unspoken thoughts and desires. Berkoff writes in his author's note to the published text: "Through their mutual catharsis the man learns how easy it is to be honest and reveal himself and how painless it is to do so since we are all afraid of revealing some shallowness we are convinced is at the bottom of all our good intentions" (*CP* I: 218).
5 The only mention made by Berkoff of his daughter located by this writer is to be found in the interview conducted by Deborah Ross in the *Independent* (2 July 2001). Ross recounts the rather odd exchange about the unnamed daughter, which terminates suddenly when Berkoff declares tersely: "I can't really talk about it."

CONCLUSIONS

Mime is a lonely art, for the mime works in a solitary world inhabited
by phantasms which take only transient form through him.(Angna
Engers, *On Mime*)

In this study I have argued that Berkoff, in his many overlapping capacities,
has been engaged in the career-long modernist project of attempting to
construct, perform and explain himself – or rather his 'self' – in and
through his multimedia *œuvre*. I have referred to this entire dynamic
process as the 'Berkoff phenomenon'. As we have seen, Berkoff has
adopted a wide range of subject positions both on and off-stage. Far from
achieving closure, however, these discursive strategies have served to
highlight the fact that the 'Berkoff phenomenon' lacks any fixed or
essential existence, and is characterised by both presence and absence to
the extent that it may be best seen, to borrow Richard Schechner's (1983:
209) apt phrase, as "a proliferation of liminalities". This being so, it is
necessary to consider in this final chapter the degree to which Berkoff
may be said to have succeeded or failed in his aims. This question is
worth posing, since Berkoff has clearly been a figure of some influence in
modern British theatre, particularly among the young up-and-coming
generation of actors, playwrights and directors. In order to search for
answers, this concluding discussion will look at the liminal quality of the
two inextricably interlinked products that Berkoff has been concerned with
constructing and commodifying, namely his dramaturgy and his identity.

The liminality that pervades the 'Berkoff phenomenon' has been a
defining characteristic of Berkoff's dramaturgical style, a style that carries
traces both of the logocentric fixity of his scripts, direction and post-
production commentaries and the apparently pure and unmediated
presence of physical performance, particularly mime. In this context it is
useful to begin by considering the distinction made by Josette Féral
between two antithetical currents in modern (that is, post-1960s) theatre,
namely *performance* and *theatre*. Performance, which she equates with the
work of conceptual performance artists such as Hermann Nitsch, Vito

Acconci, and Elizabeth Chitty, is marked by the artist's fleeting coming-into-being through performance (Féral 1982: 171). The artist achieves this ephemeral presence not through text, which, like a dramatic script, would pre-exist the event, but through the spontaneous and improvised manipulation of her or his body in a one-off event:

> Performance is meant to be a physical accomplishment, so the performer works with his [sic] body the way a painter does with his canvas. He explores it, manipulates it, paints it, covers it, uncovers it, freezes it, moves it, cuts it, isolates it, and speaks to it as if it were a foreign object. (171)

Performance, in its rejection of repetition, characterisation, narrativity, mimesis and illusion, represents the antithesis of theatre. It is indeed, Féral asserts, "the absence of meaning" (173) in so far as it "rejects form, which is immobility, and opts, instead, for discontinuity and slippage" (175). Theatre, by contrast, is aligned with logocentrism in its concern with the imitation of 'reality', the creation of narratives and characters, the repetition of performances and productions, the mediation of the playwright and director, and closure. Theatre cannot, Féral argues, "keep from setting up, stating, constructing, and giving points of view" (178). In Berkoff's dramaturgy, I suggest, performance and theatre, in the form of mime and text, permeate each other just as presence and absence, spontaneity and authorial manipulation, commingle in the 'Berkoff phenomenon'.

Berkoff formed his dramaturgy in oppositional reaction to two main aspects of conventional theatre practice that he had encountered as a drama student and a beginning actor, namely mainstream theatre's twin obsession (as he saw it) with text and naturalism. His disillusionment with a text-based approach to staging, traceable in his own accounts to Red Beard's rejection of his physical adaptation of the "The Bucket Rider", has stayed with him throughout his career. According to Berkoff, the text-based method operates most perniciously in the mainstream theatre's approach to staging Shakespeare. In *I Am Hamlet*, he complains that "DIRECTORS THINK OF THEATRE MERELY AS LITERATURE THAT HAPPENS TO BE ON STAGE, AND NOT AS A MOVING LIFE FORCE" (*IAH*: 81). By contrast, reflecting on his own work as a director, Berkoff asserts in *Coriolanus in Deutschland*: "I never presume to know in advance what might happen in rehearsal, or that the combination of elements might produce another effect to the one I imagined in advance. Theatre is a physical act" (*CID*: 41–2).

Berkoff also rejected naturalism and what he saw as its obsession with the slavish representation or imitation of reality. In his preface to *The Trial*, for example, he decries it as the "theatre of the ultra-bourgeois, so bereft of anything but the obvious, with its expensive lumbering pieces of dead weight. The fortunes spent on trying to be real, to satisfy the bloated after-supper punters" (*TT*: 6). And in his introduction to the published text of *Agamemnon*, he declares: "Naturalism, both in the writing and performing of plays, often leaves me with pangs of embarrassment, especially when witnessing actors playing this game of pretense [*sic*]" (*AFHU*: 7). Berkoff's answer was to develop a highly stylised mime-based style of acting with the aim of breaking through the constraints and constrictions of realism. This may be seen in operation in the scene in *The Trial*, for example, in which the two guards search Joseph K.'s room. Berkoff describes the ensemble in that sequence as:

> a Greek chorus turning a body into a chair or a chest of drawers, since we are what we use. When you search a person's room or cupboard you are violating him since he momentarily becomes the object. The person and his objects are wed, so by taking over the role not only of human but also the environment, the actor is able to be an outraged chest of drawers! So art rules over reality. (*TT*: 6)

Thus he used the actors' bodies and their physical performance and mime skills to assert fantastical stylisation over what he has characterised as the mainstream obsession with creating the impression of 'reality' on stage. In short, he employed performance (mime) in an attempt to undo the logocentricism of theatre (text and naturalism). It should be noted, however, that Berkoff has not always been consistent in this artistic policy, since plays such as *Harry's Christmas*, *Acapulco* and *Ritual in Blood* are naturalistic in terms of both dialogue and acting style.

Berkoff, as we have seen, drew early inspiration from what he saw as the physical approach to text taken by certain charismatic actors who created spectacular theatre by applying the full range of their physical and vocal resources and skills. In a 1977 interview he stated:

> I'm excited mainly about great performers, about Kean and Olivier, and I think we liberate the actor from the writer/director hierarchy, make him [*sic*] articulate inside his body, inside his imagination, make him capable of creating an object of fascination on the stage. (Grant 1977)

Berkoff undertook to subvert what he saw as the writer/director hierarchy and liberate his own body further by acquiring mime skills at the École Jacques Lecoq. There, he recalls, he learned how to improvise and exploit the resources of an ensemble (*FA*: 96), and how to impersonate animals and objects rather than human characters (*FA*: 103). Berkoff's first successful application of Lecoq's pedagogy, as we have seen, was *Meta-morphosis* (1969). Recalling that production, particularly his own performance in it as Gregor, he states: "I prided myself on being able to speak and move, and on the fact that I had taken the actor's body as seriously as his voice, mind and totality of his equipment" (*MOM*: 55).

One may see, therefore, that Berkoff had moved very much in the direction of employing physical practices associated with performance with the aim of escaping some of the limitations of theatre whilst – and here is the paradox – remaining connected to practices associated with theatre. For despite his overt privileging of the body it is important to note that Berkoff was not seeking entirely to divorce physical performance, particularly mime, from text but to redefine the relationship between them. As he writes in his preface to *Agamemnon*, "I was determined to see how I could bring mime together with the spoken word as its opposite partner" (*FA*: 53). His apparent aim, therefore, was to use the resources of mime to push the physical approach taken to text by the likes of Olivier, Kean, and Plummer to greater extremes of stylisation and spectacle.

Mime has been the key element of Berkoff's physical approach to acting, the hallmark of the Berkovian performance style. It has been his chief tool for dissolving what he has seen as the unyielding solidity of naturalism. Like dance, this kinetic art form hints at a presence that is apprehendable only in each passing moment of the flow of the mime's movements and gestures. As Berkoff's great idol Jean-Louis Barrault wrote, "the final aim of mime is not the visual, but presence itself, namely the moment of the theatrical present" (Barrault 1951: 73). One of the key early pre-*East* productions in which he focused on developing and show-casing a physical style of acting centred on mime was his adaptation *The Fall of the House of Usher* (Traverse Theatre, 1974). This priority is manifest in his introduction to the published version of the play, where he writes:

> The actors must be the house and its decaying fabric, must speak as stones and the memories of the house that are seared into its walls ... must be the death rattle and atmosphere, must be the environment, and since humans are born of the environment they must reflect it.
> Our bodies link, break away, dance, flow to each other passing these valuable segments of information ... must be stretched, plastic, communicative. (*AFHU*: 37–8)

Berkoff's *Usher*, like *Metamorphosis*, was an early 'performance manifesto' with which he set out the parameters of the mime-based physical approach to acting that he was taking with the LTG.

The published version of *Usher* is unique in Berkoff's *œuvre* in that it consists of a conventional dramatic text (dialogue and stage directions) and a performance text (commentary and prescriptive notes) placed side-by-side on facing pages. Thus it offers Berkoff's own best blow-by-blow account of the way he has approached text and mime in the creation of his dramaturgy and, metaphorically, of his 'self'. Taking Scene 10 (Edgar's progress through the decaying house) as a typical example, it is possible to see Berkoff's approach, as a mime-trained actor, to text in this play/production. The script in that scene runs as follows:

FRIEND: Which Way?
USHER and MADELINE. Step by step we will conduct you. [USHER *and* MADELINE *become house.* FRIEND *wanders through them.*]

FRIEND: Conducted in	MADELINE and USHER.
silence	[*Sung or whispered*]
Through dark and intricate	Insufferable
Passages. Everything I encounter	Melancholy
In this house	Half-pleasurable
Heightens vague sentiments of	Poetic
Forboding [*sic*]	Landscape
The carvings of the ceilings	Depression
Sombre tapestries of the walls	Soul
Ebony blackness of the floor	Afterdream
Phantasmagorical armorial trophies	Opium
Which rattle as I stride	Iciness
Into a large room	Sinking ...

(*AFHU*: 57)

The speech in this passage, consisting almost entirely of monologues, clearly determines the action. It does this, first, by employing two kinds of stage directions: extra-dialogic directions (e. g. "FRIEND wanders through them") and intra-dialogic directions (e. g. "Conducted in silence"; "as I stride"), and, second, by describing both what it is exactly that Usher and his sister should 'become' in the house ("Sombre tapestries", "Phantas-magorical armorial trophies", and so on) and what states of mind the three performers should embody ("Melancholy", "Depression", and so on). The performative and descriptive language here, as I have noted in the case of *Agamemnon* and *East*, may be seen to serve as a kind of choreographic score that prescribes the action.

Berkoff's commentary to this scene, which provides a further set of extra-dialogic instructions, also determines the movements of the actors.

Indeed, it does more than this, since it also sets out what he considers to be the necessary qualities both of the mimed performance and of the actors/dancers involved:

> USHER and MADELINE fluidly move through a configuration of rooms suggested by their bodies whilst again intoning the subtext which relates to the FRIEND whom USHER now calls EDGAR. The FRIEND as narrator chillingly describes the interior of the house while MADELINE and USHER create it and are 'it'. MADELINE always moves loosely and lightly – a split being, between house and 'her' – the actress like the actors should mime well and suggest advanced decay, neurosis and catalepsy, nerves stretched to their taughtest [sic] before the point of snapping, while at the same time have the vocal and physical strength to convey it. A high degree of dance skill is very valuable, if not essential – USHER becomes the doors, vibrates like the house, becomes corridors, stairs, melting out of the air until the FRIEND is led in. (AFHU: 56)

One may witness the polar demands of performance and theatre operating in this passage. On the one hand, Berkoff hints at the presence of performance in such phrases as "fluidly move", "MADELINE and USHER create it and are 'it'", and "melting out of the air". Moreover, his insistence that the actress playing Madeline should possess dance skills signals his desire to bring into play the ephemeral and kinetic qualities of *performance*. On the other hand, I suggest, these transitory and fleeting 'moments' of performance become smothered by Berkoff's logocentric concern to create theatre by narrating a story and establishing the possible world on stage.

The commentary, fossilised in published form like the stage directions of the script, aims to fix the physical performance, particularly the miming of Usher and Madeline. It is a kind of 'frozen' direction that survives the production and anticipates and determines, through the logos of Berkoff's authority as playwright and director, all repeated performances and future revivals. As Rabkin argues:

> Performance ... by its very nature denies the logocentric impulse – the body transcends the word. But the logocentric authority of the word has indeed been sustained by the evanescence of performance and the survivability of the dramatic text. (Rabkin 1983: 54)

With his physical approach to acting, I suggest, Berkoff set out to undo the competencies of theatre – particularly text and naturalism. One can see from the above, however, that Berkoff's apparently liberationist dramaturgy continued to tie performance to theatre, primarily through scripts that determine physical actions and gestures, but also through his concern, which may be seen in any of his plays, with narrativity and characterisation, and with the meticulous re-creation of original productions of these plays in revivals (see *Meditations on Metamorphosis*).

Turning now to the liminality of Berkoff's subjectivity, how does this tension between mime and text, not just in *Usher* but in the majority of Berkoff's plays and productions, relate to his constructed 'self' and to the 'Berkoff phenomenon'? Mime is, I suggest, the most apt kinetic metaphor for the way Berkoff has apparently aimed (without success) to achieve closure in his attempted construction of 'self'. Mime allows the actor, unencumbered by realistic stage properties, almost total freedom to flit freely from one representation to the next. In his commentary to Scene 7 of *Usher*, Berkoff asserts that:

> Mime renders the actor inviolable since they [*sic*] are protected by a metaphor and can stretch and expand this metaphor. Since mime acts as a metaphor one does not have to worry about dropping any real comb, etc. In other words, one does not have to suffer the limitations of the real and can expand in the imaginative and metaphoric world. (*AFHU*: 50)

The paradox of this, however, is that the signified of the mimed gesture remains elusive. The mimed 'object' – the 'motorbike' in *East*, for example, or the 'house' in *Usher* – are both present and absent. As Josette Féral argues, in performance – and here I align Berkoff's mime with Féral's performance – there is "nothing to grasp, project, introject, except for flows, networks and system. Everything appears and disappears like a galaxy of 'transitional objects' representing only the failures of representation" (Féral 179). Berkoff, as the provisional and shifting agent/actor in his construction of 'self', has flitted, free of the "limitations of the real", from one subject position to another without achieving (or desiring) closure. Thus the 'Berkoff phenomenon' may be seen metaphorically as a 'macro-mime' performed across a very diverse array of media and written in the air – present *and* absent, but never fixed or fixable.

Amid the sometimes vertiginous presence/absence of the 'Berkoff phenomenon', however, something substantial remains, namely the living presence of Berkoff's biological body on the stage and in real life. How is one to account for the moving, breathing and performing tissue of someone, as Berkoff describes himself in the *Usher* commentary, "who might have made a reasonable middle-weight or ranking welter-weight [boxer]" (*AFHU*: 46)? What, in other words, is the status of Berkoff's physical *body* in the processes of his mimed performances and his construction of 'self'? The American mime artist and dancer Angna Enders offers a clue with her assertion that the "mime [artist] is no more than the physical medium – the instrument on which the figures of his imagination play their dance of life" (Enders 1979: 134). Less mystically, but in a similar fashion, Féral sees the performance artist as

> a source of production and displacement. Having become the point of passage for energy flows – gestural, vocal, libidinal, etc. – that traverse him [sic] without ever standing still in a fixed meaning or representation, he plays at putting those flows to work and seizing networks. (174)

Seen in such a way, Berkoff's biological body is the physical raw material of his mimed performance. It is not, however, synonymous with or a marker of his identity or subjectivity, despite his attempts to create such an identification. His body, like that of the performance artist, can only "reveal places of passage" (174).

Like *Usher*, the 'Berkoff phenomenon' is characterised, I suggest, both by the spontaneity of performance and the craftedness of theatre – not in equal measure, however, but in a relationship that privileges the practices associated with the logocentricism of theatre. In his plays as well as in his autobiography Berkoff has been concerned with telling stories, creating characters – most notably his 'self' – and performing an 'act' that has been crafted, manipulated and mediated by an intentionality that has changed along with his provisional and shifting subjectivity. The paradox of the 'mimed' quality of Berkoff's constructed 'self', just like the mimed actions in *Usher* and his other plays/productions, is that neither the 'spontaneous' acts (the mimed gestures or the free associations) nor the logocentric practices employed by Berkoff to constrain them (text and direction, and authorial manipulation) achieve closure.

The clearest example of this circular process of non-signification is Berkoff's autobiography, *Free Association*. Like a mime, Berkoff apparently sought in the pages of that work to convey unmediated presence – the 'pure' presence of his 'inner self'. His stated purpose, it will be recalled, was to present his freely associated memories in a 'conversational' style, as one would relate thoughts and feelings directly, that is without the mediation of consciousness, to a psychoanalyst. Yet, as I attempted to show in the previous chapter, his purpose was evidently not to reveal his inner self spontaneously but rather to impose authorial control and structure upon his material. As a consequence, Berkoff's intended act of autopsychography became an artfully crafted and apparently teleological narrative, and the 'Berkoff' signified slipped further from his grasp. Thus *Free Association* (indeed, Berkoff's entire *œuvre*) is most interesting on account of what it can or does *not* say about 'Steven Berkoff' in factual terms and what it suggests about how he has wanted to project his 'self'.

What are the implications of this for Berkoff's overall achievement as an artist? As I mentioned in the Introduction, opinions of Berkoff's artistic worth tend to be polarised. In one camp, there are those commentators who love and respect his work. Hugh Morrison, looking back at the first half of Berkoff's career, makes the claim in his *Directing in the Theatre* that the "three directors/creators who have probably had the greatest effect on English theatre in the last two decades are Peter Brook, Joan Littlewood, and Steven Berkoff" (Morrison 1989: 151). Dominic Drumgoole (2000: 27), former artistic director of the Bush Theatre, maintains that Berkoff's influence on 1990s British theatre has been profound:

> Much of physical theatre stems from his inspiration and his experiments in the seventies. The whole cockney geezer linguistic richness you find in Jez Butterworth *et al.*, was leant from the freedom and range Berkoff found in the vernacular in his early work. Verse drama took on a new lease of life from his boldness.

Indeed, various contemporary playwrights – Mark Ravenhill (*Blood Brood*) and Harry Gibson (*Trainspotting*), for example – have openly acknowledged their debt to a single play, *East*. According to such views, Berkoff succeeded in his aim of revolutionising British theatre practice and administering shock therapy to audiences.

In the other camp, there are commentators who deride Berkoff's work. Ruby Cohn's dismissive attitude towards his writing is clear in her *ex cathedra* pronouncement that "I am tempted, like most [*sic*] critics, to dismiss Berkoff as lexically imprecise, rhythmically faltering, and naively monotonous in his 1960s-type message of love, couched in obscenity" (Cohn 1991: 94). As for his physical performance style, the *Financial Times* critic Alistair Macaulay opined in his review of *Shakespeare's Villains* (11 July 1998): "It is now many years since Berkoff became the derided British archetype of a certain kind of flashy bad acting: all selfish surface and never a moment of serious involvement in anything beyond his own ego." Whether or not one agrees with such savage appraisals, they raise the question of what, if anything, has endured beyond Berkoff's own 'self-referential' performance. It is a question that even some of his fervent admirers have felt bound to confront. Drumgoole (2000: 26), for example, states: "The fact that there is little intellectual cohesion behind [Berkoff's] work matters not a jot, there is a vivacity that works like cocaine in the system." This provocative viewpoint draws attention to three issues that I now consider along the way to setting out my own conclusions about Berkoff's achievement, namely the "vivacity" of Berkoff's brand of theatre; the lack of "intellectual cohesion" in his work; and the question of whether or not this lack should matter at all

Whether one admires or disregards Berkoff's work as a theatre artist, it can scarcely be denied that throughout his career he has created spectacles on stage that have been, by turns, shocking, hilarious, irreverent, abrasive and obscene. Berkoff's dramaturgy, based as it has been on the mime skills of the performers, has created many memorable moments of exciting and highly original theatre: the mimed motorbike ride in *East*, for example, and the grotesque acrobatics of the man-beetle in *Metamorphosis*. The spectacular effects have been brought about as much by his robust language as by the highly stylised physical performances. The polyphonic dramatic speech of *East* sticks out as the obvious example here. Thus I do not find myself in dispute with Drumgoole's suggestion that the vivacity of Berkovian theatre "works like cocaine in the system". Yet the problem suggested by such an analogy is that, as with all chemically induced highs, one must inevitably return to earth afterwards, which prompts questions about what remains after the drug of Berkoff's theatre has passed through the system. Does anything substantial and meaningful survive the sensation-inducing spectacle? And what might separate Berkovian theatre from, say, the entertaining spectacle of circus?

For a body of work to be seen as intellectually cohesive, it is reasonable to expect that it is informed and guided by principles that are deeply and rigorously thought out, consistent in integrity and engagement, and unswerving in its commitment to truth, whatever that may be for the artist in question. This is particularly so in the case of someone like Berkoff, who has set himself the high aim of revealing himself totally through his work. As we have seen, however, his interactions with the discourses that he has employed in this on-going process of manifesting and explicating his identity have lacked any such engagement and intellectual rigour. Whether Berkoff has identified himself with Jewish culture, the working class, the Kray twins, the state of Israel, Kafka, Barrault, Olivier, Kean or Freud, the multiple subject positions he has adopted in his shape-shifting career signify little of substance about the nature and development of his subjectivity. Like 'Houdini', another of his personæ, he never fails to escape. The whole process of Berkoff's construction of his 'self' through his multimedia *œuvre* has been a series of acts of *bricolage* conducted in an ad hoc manner yet retrospectively characterised by him as links in a teleological chain. There are also glaring absences in his 'intellectual life': one finds no discussion of or interaction with the ideas or practices of, for example, Brecht or Grotowski, two theatre artists with whom Berkoff shares certain superficial similarities in the perlocutionary and self-revelatory aspects of his work. Like Drumgoole, therefore, I am of the view that Berkoff's work, despite its spectacular and entertaining qualities, lacks intellectual cohesion.

Does or should this lack matter? Given Berkoff's influence on British theatre, and given that he is routinely one of the most performed playwrights at the Edinburgh Festival by young, up-and-coming and, some might suggest, impressionable theatre artists, I believe that ultimately it does matter. That, for example, he can be perceived by some people as a committed political playwright is cause enough for concern, particularly in the present troubled times, since as we have seen with his plays *Greek*, *Decadence* and *Sink the Belgrano!*, his treatment of political events in Britain has shown a shaky grasp of the issues and the solutions. For once, perhaps, Berkoff's nemesis Charles Spencer was close to the mark when he described him as "the Johnny Rotten of British theatre" (Spencer 1998). Just as the Punk bands in the 1970s kicked a bloated commercial music industry up the posterior, so too during the same period did Berkoff shake up the world of British theatre with his aggressive spectacles on and off-stage. Yet, as in the case of the Sex Pistols, what remains after Berkoff's angry posturing and snarling has fallen silent? Certainly not, in my estimation, a body of work that can tell us much about Berkoff's 'self', about his political views, about contemporary or historical events or about his engagement with key developments in modern theatre.

In conclusion, the 'Berkoff phenomenon', as I suggested above, can be seen metaphorically as a 'macro-mime': a vivacious, shocking, amusing, and spectacular career-long macro-performance that has flitted enticingly and entertainingly from one invisible and intangible representation to another. Yet it is a performance that has created very little of substance. To be sure, Berkoff has certainly shocked and delighted his audiences, but I for one find it difficult to agree with Paul Currant's (1991: 183) assertion that Berkoff's intention, like Artaud's, has been "to go beyond the comfort zone established by conventional theatre to shock the audience into new self-revelations". The alpha and omega of Berkoff's project has consistently been the construction and projection of himself through his *œuvre*. He has not, I would argue, been motivated by a wish to change the views or ideas of the members of his audiences but by his desire to perform his 'self' into existence in ways that have been coloured by his unquenchable anger and bitterness, his need for personal power and control, and his own obsession with self-justification. In that sense, Alistair Macaulay may be correct in his assertion that Berkoff has not been involved seriously in anything beyond his own ego.

REFERENCES

I list here only the works that are cited in the text of this study. For clarity, published interviews with Berkoff are listed under the name of the interviewer.

Abbott, H. Porter (1988) 'Autobiography, autography, fiction: Groundwork for a taxonomy of textual categories', *New Literary History*, vol. 19, no. 3 (Spring), 597–615.

Alter, Jean (1990) *A Sociosemiotic Theory of Theatre*. Philadelphia: University of Pennsylvania Press.

Anderegg, Michael (1999) *Orson Welles, Shakespeare and Popular Culture*. New York: Columbia University Press.

Ansorge, Peter (1975) *Disrupting the Spectacle: Five Years of Experimental and Fringe Theatre in Britain*. London: Pitman.

Appleyard, Brian (1989) 'Beware of Berkoff'. Interview with Steven Berkoff. *Sunday Times Magazine*, 12 November.

Artaud, Antonin (1977) *The Theatre and Its Double*. Translated by Victor Corti. London: John Calder.

—— (1989) *Artaud on Theatre*. Edited by Claude Schumacher. London: Methuen.

Aston, Elaine and George Savona (1991) *Theatre as Sign-System. A Semiotics: A Semiotics of Text and Performance*. London: Routledge.

Auslander, Philip (1997) *From Acting to Performance: Essays in Modernism and Postmodernism*. London: Routledge.

Bakhtin, Mikhail (1981) *The Dialogic Imagination*. Translated by Caryl Emerson and Michael Holquist. Austin: University of Texas Press.

—— (1984) *Rabelais and His World*. Translated by Hélène Iswolsky. Bloomington: Indiana University Press.

Banham, Martin (1990) *The Cambridge Guide to World Theatre*. 2nd edn. Cambridge: Cambridge University Press.

Barba, Eugenio and Nicola Savarese (eds) (1991) *A Dictionary of Theatre Anthropology: The Secret Life of the Performer*. Translated by Richard Fowler. London: Routledge.

Barber, Lynn (1996) 'The loneliness of Berkoff'. Interview with Steven Berkoff. *The Daily Telegraph*, 22 April.

Barker, Clive (1969) 'Contemporary Shakespearean parody in British theatre'. *Shakespeare Jahrbuch*, vol. 105, 104–20.

—— (1978) 'From fringe to alternative theatre'. *Zeitschrift für Anglistik und Amerikanistik*, vol. XXVI, no. 1, 48–62.

Barnes, Philip (1986) *A Companion to Post-War British Theatre*. London: Croom Helm.

Barnett, Anthony (1982) *Iron Britannia: Why Parliament Waged the Falklands War*. London: Allison & Busby.

Barrault, Jean-Louis (1951) *Reflections on the Theatre*. Translated by Barbara Wall. London: Rockliff.

—— (1961) *The Theatre of Jean-Louis Barrault*. Translated by Joseph Chiari. London: Barrie & Rockliff.

—— (1974) *Memories for Tomorrow*. Translated by Jonathan Griffin. London: Thames & Hudson.

Barrault, Jean-Louis and Andre Gide (1950) *The Trial, from the Novel by Franz Kafka*. Translated by Jacqueline and Frank Sundstrom. London: Secker & Warburg.

Barthes, Roland (1976) *The Pleasure of the Text*. Translated by Richard Miller. London: Jonathan Cape.

—— (1977) *Image Music Text*. Translated by Stephen Heath. London: Fontana.

Bate, Jonathan and Russell Jackson (1996) *Shakespeare: An Illustrated Stage History*. Oxford: Oxford University Press.

Bawden, Liz-Anne (ed.) (1976) *The Oxford Companion to Film*. London: Oxford University Press.

Beck, Evelyn Torton (1971) *Kafka and the Yiddish Theatre*. Madison: Wisconsin University Press.

Benson, Mary (1976/77) 'Steven Berkoff: What theatre can be'. *London Magazine*, December 1976/January 1977, 83–9.

Bentley, Eric (1950) 'Jean-Louis Barrault'. *Kenyon Review*, 12, 224–42.

Berkoff, Steven (1978) 'Three theatre manifestos', *Gambit*, vol. 8, no. 32, 7–21.

—— (1981) *The Trial. Metamorphosis. In the Penal Colony*. Charlbury: Amber Lane.

—— (1989a) *I Am Hamlet*. London: Faber & Faber.

—— (1989b) 'My favourite films'. *Sunday Telegraph, 7 Days* Journal, 22 October.

—— (1989c) *A Prisoner in Rio*. London: Hutchinson.

—— (1989d) 'Steven Berkoff on Laurence Olivier'. *The Independent Magazine*, 29 July.

—— (1990a) *Agamemnon. The Fall of the House of Usher*. Charlbury: Amber Lane.

—— (1990b) 'The coffee we deserve'. *Weekend Guardian*, 19–20 March.

—— (1990c) 'The ghost at the feast'. *Guardian*, 6 December.

—— (1990d) 'Schnozzles in the sand'. *Guardian*, 17 March.

—— (1990e) 'Treasures of the East: Why I live in Limehouse'. *Evening Standard*, 28 March.

—— (1991) 'The leavings of Liverpool'. *Weekend Guardian*, 4–5 May.

—— (1992a) 'Berkoff's East Enders'. *Evening Standard*, 5 May.

—— (1992b) *Coriolanus in Deutschland*. Charlbury: Amber Lane.

—— (1992c) 'From balcony to bedlam'. *Guardian*, 25 July.

—— (1992d) 'Rumblings of the thoroughfare'. *Guardian*, 4 June.

—— (1992e) *The Theatre of Steven Berkoff*. London: Methuen.

—— (1993a) *Gross Intrusion and Other Stories*. London: John Calder, 1979; reprint, London: Quartet.

—— (1993b) 'Herd in camera'. *The Sunday Times*, 30 May.

—— (1994a) *The Collected Plays*. Vol. I. London: Faber & Faber.

—— (1994b) *The Collected Plays*. Vol. II. London: Faber & Faber.

—— (1994c) *Overview*. London: Faber & Faber.

—— (1994d) 'Surreal fringe benefits'. *Guardian*, 3 September.

—— (1995a) 'The worst days of my life'. *Independent on Sunday*, 5 November.

—— (1995b) *Meditations on Metamorphosis*. London: Faber & Faber.

—— (1996a) *Free Association: An Autobiography*. London: Faber & Faber.

—— (1996b) 'A slow jog in Venice; a sambo in Rio'. *Sunday Telegraph*, 12 May.

—— (1998) *Graft. Tales of an Actor*. London: Oberon.

—— (1999) 'Finding a ready market for a Hebrew Hamlet'. *Independent*, 1 March.

—— (2000a) 'My inspiration'. *Guardian*. 28 November.

—— (2000b) *Plays One*. London: Faber & Faber.

—— (2000c) *Plays Two*. London: Faber & Faber.

—— (2000d) *Plays Three*. London: Faber & Faber.

—— (2000e) *Shopping in the Santa Monica Mall. The Journals of a Strolling Player*. London: Robson Books.

—— (2001) *The Secret Love Life of Ophelia*. London: Faber & Faber.

—— (2002) 'Requiem for Ground Zero'. www.east-productions.demon.co.uk/requiem.htm

Bigsby, C. W. E. (1981) 'The language of crisis in British theatre'. In *Contemporary English Drama*, edited by C. W. E. Bigsby, 11–51. London: Edward Arnold.

Billig, Michael (1990) 'Rhetoric of social psychology'. In *Deconstructing Social Psychology*, edited by Ian Parker and John Shotter, 47–60. London: Routledge.

Birch, David (1991) *The Language of Drama: Critical Theory and Practice*. Basingstoke: Macmillan.

Boireau, Nicole (1996) 'Steven Berkoff's orgy: The four-letter ecstasy'. *Contemporary Theatre Review*, vol. 5, no. 1, 77–89.

Bourdieu, Pierre (1984) *Distinctions: A Social Critique of the Judgement of Taste*. Translated by Richard Nice. Cambridge, MA: Harvard University Press.

Bourke, Joanna (1994) *Working-Class Cultures in Britain 1890–1960*. London: Routledge.

Brake, Michael (1985) *Comparative Youth Culture: The Sociology of Youth Cultures and Youth Subcultures in America, Britain and Canada*. London: Routledge.

Brecht, Bertolt (1964) *Brecht on Theatre*. Edited and translated by John Willett. London: Eyre: Methuen.

Brook, Peter (1968) *The Empty Space*. Harmondsworth: Penguin.

Brown, Allen (1994) 'Spittle big man'. *Sunday Times*, 24 July.

Brown, Mick (1986) 'A monstrous megalomaniac does battle at the box office'. Interview with Steven Berkoff. *Sunday Times*, 7 September.

Bruss, Elizabeth (1976) *Autobiographical Acts*. Baltimore: Johns Hopkins University Press.

Bull, John (1994) *New British Political Dramatists*. Basingstoke: Macmillan.

Burgess, Anthony (1984) *A Clockwork Orange*. Harmondsworth: Penguin.

Burns, Elizabeth (1972) *Theatricality: A Study of Convention in the Theatre and in Social Life*. London: Longman.

Burr, Vivien (1995) *An Introduction to Social Constructionism*. London: Routledge.

Callaghan, Dympna (1996) '"Othello was a white man": Properties of race on Shakespeare's stage'. In *Alternative Shakespeares*. Vol. 2, edited by Terence Hawkes, 192–215. London: Routledge.

Callois, Roger (1961) *Man, Play and Games*. Translated by Meyer Barash. New York: Free Press.

Campbell, Patrick (ed.) (1996) *Analysing Performance: A Critical Reader*. Manchester: Manchester University Press.

Carlson, Marvin (1996) *Performance: A Critical Introduction*. London: Routledge.

Caughie, John and Kevin Rockett (1996) *The Companion to British and Irish Cinema*. London: British Film Institute.

Cave, Richard Allen (1987) *New British Drama in Performance on the London Stage 1970–1985*. Gerrards Cross: Colin Smythe.

Chaillet, Ned (1980) 'Steve Berkoff's cultural assault'. Interview with Steven Berkoff. *The Times*, 16 February.

Chalmers, Robert (1991) 'The Devil comes in from the cold'. Interview with Steven Berkoff. *Daily Telegraph*, 22 November.

Chambers, Colin (1980) 'Product into Process: Actor-based workshop'. In *Dreams and Deconstructions, Alternative Theatre in Britain*, edited by Sandy Craig, 105–15. Ambergate: Amber Lane Press.

Chambers, Colin and Mike Prior (1987) *Playwrights' Progress: Patterns of Postwar Drama*. Oxford: Amber Lane Press.

Christopher, James (1993) 'Uneven Steven'. Interview with Steven Berkoff. *Time Out*, 17–24 November.

Church, Michael (1994) 'Mr Nasty craves affection'. Interview with Steven Berkoff. *The Times*, 14 January.

Clarke, Peter (1996) *Hope and Glory: Britain 1900–1990*. London: Penguin.

Cohen, Stanley and Paul Rock (1970) 'The Teddy Boy'. In *The Age of Affluence*, edited by Vernon Bogdanor and Robert Skidelsky, 288–318. Basingstoke: Macmillan.

Cohn, Ruby (1991) *Retreats from Realism in Recent English Drama*. Cambridge: Cambridge University Press.

Collier, Susanne (1992) 'Post-Falklands, post-Colonial: Contextualizing Branagh as Henry V on stage and on film'. *Essays in Theatre/Études théatrales*, Vol. 10, no. 2 (May), 141–54.

Connor, Steven (1996) 'Postmodern performance'. In *Analysing Performance: A Critical Reader*, edited by Patrick Campbell, 107–24. Manchester: Manchester University Press.

—— (1997) *Postmodern Culture: An Introduction to Theories of the Contemporary*. 2nd edn. Oxford: Blackwell.

Corner, John and Sylvia Harvey (eds) (1991) *Enterprise and Heritage: Crosscurrents of National Culture*. London: Routledge.

Cottam, Francis (1992) 'Being Berkoff'. Profile of Steven Berkoff. *For Him Magazine*, (February).

Counsell, Colin (1996) *Signs of Performance: An Introduction to Twentieth-Century Theatre*. London: Routledge.

Coveney, Michael (1996) 'Berkoff bites back'. Review of *Free Association* by Steven Berkoff. *Observer*, 19 May.

Craig, Sandy (1980a) 'Reflexes of the future: The beginnings of the fringe'. In *Dreams and Deconstructions, Alternative Theatre in Britain*, edited by Sandy Craig, 9–29. Ambergate: Amber Lane Press.

—— (1980b) 'Unmasking the lie: Political theatre'. In *Dreams and Deconstructions, Alternative Theatre in Britain*, edited by Sandy Craig, 30–48. Ambergate: Amber Lane Press.

Currant, Paul Brian (1991) *The Theatre of Steven Berkoff*. PhD dissertation, University of Georgia.

Curtis, Nick (1993) 'Words shall never hurt him'. Interview with Steven Berkoff. *Independent*, 23 August.

Davies, Andrew (1987) *Other Theatres: The Development of Alternative and Experimental Theatre in Britain*. Basingstoke: Macmillan.

Davies, Bronwyn and Rom Harré (1990) 'Positioning: The discursive production of selves'. *Journal for the Theory of Social Behaviour*, vol. 20, no. 1, 43–63.

Davies, Russell (1973) 'Joseph K in a strait-jacket'. Review of *The Trial*, adapted by Steven Berkoff. *Observer*, 25 November.

de Jongh, Nicholas (1969) 'Kafka plays'. Reviews of *In the Penal Colony* and *Metamorphosis*, adapted by Steven Berkoff. *Guardian*, 16 April.

—— (1989) '"Hello Nick, I'm going to kill you"'. Profile of Steven Berkoff. *The Guardian*, Aug. 11.

de Man, Paul (1979) 'Autobiography as de-facement'. *Modern Language Notes*, vol. 94, no. 5 (December), 919–30.

Demastes, William W. (ed.) (1996) *British Playwrights, 1956–1995: A Research and Production Sourcebook*. Westport, Connecticut: Greenwood Press.

Derrida, Jacques (1977) *Of Grammatology*. Translated by G. C. Spivak. Baltimore: Johns Hopkins University Press

—— (1978) *Writing and Difference*. Translated by Alan Bass. London: Routledge & Kegan Paul.

Dodd, Stephen (1996) 'Basking in shock and sensation'. Interview with Steven Berkoff. *Sunday Independent*, 12 May.

Dort, Bernard (1982) 'The liberated performance'. *Modern Drama*, vol. 25, no. 1, 60–8.

Drakakis, John (1997) 'Shakespeare in quotations'. In *Studying British Cultures. An Introduction*, edited by Susan Bassnett, 152–72. London: Routledge.

Drumgoole, Dominic (2000) *The Full Room: An A-Z of Contemporary Playwriting*. London: Methuen.

D'Silva, Beverley (1990) 'Theatrical moves to a maverick beat'. Interview with Steven Berkoff. *Sunday Times*, 4 March.

Dunn, Tony (1996) 'Sated, starved or satisfied: The languages of theatre in Britain today'. In *Contemporary British Theatre*, edited by Theodore Shank, 19–40. Basingstoke: Macmillan.

Dyer, Richard (1986) *Heavenly Bodies: Film Stars and Society*. London: British Film Institute.

Elam, Keir (1991) *The Semiotics of Theatre and Drama*. London: Methuen, 1980; reprint, London: Routledge.

Elder, Bruce (1978) '"Doing the inexpressible uncommonly well": The theatre of Steven Berkoff'. Interview with Steven Berkoff. *Theatre Quarterly*, vol. 8, no. 30 (Summer), 37–43.

Elsom, John (1979) *Post-War British Theatre*. London: Routledge & Kegan Paul.

—— (ed.) (1992) *Is Shakespeare Still Our Contemporary?* London: Routledge.

Engers, Angna (1979) 'On mime'. In *Mimes on Miming*, edited by Bari Rolfe. London: Millington, 133–4.

Esslin, Martin (1983) *The Theatre of the Absurd*. Harmondsworth: Penguin.

—— (1996) *The Field of Drama: How the Signs of Drama Create Meanings on Stage and Screen*. London: Methuen.

Eyre, Richard and Nicholas Wright (2000) *Changing Stages: A View of British Theatre in the Twentieth Century*. London: Bloomsbury.

Féral, Josette (1982) 'Performance and theatricality: The subject demystified'. *Modern Drama*, vol. 25 , 170–81.

Fishman, William J. (1979) *The Streets of East London*. London: Duckworth.

Fiske, John (1989a) *Reading the Popular*. London: Routledge.

——(1989b) *Understanding Popular Culture*. London: Routledge.

Fortier, Mark (1997) *Theory/Theatre: An Introduction*. London: Routledge.

Foss, Roger (1991) 'East'. Review of *East*, by Steven Berkoff. *What's On*, 11 September.

Foucault, Michel (1972) *The Archaeology of Knowledge*. London: Tavistock.

—— (1979) *Discipline and Punish: The Birth of the Prison*. Translated by Alan Sheridan. Harmondsworth: Peregrine.

—— (1990) *The History of Sexuality. An Introduction*. Vol. I. Translated by Robert Hurley. New York: Vintage Books.

Freud, Sigmund (1973) *New Introductory Lectures on Psychoanalysis*. Translated by James Strachey, edited by James Strachey and Angela Richards. The Pelican Freud Library, vol. 2. Harmondsworth: Penguin.

Frost, Anthony and Ralph Yarrow (1990) *Improvisation in Drama*. Basingstoke: Macmillan.

Frye, Northrop (1957) *Anatomy of Criticism*. Princeton: Princeton University Press.

Gamble, Andrew (1994) *Britain in Decline. Economic Policy, Political Strategy and the British State*. London: St Martin's Press.

Gardner, Lyn (1999) 'Anyone of any quality feels an outsider'. Interview with Steven Berkoff. *Guardian*, 15 September.

Garner, Stanton B. (1994) *Bodied Spaces: Phenomenology and Performance in Contemporary Drama*. Ithaca: Cornell University Press.

Gavshon, Arthur and Desmond Rice (1984) *The Sinking of the Belgrano*. London: New English Library.

Gergen, Kenneth J. (1973) 'Social psychology as history'. *Journal of Personality and Social Psychology*, vol. 26, 309–20.

—— (1989) 'Warranting voice and the elaboration of the self'. In *Texts of Identity*, edited by John Shotter and Kenneth J. Gergen, 70–81. London: Sage.

Gergen, Mary (1994) 'The social construction of personal histories: Gendered lives in popular autobiographies'. In *Constructing the Social*, edited by Theodore R. Sarbin and John I. Kitsuse, 19–44. London: Sage.

Gibb, Eddie (1999) 'East and Eden'. *Sunday Herald*, 8 August.

Gilmour, Ian (1992) *Dancing with Dogma: Britain under Thatcherism*. London: Simon & Schuster.

Glaister, Dan (1998) 'A drama in one act: angry scenes as Berkoff takes the burger shilling'. *Guardian*, 13 January.

Goorney, Howard (1981) *The Theatre Workshop Story*. London: Eyre Methuen.

Gordon, Giles (1983) Review of *Decadence*, by Steven Berkoff. Arts Theatre, London. *The Spectator*, 13 January.

Grant, Steve (1977) 'Gulp!' Interview with Steven Berkoff. Reprinted in *Time Out Interviews 1968–1998*, edited by Frank Broughton. Harmondsworth: Penguin, 1998.

—— (1985) 'Lonely Harry's brush with Berkoff'. Interview with Steven Berkoff. *Guardian*, 7 December.

Gray, Ronald (1973) *Franz Kafka*. Cambridge: Cambridge University Press.

Grotowski, Jerzy (1992) *Towards a Poor Theatre*. Edited by Eugenio Barba. London: Methuen Drama.

Hall, Anthea (1992) 'An eye for everyday brutality'. Interview with Steven Berkoff. *Daily Telegraph*, 10 May.

Halsey, A. H. (1989) *Change in British Society*. Oxford: Oxford University Press.

Halton, Kathleen (1965) 'Seven actors in search of a character'. Profile of Steven Berkoff. *Sunday Times Magazine*, 25 April, 28–35.

Hammond, Jonathan (1973) 'A potted history of the fringe'. *Theatre Quarterly*, vol. 3, no. 12 (October–December), 37–46.

—— (1974) 'London Theatre Group'. Reviews of *Agamemnon* and *The Trial*, adapted by Steven Berkoff. *Plays and Players* (January), 53–4.

Hartnoll, Phyllis (1989) *The Theatre: A Concise History*. London: Thames & Hudson.

—— (ed.) (1993) *The Oxford Companion to the Theatre*. Oxford: Oxford University Press.

Haynes, Jim (1984) *Thanks for Coming!* London: Faber & Faber.

Hebdige, Dick (1979) *The Meaning of Style*. London: Methuen.

Heelas, Paul (1991) 'Reforming the self: Enterprise and the characters of Thatcherism'. In *Enterprise Culture*, edited by Russell Keat and Nicholas Abercrombie, 72–90. London: Routledge.

Hern, Anthony (1969) 'Triple honours for busy Berkoff'. Reviews of *In the Penal Colony* and *Metamorphosis*, adapted by Steven Berkoff. *Evening Standard*, 15 July.

Hewison, Robert (1987) *Too Much: Art and Society in the Sixties 1960–75*. New York: Oxford University Press.

—— (1995) *Culture and Consensus: England, Art and Politics Since 1940*. London: Methuen.

—— (2001) Review of *The Secret Love Life of Ophelia*, by Steven Berkoff. *Sunday Times*, 8 July.

Hicklin, Aaron (1997) 'Noble savage'. *Thud.* 5 September.

Hill, Charles G. (1992) *Jean-Paul Sartre: Freedom and Commitment*. New York: Peter Lang.

Hobson, Harold (1969) 'Kafka's nightmare'. Reviews of *In the Penal Colony* and *Metamorphosis*, adapted by Steven Berkoff. *Sunday Times*, 20 July.

Holderness, Graham (ed.) (1992) *The Politics of Theatre and Drama*. Basingstoke: Macmillan.

Hoyle, Martin (1986) Review of *Sink the Belgrano!*, by Steven Berkoff. *Financial Times*, 10 September.

Huitzinga, Johan (1955) *Homo Ludens: A Study of the Play-Element in Culture*. Boston: The Beacon Press.

Husbands, C. (1983) 'East End racism, 1900–1980: Geographical continuities in vigilantist and extreme right-wing political behaviour'. *London Journal*, vol. 8, no. 1, 3–26.

Hutcheon, Linda (1988) *A Poetics of Postmodernism*. London: Routledge.

Iley, Chrissy (1993) 'The Beast of Burden'. *Sunday Times*, 5 December.

Innes, Christopher (1992) *Modern British Drama, 1800–1992*. Cambridge: Cambridge University Press.

—— (1993) *Avant Garde Theatre 1892–1992*. London: Routledge.

Irvine, Ian (1991) 'The Kennedy effect'. *Evening Standard*, 13 June.

Itzin, Catherine (ed.) (1976) *Alternative Theatre Handbook 1975–76*. London: Theatre Quarterly Publications.

—— (1980) *Stages in the Revolution*. London: Eyre Methuen.

Jackson, Anthony and George Rowell (1984) *The Repertory Movement*. Cambridge: Cambridge University Press.

Jay, Paul (1984) *Being in the Text: Self-Representation from Wordsworth to Barthes*. Ithaca: Cornell University Press.

Jencks, Charles (1977) *The Language of Postmodern Architecture*. New York: Rizzoli.

Kafka, Franz (1961) *Metamorphosis and Other Stories*. Harmondsworth: Penguin Books.

Keat, Russell, Nicholas Abercrombie and Nigel Whiteley (eds) (1994) *The Authority of the Consumer*. London: Routledge.

Keating, P. J. (ed.) (1976) *Into Unknown England 1866–1913. Selections from the Social Explorers*. London: Fontana/Collins.

Kellaway, Kate (1994) 'Taking a walk in the wild East End'. *Observer*, 3 April.

Kershaw, Baz (1992) *The Politics of Performance: Radical Theatre as Cultural Intervention*. London: Routledge.

—— (1994) 'Framing the audience'. In *The Authority of the Consumer*, edited by Russell Keat, Nicholas Abercrombie and Nigel Whiteley, 166–86. London: Routledge.

Kiefer, Elisabeth (1989) 'Theaterspuren in Kafkas Werk: Eine Analyse der Erzählung "Die Verwandlung" im Hinblick auf ihre theatralen Elemente'. *Neophilologus*, vol. 73, no. 2, 263–80.

Kirby, E. T. (ed.) (1969) *Total Theatre: A Critical Anthology*. New York: E. P. Dutton.

Kitchin, Laurence (1966) *Drama in the Sixties: Form and Interpretation*. London: Faber & Faber.

Kitzinger, Celia (1992) 'The individuated self concept: Critical analysis of social-constructionist writing on individualism'. In *Social Psychology of Identity and the Self Concept*, edited by G. Breakwell, 221–50. London: Surrey University Press/Academic Press.

Klinger, Kurt (1983) 'Kafka auf der Bühne'. *Newsletter of the Kafka Society America*, no. 1 (June), 56–70.

Knapp, Bettina (1994) *Antonin Artaud, Man of Vision*. Chicago: Swallow Press.

Kohn, Marek (1989) 'A workers' bard'. Interview with Steven Berkoff. *Observer*, 13 August.

Lambert, Angela (1989) 'Dramatic passions of a Beverley Hills Cop'. Interview with Steven Berkoff. *Independent*, 13 November.

Leabhart, Thomas (1989) *Modern and Post-Modern Mime*. Basingstoke: Macmillan.

Lecoq, Jacques (2002) *The Moving Body*. London: Methuen.

Lewis, Peter (1978) *The Fifties*. London: Heinemann.

Lipman, V. D. (1954) *Social History of the Jews in England 1850–1950*. London: Watts.

Lister, David (1989) 'Berkoff admits threatening to murder "sadistic" critic'. *Independent*, 16 August.

Logan, Brian (2002) 'Requiem for Ground Zero'. Review of *Requiem for Ground Zero*, by Steven Berkoff. *Guardian*, 19 August.

MacDonald, Marianne (1996) 'A different step'. Interview with Steven Berkoff. *Independent on Sunday*, 16 June.

Marcus, Laura (1994) *Auto/biographical Discourses: Criticism, Theory, Practice*. Manchester: Manchester University Press.

Marquand, David (1991) *The Progressive Dilemma*. London: Heinemann.

Martin, Randy (1990) *Performance as Political Act*. Westport, Connecticut: Bergin & Garvey.

Marwick, Arthur (1990) *British Society since 1940*. Harmondsworth: Penguin.

Masters, Brian (1970) *A Student's Guide to Sartre*. London: Heinemann.

McAfee, Annalena (1989) 'Bovver craft'. Interview with Steven Berkoff. *Evening Standard*, 10 August.

—— (1991) 'Berkoff among the misfits'. Interview with Steven Berkoff. *Evening Standard*, 28 February.

—— (1996) 'Cockney rebel turned impresario'. Interview with Steven Berkoff. *Financial Times*, 8–9 June.

Melly, George (1989) *Revolt into Style: The Pop Arts in the 50s and 60s*. Oxford: Oxford University Press.

Morley, Sheridan (1975) 'Punk plays'. Profile of Steven Berkoff. *Sunday Telegraph*, 30 October.

Morrison, Hugh (1989) *Directing in the Theatre*. London: A & C Black.

Nathan, David (1991) Review of *Kvetch*, by Steven Berkoff. *The Jewish Chronicle*, 4 October.

Nightingale, Benedict (2001) 'More missive than hit'. Review of *The Secret Love Life of Ophelia*, by Steven Berkoff. King's Head Theatre Club, London. *The Times*, 6 July.

Norris, Christopher (1991) *Deconstruction: Theory and Practice*. London: Routledge.

Olivier, Laurence (1982) *Confessions of an Actor: An Autobiography*. New York: Simon & Schuster.

O'Reilly, John (1997) 'Lord of the trance'. *Independent*. 26 April.

Orr, John (1991) *Tragicomedy and Contemporary Culture: Play and Performance from Beckett to Shepard*. Basingstoke: Macmillan.

Paget, Derek (1992) 'Oh what a lovely post-modern war: Drama and the Falklands'. In *The Politics of Theatre and Drama*, edited by Graham Holderness, 154–79. Basingstoke: Macmillan.

Palmer, Alan (1989) *East End: Four Centuries of London Life*. London: John Murray.

Pavis, Patrice (1982) *Languages of the Stage: Essays in the Semiology of the Theatre*. New York: Performing Arts Journal.

—— (1998) *Dictionary of the Theatre: Terms, Concepts and Analysis*. Toronto: University of Toronto Press.

Peacock, D. Keith (1999) *Thatcher's Theatre: British Theatre and Drama in the Eighties*. Westport, Connecticut: Greenwood Press.

Peter, John (1991) 'The classical problem of staging time'. *Sunday Times*, 10 March.

Phillips, Caroline (1991) 'The gentle outlaw'. Interview with Steven Berkoff. *Evening Standard*, 11 March.

Playfair, Giles (1950) *Kean: The Life and Paradox of the Great Actor*. New York: E. P. Dutton, 1939; London: Reinhardt & Evans.

Politzer, Heinz (1962) *Franz Kafka: Parable and Paradox*. Ithaca: Cornell University Press.

Potter, Beatrice (1904) 'The Jewish community'. In *Life and Labour of the People of London*, edited by Charles Booth, 166–92. London: Macmillan.

Prunet, Monique (1996) 'The outrageous 1980s: Conservative policies and the Church of England under fire in Steven Berkoff's *Sink the Belgrano* and David Hare's *The Secret Rapture* and *Racing Demon*'. *Contemporary Theatre Review*, vol. 5, no. 1, 91–102.

Quinn, Michael L. (1990) 'Celebrity and the Semiotics of Acting'. *New Theatre Quarterly*, vol. 6, no. 22 (May).

Rabkin, Gerald (1983) 'The play of misreading: Text/theatre/deconstruction'. *Performing Arts Journal*, vol. 26, no. 27: 42–59.

Rees, Roland (1992) *Fringe First: Pioneers of Fringe Theatre on Record*. London: Oberon Books.

Rees-Mogg, William (1985) *The Political Economy of Art*. London: Arts Council of Great Britain.

Renza, Louis A. (1977) 'The veto of the imagination: A theory of autobiography'. *New Literary History*, vol. 9 (1977), 1–26.

Reynolds, Nigel (1998) 'Berkoff attacks British audiences'. *Daily Telegraph*, 10 July.

Rolleston, James (1974) *Kafka's Narrative Theater*. University Park & London: Pennsylvania State University Press.

Rosen, Craig (n.d.) 'Creating the Berkovian aesthetic: An analysis of Steven Berkoff's performance style'. Reproduced at www.iainfisher.com/berkoff.html.

Ross, Deborah (2001) 'Are you looking at me?' *Independent*, 2 July.

Rudlin, John (1986) *Jacques Copeau*. Cambridge: Cambridge University Press.

Rycroft, Charles (1968) *A Critical Dictionary of Psychoanalysis*. Harmondsworth: Penguin.

Salter, Denis (1996) 'Acting Shakespeare in postcolonial space'. In *Shakespeare, Theory and Performance*, edited by James Bulman, 113–32. London: Routledge.

Sampson, Edward (1989) 'The deconstruction of the self'. In *Texts of Identity*, edited by John Shotter and Kenneth J. Gergen, 1–19. London: Sage.

Sawicki, J. (1991) *Disciplining Foucault: Power and the Body*. London: Routledge.

Scarry, Elaine (1985) *The Body in Pain: The Making and Unmaking of the World*. New York: Oxford University Press.

Schechner, Richard (1983) 'News, sex, and performance theory'. In *Innovation/ Renovation: New Perspectives on the Humanities*, edited by Ihab Hassan and Sally Hassan, 189–210. Madison: University of Wisconsin Press.

Schwartz, Bill (1991) 'Where horses shit a hundred sparrows feed: Docklands and East London during the Thatcher years'. In *Enterprise and Heritage:*

Crosscurrents of National Culture, edited by John Corner and Sylvia Harvey, 76–92. London: Routledge.

Shakespeare, William (1988) *The Complete Works*. Edited by Stanley Wells and Gary Taylor. Oxford: Clarendon Press.

Shank, Theodore (1982) *American Alternative Theatre*. Basingstoke: Macmillan.

Shellard, Dominic (1999) *British Theatre Since the War*. New Haven and London: Yale University Press

Shepherd, Simon and Peter Womack (1996) *English Drama: A Cultural History*. Oxford: Blackwell.

Sierz, Aleks (2001) *In-Yer-Face Theatre: British Drama Today*. London, Faber & Faber.

Sinfield, Alan (1988) 'Making space: Appropriation and confrontation in recent British plays'. In *The Shakespeare Myth*, edited by Graham Holderness. Manchester: Manchester University Press, 128–44.

Sked, Alan and Chris Cook (1990) *Post-War Britain: A Political History*. Harmondsworth: Penguin.

Smith, Godfrey (1985) 'Of plays and players.' *Sunday Times*, 29 December.

Smith, Paul (1988) *Discerning the Subject*. Minneapolis: University of Minnesota Press.

Smurthwaite, Nick (1996) 'Steven Berkoff . . . feeling mad all over'. Interview with Steven Berkoff. *Midweek*, 10–13 June.

Spencer, Charles (1996) 'Histrionic skinhead'. Review of *Free Association* by Steven Berkoff. *Sunday Telegraph*, 7 April.

—— (1998) Review of *Shakespeare's Villains*, by Steven Berkoff. *Daily Telegraph*. 7 October.

—— (1999) 'Unforgettable . . . sadly'. Review of *East*, by Steven Berkoff. *Daily Telegraph*. 17 September.

Stamp, Terence (1988) *Coming Attractions*. London: Bloomsbury.

Stead, Peter (1989) *Film and the Working Class: The Feature Film in British and American Society*. London: Routledge.

Stefanova, Kalina (2000) *Who Keeps the Score on the London Stages?* Amsterdam: Harwood.

Street, Sarah (1997) *British National Cinema*. London: Routledge.

Sturrock, John (1993) *The Language of Autobiography: Studies in the First Person Singular*. Cambridge: Cambridge University Press.

Tennenhouse, Leonard (1985) 'Strategies of State and political plays: *A Midsummer Night's Dream, Henry IV, Henry V, Henry VIII'*. In *Political Shakespeare: New Essays in Cultural Materialism*, edited by Jonathan Dollimore and Alan Sinfield, 109–28. Manchester: Manchester University Press.

Thatcher, Margaret (1993) *The Downing Street Years*. London: HarperCollins.

Thompson, John B. (1990) *Ideology and Modern Culture*. Cambridge: Polity Press.

Thorlby, Anthony (1972) *A Student's Guide to Kafka*. London: Heinemann.

Time Out. (1971) 'Guide to Underground Theatre'. *Theatre Quarterly*, vol. 1, no. 1 (January–March), 61–65.

Tynan, Kenneth (1975) *A View of the English Stage 1944–63*. London: Davis-Poynter.

Usher, Shaun (1999) 'Berkoff's sun, still rising in the East'. Review of *East* by Steven Berkoff. *Daily Mail*, 16 September.

Vanden Heuvel, Michael (1993) *Performing Drama/Dramatizing Performance: Alternative Theater and the Dramatic Text.* Ann Arbor: University of Michigan Press.

Veltrusky, Jiri (1964) 'Man and object in the theater'. In *A Prague School Reader on Esthetics, Literary Structure and Style*, edited by Paul L. Garvin, 83–91. Washington: Georgetown University Press.

Vigouroux-Frey, Nicole (1997) 'Greeks in drama: Four contemporary issues'. In *Drama on Drama: Dimensions of Theatricality on the Contemporary British Stage*, edited by Nicole Boireau, 3–14. Basingstoke: Macmillan.

Wallis, Bill (1971) 'Jean-Louis Barrault's "Rabelais"'. *Theatre Quarterly*, vol. 1, no. 3 (July–September), 83–97.

Walsh, John (1991) 'Anti-hero with an East Side story'. Interview with Steven Berkoff. *Sunday Times*, 10 February.

Weedon, Chris (1987) *Feminist Practice and Poststructuralist Theory.* Oxford: Blackwell.

Weiss, William (1979) 'An Interview with Jean-Louis Barrault'. *Mime, Mask and Marionette*, vol. 2 (1979), no. 1, 1–11.

Wiles, Timothy (1980) *The Theater Event: Modern Theories of Performance.* Chicago: University of Chicago Press.

Willett, John (1959) *The Theatre of Bertolt Brecht: A Study from Eight Aspects.* London: Methuen.

Willis, Paul (1977) *Learning to Labour: How Working Class Kids Get Working Class Jobs.* London: Saxon House.

Wollen, Tana (1991) 'Over our Shoulders: Nostalgia screen fictions for the 1980s'. In *Enterprise and Heritage: Crosscurrents of National Culture*, edited by John Corner and Sylvia Harvey, 178–93. London: Routledge.

Woolf, Michael (1995) 'Negotiating the self: Jewish fiction in Britain since 1945'. In *Other Britain, Other British: Contemporary Multicultural Fiction*, edited by A. Robert Lee, 124–41. London: Pluto Press.

Wunderlich, Heinke (1979) 'Dramatisierungen und Verfilmungen'. In *Kafka-Handbuch*, edited by Harmut Binder, 825–41. Stuttgart: Alfred Kröner Verlag.

INDEX